Has Semantics Rested on a Mistake?
And Other Essays

STANFORD SERIES IN PHILOSOPHY

Editorial Board

Jon Barwise
Michael Bratman
John Dupré
John Etchemendy
Solomon Feferman
Dagfin Føllesdal
Eckart Förster
Peter Galison
Stuart Hampshire
Julius Moravcsik
David Nivison
John Perry
Thomas Wasow

HAS SEMANTICS RESTED ON A MISTAKE?
And Other Essays

Howard K. Wettstein

Stanford University Press, Stanford, California

Stanford University Press
Stanford, California
© 1991 by the Board of Trustees of the Leland Stanford Junior University

CIP data appear at the end of the book

Stanford University Press publications are distributed exclusively by Stanford University Press within the United States, Canada, Mexico, and Central America; they are distributed exclusively by Cambridge University Press throughout the rest of the world.

Original printing 1991
Last figure below indicates year of this printing:
04 03 02 01 00 99 98 97 96 95

FOR MY PARENTS,
HY AND ROSALIE WETTSTEIN

Acknowledgments

PHILOSOPHERS—at least nowadays—refuse to constitute much of a community. There is all too much competition, too little genuine sharing of ideas and enthusiasms. In light of this, a friend once noted, one needs to create one's own community. One needs to seek out philosophers with whom one can talk freely, with whom one can try out ideas, even if half-baked, even if still-born. It has been my great fortune to have found such philosophical friends, to have been supported, encouraged, and instructed by them. One does not often find oneself in a setting appropriate to the expression of this sort of gratitude. I thus seize on the present occasion to thank Tom Blackburn, Michael Bratman, Arthur Collins, Keith Donnellan, Richard Foley, Richard Fumerton, Eli Hirsch, David Kaplan, (the late) Dean Kolitch, Ernie LePore, Genoveva Marti, Richard Mendelsohn, John Perry, and Larry Simon. I am fortunate to find myself in a department that is growing, not only in quantity and quality, but also in its view of itself as a philosophic community. I thank the members of the Philosophy Department at the University of California, Riverside, for their support and stimulation. My debt to Joseph Almog is a special one. For the past few years, we have talked and talked and talked, and while it has not always been, let us say, totally relaxed, it has always been extremely profitable. Finally, to my family—to my wife, Barbara Wettstein, and to my children, Eve and Jonathan Wettstein—I owe more than I can begin to express.

H.K.W.

Contents

	Introduction	1
ONE	Can What Is Asserted Be a Sentence?	9
TWO	Indexical Reference and Propositional Content	20
THREE	Proper Names and Propositional Opacity	28
FOUR	Demonstrative Reference and Definite Descriptions	35
FIVE	The Semantic Significance of the Referential-Attributive Distinction	50
SIX	Did the Greeks Really Worship Zeus?	59
SEVEN	How to Bridge the Gap Between Meaning and Reference	69
EIGHT	Frege-Russell Semantics?	86
NINE	Has Semantics Rested on a Mistake?	109
TEN	Cognitive Significance Without Cognitive Content	132
ELEVEN	Turning the Tables on Frege, or How Is It That "Hesperus Is Hesperus" Is Trivial?	159
	Notes	179
	Index	229

Has Semantics Rested on a Mistake?
And Other Essays

Introduction

I WAS once asked by a friend whether I agreed with Frege that philosophy of language was *first philosophy*, that it might supply the very foundation of philosophy that some have sought. My friend should have added that he was speaking of Frege-as-interpreted-by-Michael Dummett. Foundational, I responded, is not the same thing as fundamental. What is clear is that Frege directed our attention to a domain he saw as *fundamental*. Frege's vision of what was fundamental, moreover, altered the philosophical landscape. I doubt that the philosophy of language is nowadays taken to be foundational, but its issues are surely fundamental.

Frege's concerns are with matters intellectually basic though abstract, matters about which something very much like common sense seems to lead in conflicting directions. Such concerns seem paradigmatically philosophical. I originally turned to Frege for help with one such question: what is it that is true or false in the most fundamental sense? Frege defends the ostensibly quite reasonable idea that the things that are, in the most basic sense, true or false ought to be distinguished from the symbols we use to express them. Something seems almost perverse about the thought that the very marks on paper are what are right or wrong. Rather, what is right or wrong in this most fundamental sense is *what we say* by the use of these symbols. The things said—often called *propositions* (Frege calls them *thoughts*)—are thus distinct from the sentences used to assert those propositions.

This distinction between sentences and propositions seemed to me, at first, quite natural. This is not to say that there was no philosophical discomfort associated with it. What, after all, are these propositions? Are they, in some important sense, in the head (or the mind)? If not, what are we to make of them? While it is thus plausible enough to distinguish propositions from sentences, it is equally reasonable to wonder about whether there really are any such things.

There are a host of related questions, some arguably even more fundamental, concerning which Frege may be a source of stimulation and insight. One is Wittgenstein's query about the vitality of language. What, Wittgenstein asks, brings language to life? What makes these molecules, the inscription on paper, *mean* something? What sort of fact is it that symbols mean things? Is it a psychological fact, or what? Still another closely related question concerns the reference of linguistic expressions. In virtue of what do certain expressions connect with, refer to, denote, various things? Take the name 'Gottlob Frege'. In virtue of what does that name connect to the particular person of whom we speak?

I was drawn to the work of Frege early in my graduate studies, for Frege seemed focused on the most basic issues in philosophy. Long-term study of Frege persuaded me, however, that his pivotal distinction between sense and reference, and his attendant philosophical views about language and thought, were unsatisfactory.[1] The first of the essays in this volume, "Can What Is Asserted Be a Sentence?," defends the Fregean distinction between sentences and propositions. The rest represent my developing feeling that the Fregean outlook in the philosophy of language—as well as its implications for the philosophy of mind—is unacceptable, and not only in detail. Not that Frege's orientation is indefensible. Frege's views have been defended by many able philosophers and will, no doubt, continue to be defended. It seemed, though, that the attempt to defend even a broadly Fregean perspective violated the sort of naturalness that we should demand from philosophy.

I am, of course, not alone in rejecting Frege's philosophy of language. The past quarter of a century has seen significant movement away from the Fregean orientation for a variety of reasons. My approach certainly overlaps with others', but it may be useful to briefly note some differences. My approach, unlike that of, say, Saul Kripke and, to some extent, David Kaplan, was not fuelled by modal considerations. Imagine, contrary to fact, that Frege's approach provides an extremely natural account of the semantics of a host of kinds of expressions, until, that is, we get to modality. Perhaps it would be noted that Frege's view has difficulties with modal discourse, or with the truth conditions for ordinary non-modal propositions evaluated with respect to counterfactual circumstances, or whatever. Given that modality is itself so philosophically controversial, one would naturally hesitate before concluding that Frege's view is hopeless, or even in deep trouble.[2] My own sense that Frege was in deep trouble reflected my view that Frege's difficulties begin before one gets to modality, with ordinary, garden-variety talk that he cannot naturally accommodate.

Considerations about indexicals and demonstratives, not about proper names, were the ones that figured prominently in my own rejection of Frege, as they did for David Kaplan. Kaplan's famous distinction between character and content, however, was no part of what I had in mind. As I now see it (see "Has Semantics Rested on a Mistake?"), Kaplan's notion of character, even aside from its failure to do some of the work asked of it, is a not too distant relative of Frege's notion of sense, and what I have in mind is a more radical rejection of the Fregean outlook. (See "Cognitive Significance Without Cognitive Content" and "Turning the Tables on Frege.")

Let me try to create a sense of what, from my point of view, is wrong with Frege's outlook. I pointedly say "a sense of what is wrong," rather than "an argument against Frege." A number of arguments will follow in the papers contained herein. I want to begin, though, with a more impressionistic rendering.

Here is an analogy. If one wants to provide an account of what might be called the spiritual dimension of human existence, it may seem natural, at a certain stage of the development of reflection on these matters, to posit a spirit, some entity perhaps "purely spiritual," an entity uncorrupted, unpolluted, uncomplicated, in the ways that we are. Our own spiritual aspect, on such a view, is a product of some special relation in which we stand to this pure spirit. Such moves, not only with regard to spirituality, are familiar in the history of philosophy and, to many of us, never yield substantial progress. Frege's answer to Wittgenstein's query about the vitality of language is not dissimilar. If one wants to account for the significance, the meaningfulness, of symbols, one should posit a meaning, a pure meaning if you like, something intrinsically meaningful, something whose representational character is not a matter of anything like human convention or practice. Such meanings—Frege calls them *senses* and takes them to be abstract, nonmental representations—are Frege's key to understanding the vitality of symbols. Pieces of language come to life when they are associated with senses by agents that apprehend the latter.

It is one thing to feel such intuitive discomfort with the Fregean outlook and quite another to provide an alternative. Even if one rejects the details of Frege's philosophy of language, needn't one accept something like Frege's approach to the vitality of language? What else could account for the significance of a symbol other than some sort of tie to a representation of some sort? Isn't Frege's virtually "the only game in town"? The challenge, then, is to provide at least a sketch of a positive alternative—not a trivial matter. Given the inherent difficulty of the subject, however, we need to be very patient concerning positive answers. It seems more important to hold onto a sense of what seems the wrong direction—to know what we do not want to say—than to know, early on, what we ought to say. My preferred alternative is one that I have come to slowly, in small steps. Those steps are recounted in the papers collected here, but I will, for the moment, skip the steps and jump to the alternative picture.

I want to approach the vitality of language not by positing a realm of intrinsically meaningful representations—mental, objective, or whatever—but rather by emphasizing the embeddedness of linguistic symbols in social practice. This, of course, is the path suggested by Wittgenstein, but it has looked hopeless to many. How might embeddedness in social practice possibly confer as singular a thing as *meaningfulness* on a word? How could a bunch of people making noises give *significance* to the noises any more than could individual people making noises in isolation?

Formulated in such large terms, the matter seems unmanageable, so let me shrink its proportions. Consider a hypothetical linguistic community (not altogether unlike ours) in which numbers are assigned to individuals at birth. These numbers are used as official tags, as publicly available devices for making the relevant individuals subjects of discourse. These tags—roughly comparable to our social security numbers—do not depend for their functioning on a speaker's knowledge of the tagged individuals. Thus one can ask questions like "Who is 659-48-8840?" and "Has 022-22-0922 paid his or her taxes this year?" without any idea of the identity of the relevant individual.

This practice, as I have described it, arguably overlaps in interesting ways with our practice with proper names. Proper names, once bestowed upon individuals, function as publicly available devices for making those individuals subjects of discourse. As was the case with the official numbers, one can use a proper name to refer to its bearer in the absence of anything close to individuating knowledge of the bearer. This, in fact, is an important feature of our practice, since it allows for questions like "Who was Aristotle?" from people who really have no idea who he was.

Let us return to Wittgenstein's question about the vitality of language. When considering that question in an abstract and general way, we might be tempted to assume that words are meaningful only insofar as we associate them with meanings, that symbols can represent only insofar as we associate them with mental or abstract representations. It is not at all tempting, however, to tell any such story about the official numbers, or about proper names (if my John Stuart Mill–inspired sketch of our practices with names has merit). Indeed, if God, to use Wittgenstein's metaphor, were to scrutinize the speaker's consciousness, searching for an associated representation, God would search in vain. The vitality of the respective symbols, the fact that these symbols are significant at all, and the specific significance they have are clearly not a matter of some meaning-entity associated with the symbol. The significance of the official numbers, and arguably of ordinary proper names, is rather a function of the linguistic practices sketched above.

Such a social practice conception was implicit, and at times verged on becoming explicit, in Kripke's remarks on the historical chains of communication that ground, according to Kripke and Keith Donnellan, our use of proper names. Do not think, Kripke tells us in lecture 2 of *Naming and Necessity*, of the significance of names as something bestowed upon names in the privacy of our studies. We name-users do not intellectually give meaning to names, or associate meanings, or senses, with them. Rather, a baby is born (or as Kripke says, "Someone, let's say a baby, is born . . ."), a name is assigned and subsequently used, and the name thereby becomes public currency in the community as a name for this individual. One speaker picks up the name from another, and so later users of the name are connected by a "historical chain of communication" with the referent. Later users, though, may know very little of the actual properties of the referent. Indeed, their beliefs about the referent may be substantially mistaken. God, to return to Wittgenstein's metaphor, in her efforts to find the referent, will look, not into the head of the speaker, but rather at the role of this name in the public practice, specifically at the historical chain of communication.[3]

It is usually supposed that contemporary anti-Fregeans and Wittgenstein, insofar as they make contact at all, occupy fundamentally opposed positions. Notice, though, that the anti-Fregean approach to proper names sketched above provides a relatively painless grasp of Wittgenstein's idea, elusive as it has seemed, that significance is a matter of embeddedness in practice. Nor does aid flow only in one direction. Wittgenstein provides, perhaps even more significantly and certainly more surprisingly, a larger (dare I say) theoretical perspective on anti-Fregean insights about language. Although anti-representationalist tendencies are present, albeit scattered, in the works of leading anti-Fregeans, they are never attended to with sufficient care, nor considered in a sustained way.

I believe that embedding the insights of contemporary anti-Fregeans in a larger social practice conception pays great dividends. Whether or not I am right about the dividends, things certainly look very different from the vantage point of such a larger perspective. It was not until relatively late that I came to occupy such a vantage point. The beginnings of my own transition can be found in "How to Bridge the Gap Between Meaning and Reference," a paper in which I began to sort out the differences between my own approach and those of my fellow anti-Fregean travelers. In "Has Semantics Rested on a Mistake?" I explore what I now see as a hallmark of the new outlook, a different way of thinking about the task of semantics. I review this latter conception of the semantic enterprise and contrast it with the more traditional, Frege-inspired conception, in "Cognitive Significance Without Cognitive Content," a paper in which the larger perspective of which I have been speaking becomes explicit.

Wittgenstein maintained that philosophical problems, at least some of them, require not solution but dissolution. A dark reading of this, encouraged by Wittgenstein in his darker moments, amounts to an indictment of philosophy, the idea that there is virtually no positive philosophical work worth doing. A very different reading is also encouraged by Wittgenstein: philosophical puzzles, at least some of them, bespeak the grip on us of inadequate pictures of domains under investigation. Given an inadequate, constricting picture, philosophers twist and turn to find solutions to the puzzles as posed. What is needed, at least in such cases, is not new, more ingenious solutions but the replacement of the constricting overall conception by a more adequate one.[4] The new picture, in reconceptualizing the domain in a more natural fashion, may not yield anything that can be called *a solution* to the puzzle. Yet the puzzle disappears, in the sense that the phenomena seem to fall into place and cease to confound in the old ways.

I suggested above that contemporary anti-Fregean philosophy of language looks very different when seen, as it usually is, as a series of incursions into Frege's home territory than it does when set in a larger social practice perspective. Here is what I have in mind. It is generally allowed that anti-Fregeans have offered telling criticisms of the traditional views of Frege (and Russell), particularly as those views bear on actual linguistic practice. Defenders of a broadly Fregean outlook allege, however, that the anti-Fregean orientation is ill equipped to handle any number of crucial puzzles that are central for philosophical semantics. These puzzles concern the "cognitive significance of language," the most famous being Frege's famous puzzle about informative identities. Anti-Fregeans typically respond by accepting the challenge to provide solutions to the puzzles, solutions that proceed by invoking various pieces of apparatus that mimic the behavior of the rejected Fregean apparatus. It is precisely here that Wittgenstein's dissolution point, in its more positive—less dark—guise, can be brought to bear.

My thesis is that when we reconceptualize the domain along the lines I am suggesting, what has been taken to be *the* challenge falls away. Frege's perspective, as I argue in "Has Semantics Rested on a Mistake?" imposes upon us a distinctive and controversial way of thinking about semantics, specifically about the centrality of cognitive significance puzzles for semantics. Freed from Frege's perspective, we will, I contend, no longer find it natural to think about semantics in this way. And so it will no longer seem a decisive objection to the anti-Fregean semantical work that no immediate solution to the cognitive significance puzzles falls out of that work.

There is, though, an even more important application of the Wittgenstein dissolution idea, an even more important way in which the challenge from cognitive significance falls away: it is not at all clear that there really are the puzzles that there have been thought to be, that the phenomena in question are puzzling in the ways they have been taken to be. This sounds too good to be true. Indeed, when I first realized that the new perspective obviates the need for the sort of solution we anti-Fregeans had been seeking, it seemed to me that something in my thinking must have gone very wrong. I believe that this is a case where with the help of a more adequate picture, we can reconceptualize the domain in a more natural fashion. What emerges is not *a solution* to the puzzle, but the formerly puzzling phenomena are well understood and the puzzle disappears. So I argue, at least for the most famous of the cognitive significance puzzles, Frege's famous puzzle about informative identities. (See "Cognitive Significance Without Cognitive Content" and "Turning the Tables on Frege.") I believe that the same sort of point holds for the other renowned puzzles, for example, those concerning substitutivity and belief reports, empty names, and negative existentials. Each of these needs detailed treatment. It would be more than enough, though, if I am able to convince you of the thesis in the case of Frege's puzzle about informative identities.[5]

ONE

Can What Is Asserted Be a Sentence?

IN DISCUSSING the question of what it is that has a truth-value, philosophers have often gone to great lengths to avoid assuming that propositions exist, that is, that there are abstract entities which are "expressed" by sentences (or by utterances of sentences) but which are not themselves part of any language. One might want to avoid such an assumption for any of a host of reasons: because propositions are *abstract* entities, or because their identity conditions are unclear, or because their assumption is not necessary for an adequate semantical account of a language. At the same time it seems quite plausible that *what a person asserts* is what can properly be said to be true or false.[1] Those who hope to make do without propositions need not deny that things asserted are the truth-bearers; a natural move on their behalf would be to claim that what a person asserts is nothing other than a sentence.[2] In this paper I hope to make a contribution to the perennial problem of the nature of the bearers of truth and falsity. I will do this by laying to rest the claim that sentences are what we assert.[3]

It may seem natural for those tempted to identify things asserted and sentences to take *the sentence a speaker utters* to be what he asserts. But that cannot, in general, be the case. For one

Reprinted by permission from *The Philosophical Review* 85, no. 2 (April 1976): 196–207.

thing, the same sentence[4] may be used to assert many different things. Hence it cannot be that what each of the speakers (who assertively utter some sentence) assert is identical to the (single) sentence which they all utter. For another, *different* sentences may be used to assert the *same* thing; hence the *one* thing asserted cannot be identical to *each* of the *nonidentical* sentences uttered in asserting it.

Richard Cartwright, in "Propositions," has pointed out that these two arguments are often thought to show more than they actually do. They do show that it is false that, in general, what a speaker asserts is the sentence he utters. They do not show that no one ever asserts what he utters. With respect to the first argument mentioned above, given that the same sentence can be used to assert different things, it does follow that the single sentence in question cannot be identical to *more than one* of the things asserted; it does not follow, however, that the single sentence is not identical to any of the things asserted. Similarly with regard to the second argument, given that one thing was asserted by the use of different sentences, it surely follows that what was asserted cannot be identical to more than one of the sentences uttered. Still, what was asserted *can* be identical to one of those sentences.

Thus what needs to be shown is that, with respect to the first argument, the single sentence uttered could not be identical to even one of the things asserted and, with respect to the second argument, it could not be that even one of the sentences is identical to the thing asserted.[5] (In what follows I will deal only with the second argument, though what I have to say is applicable to the first as well.)

Consider the hypothesis that one of the sentences usable to assert something *is identical to* the thing asserted.[6] If this were true, then the single sentence which *is* identical to what is asserted would presumably have to have something about it which distinguishes it from all the other sentences which could be used to make that assertion. Furthermore, the distinguishing feature(s) would have to be such that the possession of this feature by the sentence in question gives us a reason to take *this* sentence and not some other to be the thing asserted. Of course, it is logically possible that there is no such distinguishing feature of any sentence (the possession of which would give us grounds for singling out *that* sentence as identical to the thing asserted) and that nevertheless one of the sentences is, *as a matter of brute fact*, identical to what is asserted. But surely it is absurd to suppose that of all the sentences which could be used to assert that, for example, Gerald Ford is President, one and only one of those sentences is, as a matter of brute fact, identical to that which is asserted, and yet there is *nothing* about that sentence which indicates that it and not one of the other sentences is the thing asserted. I do not have an argument to show that this logical possibility may be discounted. It seems obvious, however, that *if* one of the sentences really is the thing asserted, there must be some reason for its being so privileged.

What could possibly be a reason for distinguishing one such sentence? It might be urged that eternal sentences are likely candidates for things asserted since they have the relevant feature of being *complete formulations*. Imagine a number of speakers all of whom assert that Gerald Ford is President but each of whom utters a different sentence. One utters, "He is President," a second utters, "The man at the podium is President," and a third utters, "Gerald Ford is President of the United States on August 23, 1975."[7] While each of the speakers asserted the same thing, *only the sentence uttered by the last speaker*, it might be claimed, "completely expresses" this or puts it into words. Accordingly, it might seem plausible to take this sentence as the thing asserted.

The feature of completeness of formulation, however, fails to supply us with a single sentence per thing asserted. For anything assertible there is *more than one* eternal sentence, that is, more than one "complete formulation," which can be used to assert it. First, eternal sentences often include information (for example, spatial, temporal) not explicit in those non-eternal sentences which can be used to assert the same thing. This information can be included at the beginning of the sentence, the end, and so on. Each different ordering clearly yields a different (but equivalent) sentence. Second, given some eternal sentence, we can often generate an eternal sentence which can be used to assert the same thing by altering the grammatical structure, by, for example, changing from active to passive construction. Third, there can be eternal sentences of different languages, the utterance of which issue in the same thing asserted. Accordingly, completeness of formulation, although an intuitively plausible candidate for the discriminating characteristic for which we are searching, will not suffice.

Moreover, it is difficult to see how the ways in which (eternal)[8] sentences differ from one another could possibly be grounds for picking one of them as the thing asserted. Think of the many eternal sentences "corresponding to" some thing asserted, and consider some of the ways in which these sentences differ from one another. Some will be in English, some in French, and some will have an active construction, some passive, and so on. It certainly appears to be the case that these kinds of differences are irrelevant for the purposes considered here. Accordingly, Cartwright, although he apparently does not think that the line of reasoning which I am employing is conclusive, states that "if we sought to identify the statement made with one of these complete sentences[9] we should have absolutely no reason for picking one of them rather than any other. None is in any way a more natural or reasonable choice than any other."[10]

Furthermore, *even if it were possible* to identify other features which were plausible candidates for distinguishing features, still it *could not* be the case that exactly one sentence per thing asserted had such features. Let us imagine that we discover some feature F of certain eternal sentences which seems to us to be a plausible candidate. Let us further imagine that for each thing asserted, one and only one of the *currently available* formulations has the property F. Even so, for each eternal sentence which had F we could always formulate another sentence which had F but which differed only in vocabulary from the currently available one. The idea is that the relevant property could not be the particular words used. So we could always invent a new sentence which contained different words—new ones—but which had the same relevant feature.

I conclude that there are no such features possessed by exactly one sentence per thing asserted, the possession of which would make it plausible to single out that sentence as the thing asserted. But if one of those sentences really was the thing asserted, then, as stated before, there would be something about it which would give us grounds for singling it out as the thing asserted. It follows that none of the eternal (or, for that matter, non-eternal) sentences which can be used to make an assertion is identical to what is asserted.

If the foregoing is correct, then we must distinguish, in every act of assertion, between the sentence uttered and what is asserted; what is asserted is in no case the sentence uttered. Furthermore, we can now arrive at the (stronger) conclusion that what one asserts is not any sentence (neither the one uttered nor any other), for we have seen that what someone asserts could not be identical to any of the sentences which could be used to assert it. It follows that what one asserts could be a sentence only if it were a sentence which could not be used to assert it. But surely this is absurd. What is asserted surely is not identical to a sentence which could not be used to make that assertion.

Cartwright's own attempt to show that what is asserted is in no case a sentence proceeds along rather different lines. He points out that *if* it were the case that only one of the speakers (call him *A*) asserted what he uttered, then since all the speakers asserted the same thing, it follows that each speaker asserted what *A* asserted, which is, *ex hypothesi*, *A*'s sentence. Thus, on the hypothesis that only one of the speakers asserted the sentence that he uttered, we get the consequence that each of the other speakers asserted a sentence which he did not even utter. And this consequence Cartwright thinks is absurd.

It seems to me, on the contrary, that if we could not show independently of Cartwright's approach that sentences are not what we assert, then it would not be absurd to suppose that someone could assert a sentence without uttering it. The following view would seem, at least prima facie, quite plausible if we could not show that, for example, eternal sentences are not what we assert. While what we utter are, for the most part, non-eternal sentences, what we assert are the "eternal sentence counterparts"[11] of the uttered sentences. When we happen to utter an eternal sentence, what we assert may indeed be identified with what we utter. And when we utter a non-eternal sentence, what we assert *is* a sentence other than the one uttered; that is, we assert the corresponding eternal sentence. Such a view has plausibility because the eternal sentence counterparts *more completely formulate* what we assert than do our uttered sentences.

If Cartwright were correct in his absurdity claim, then it should seem patently unacceptable to suppose that in uttering a non-eternal sentence, what one asserts is an eternal sentence *simply because* the sentence uttered was not the eternal sentence supposedly asserted. In fact, contra Cartwright, it seems intuitively appealing to suppose that in uttering a non-eternal sentence what is asserted is the eternal sentence which more fully formulates what was incompletely formulated by the non-eternal sentence.[12]

Cartwright was aware of the line of reasoning I have employed as an alternative to his:

> If we sought to identify the statement made with one of these complete sentences, we should have absolutely no reason for picking one of them rather than any other. None is in any way a more natural or reasonable choice than any other. I take it that this consideration by itself will appear to some to be sufficient reason for refusing to identify the statement made with any of the (complete) sentences which can be used to assert it. It cannot be a perfectly arbitrary manner, they will say, which, if any, of a number of *distinct* things is identical to some *one* thing.
> This move is one of a kind which is familiar in philosophy and with which I feel a good deal of sympathy. Yet, I doubt whether by *themselves* arguments of this sort ever accomplish much.[13]

Cartwright explains why he takes the argument to be inconclusive via an analogy between the natural numbers and "statements" (things asserted).

> Peano's axioms evidently do embody at least some of the features of the natural numbers; and they are in addition categorical, that is, any two models are isomorphic. Some have accordingly been led to say that the concept of a natural number is adequately represented by those axioms; and they have gone on to conclude that that concept is insufficiently determinate to permit a reasonable identification of the system of natural numbers with one rather than another of the various distinct (but isomorphic) models. Each, they say, may quite legitimately be "taken as" the system of natural numbers. The concept of a natural number might, on this view, be said to be *open*, in the sense that distinct sets of things may equally legitimately be identified as the set of natural numbers. Now anyone who proposed to identify statements with some set of representative sentences is presumably prepared to say that the concept of statement is, similarly, open.[14]

Cartwright's point is that someone may argue as follows:

(1) We can formulate a set of conditions which play a role with respect to the concept of thing asserted analogous to the role of Peano's axioms with respect to the concept of a natural number.

(2) Sentences do satisfy those conditions; that is, such conditions do not exclude sentences as things asserted.
(3) Those conditions are not such as to specify which particular sentence is the thing asserted for any particular assertive utterance.

Given (1), (2), and (3), it would be reasonable to select one eternal sentence for each thing asserted and "take that as" the thing asserted. Yet *ex hypothesi,* there is nothing that dictates which eternal sentence we are to choose (for each thing asserted). Indeed, any number of sets of eternal sentences may legitimately be "taken as" the things asserted.

Cartwright does not claim, however, that the concept of thing asserted is "open." Rather, his point is that before one can disqualify eternal sentences as things asserted, one must *first show* that the concept of thing asserted is not open. I have not shown this, hence I have, according to Cartwright, begged a crucial question. If this *is* Cartwright's objection, then I do not think he is correct, for I think that my line of reasoning is entirely neutral with respect to the question of whether the concept is open.

In order to see that this is so, let us take a somewhat closer look at the notion of an "open" concept. When the claim is made that a concept is open, the point being made is that although the term in question, 'the natural numbers' or 'what is asserted', for example, "purports" to designate some unique entity (set of entities), when necessary and sufficient conditions for a correct account of the entity in question are specified, it turns out that there is not one but several (sometimes infinitely many) different accounts, each of which satisfies the conditions specified.

For example, Cartwright makes reference to the view that the concept of a natural number is open since (1) that concept is "adequately represented" by Peano's axioms, that is, satisfaction of the axioms by the entities specified in an account is a necessary and sufficient condition for a correct account, and yet (2) there exist different sets of entities each of which satisfies the axioms.

Paul Benacerraf, in "What Numbers Could Not Be," agrees that the concept of natural number is open but presents a different *analysis* of the concept. Benacerraf argues that the following conditions are necessary and sufficient for any correct account of the natural numbers: (1) definitions of "1," "number," and "successor," as well as "+," "×," and so on, must be provided on the basis of which the laws of arithmetic could be derived and (2) an explanation of the "extra-mathematical" uses of number, for example, in counting and measurement, must be provided. Benacerraf points out that even given such conditions, infinitely many different set-theoretic accounts may be given, each of which satisfies these conditions. Furthermore, these accounts are not even extensionally equivalent, for each takes the natural number series to be a different set of sets.

Assuming that the conditions stated by, for example, Benacerraf are really necessary and *sufficient* for a correct account of the natural numbers, what ought we to say about the correctness of any of the competing set-theoretic accounts of the numbers? It seems clear that if the conditions stated really are sufficient, then every one of the contending accounts has as much claim to being considered *the* correct account as every other. However, *not more than one* of these accounts can be uniquely correct. That is, not more than one of these can correctly specify which set of sets the numbers *really are*, for, as Benacerraf points out, "if the number 3 is in fact some particular set b, it cannot be that two correct accounts of the meaning of 3—and therefore also of its reference—assign two different sets to 3. For if it is true that for some set b, $3 = b$, then it cannot be true that for some set c, different from b, $3 = c$."[15]

At this point the following question might be raised: is it possible that one of these accounts is, in fact, the uniquely correct one but that there is no argument which could show it to be so? In other words, is it possible that the numbers are really some particular set of sets but that no reason could ever be given for singling out that set as the set of natural numbers? Benacerraf rejects such a possibility as absurd (and I concur).[16] If the numbers are really one particular set of sets, then it must be that there is something about that particular set which distinguishes it from the other contenders and which would give us grounds to single it out as the set of natural numbers.

We have seen that *at most* one of the competing accounts can be *the* correct one and further that *if* one is the correct one, then there must be some reason for singling it out. But *if* the conditions stated really are sufficient for a correct account, then it cannot be that *even* one of the accounts is *the* correct one. For if one were uniquely correct, then that set of sets (specified in the correct account) would have had some distinguishing feature which would have furnished us with a reason for selecting that set as the set of natural numbers. But that distinguishing feature would then necessarily find itself in our list of conditions which are sufficient for any correct account of the natural numbers. Thus if our conditions, for example, those stated by Benacerraf, *were* sufficient, it would follow that there is no such discriminating feature. In short, none of the accounts is uniquely correct. That is, none specifies that set of sets which is, in fact, identical to the natural numbers.

If the preceding line of reasoning is correct, then it would seem that if a concept is open, there will always be competing accounts all of which satisfy the necessary and sufficient conditions for being a correct account but none of which is the uniquely correct account. That is, none of the accounts specify that entity which is, as a matter of fact, the referent of the term in question.

I argued previously that what someone asserts could not be identical with *any* of the sentences which could be used to assert it. Cartwright would counter (apparently) that my argument presupposed that the concept of *thing asserted* was not open. That is, if the concept *was* open in such a way that among the competing accounts of the concept of *the thing asserted* were accounts each of which specified a different set of eternal sentences, then my argument would fail. But if the concept of thing asserted *is* open in the respect in question, then each of these competing accounts fails to be uniquely correct. Hence what someone asserts is not identical to any of the sentences in question.

To recapitulate, the line of reasoning by which I attempted to show that what someone asserts could not be identical with any sentence was entirely neutral with respect to the question of whether the concept of *the thing asserted* is open. I surely did not assume it was open. But even if it turns out that the concept is an open one, the same conclusion follows.

In the foregoing I have assumed that Cartwright's objection to my line of reasoning was that my argument presupposed that the concept of thing asserted was not open. It seems to me, however, that Cartwright may have had something different in mind.

I will now explore an alternative account of what Cartwright's objection really was and try to see whether there is, in the end, any disagreement between his point and what I have been arguing for.

It should be clear that one who takes the concept of, for example, a natural number, to be open and goes on "to conclude that the concept is insufficiently determinate to permit a reasonable identification of the system of natural numbers with one rather than another of the various distinct (but isomorphic) models"[17] is not one who is likely (to say the least) to claim to have *discovered* which set is really the set of natural numbers. Accordingly (as Benacerraf points out),[18] when someone chooses to "identify" the numbers with one particular model, he is not claiming to have discovered which set the numbers really were all along. Similarly, when someone claims that each of the models "may quite legitimately be 'taken as' the system of natural numbers,"[19] he is not making the (absurd) claim that each of the models is identical to the natural numbers[20] but "explicating" the concept of a natural number. To "identify" the numbers with some particular set of sets is to take that particular set of sets as "natural number surrogates" for some particular purpose. Indeed, one may "identify" the numbers with different sets of sets for different purposes. Without giving any precise account of explication, one can still say that to explicate, for example, the natural number series in terms of some particular set is not to claim that the numbers are "identical" to that set.

We should, therefore, clearly distinguish two similar-sounding but radically different claims: (1) the natural numbers are identical to some particular set of sets (or what someone asserts is identical to some particular sentence), and (2) the natural numbers may be *identified with* (that is, explicated in terms of) some particular set of sets (or what someone asserts may be identified with some particular sentence).[21]

Returning to Cartwright's discussion of the openness of concepts, we can say that if the concept of thing asserted is indeed open, then things asserted are of a kind with natural numbers (on the view of natural numbers we have been considering) and various explications might be expected.[22] If one were to believe that the concept of the thing asserted is open and were to proceed to identify things asserted with some set of eternal sentences, one would not be claiming to have discovered which sentence was really the one asserted on any given occasion or even that what we really assert are sentences. Thus *if* the concept of the thing asserted is open, we may end up after all with arbitrarily chosen *representative eternal sentences* as *things asserted* (more accurately, as *surrogates* for things asserted) and thus as truth-bearers.

It may be that Cartwright's point was not that the line of reasoning I employed fails to show that things asserted are not *identical* to sentences. His point may be that since I did not argue that the concept is not open, my argument was not sufficient to show that we do not end up with eternal sentences as surrogates for things asserted (and thus as truth-bearers). If this was his point, I fully agree. My claim was only that what someone asserts is never *identical* with a sentence. And this point is correct whether or not the concept is open. Of course, if the concept is open, explication is a natural move, and then it may be that we would want to *identify* what someone asserts with some eternal sentence. But that is another matter.[23]

TWO

Indexical Reference and Propositional Content

THE QUESTION of whether proper names have sense (alternatively, are equivalent to definite descriptions) or whether, on the contrary, they are "purely denotative" has recently received a great deal of attention. What is really at issue is a more general, more fundamental topic: singular reference. The debate over whether names have sense is motivated by conflicting paradigms of singular reference.

On Fregean accounts, a definite description, say, 'the first prime number', is a model referring expression, a paradigm referring expression. An object is referred to in virtue of its possessing uniquely the properties specified in the description. Reference, on Frege's view, is thus impossible without *sense*; and if we do refer by our utterances of proper names, which we surely do, then such names *must* possess sense or descriptive content.[1]

On John Stuart Mill's alternative view, a view developed by Saul Kripke and Keith Donnellan, a proper name is thought of as devoid of sense or descriptive content. Reference is achieved by an utterance of a proper name but not by the specification of properties uniquely possessed by one's intended referent. Reference, on this view, is thought of, not on the model of *describing*, but on the model of *pointing*. As Ruth Barcan Marcus puts it, proper names are "the long finger of ostension."[2]

Reprinted by permission from *Philosophical Studies* 36 (1979): 91–100. Copyright 1979 by D. Reidel Publishing Co.

In this paper I shall defend an account of indexical expressions which sides with Mill against Frege with regard to its model of singular reference. I shall begin with an examination of considerations which militate against the view I wish to defend.

Frege, in his discussion of sentences containing indexical expressions and/or tensed verbs, states: "The mere wording, as it is given in writing, is not the complete expression of the thought, but the knowledge of certain accompanying conditions of utterance, which are used as a means of expressing the thought, are needed for its correct apprehension."[3] We may express Frege's point by saying that many of the sentences we utter,[4] in particular the non-eternal sentences, fail to make explicit or completely formulate what is asserted by their utterance. When one utters the sentence "He is bald," this sentence does not make explicit, for example, the identity of the referent. By contrast when one utters an eternal sentence, "Gerald Ford is bald on March 27, 1976," or "2 + 2 = 4," the sentence uttered does appear to completely formulate what was asserted.

To say that only eternal sentences make explicit what is asserted is to imply that *what is asserted*, what Frege calls "the thought," is, in an important sense, *complete* and *determinate*; that is, it includes the kind of information which is often not explicit in the sentences we utter but is explicit in eternal sentences. That for Frege, a "thought" *is* complete and determinate emerges particularly clearly in his defense of the thesis that the truth-bearers (Frege's "thoughts") possess truth-values eternally.

> But are there not thoughts which are true today but false in six months time? The thought, for example, that the tree is covered with green leaves, will surely be false in six months time. No, for it is not the same thought at all. The words "this tree is covered with green leaves" are not sufficient by themselves for the utterance; the time of utterance is involved as well. Without the time-indication this gives we have *no complete thought, i.e. no thought at all*. Only a sentence supplemented by a time indication and complete in every respect expresses a thought. But this [the thought expressed], if it is true, is true not only today or tomorrow but timelessly.[5]

According to Frege, we are tempted to think that something can possess one truth-value now and another later because we fail to note that *every thought is necessarily a complete thought*. While the sentence uttered may or may not be "complete," whatever is required for the thought to be a complete one, a time indication or the identification of some individual, for example, must be supplied either by the sentence or in some other way, most notably by the context of utterance, in order for an act of assertion to have been performed at all.

Taking things asserted to be *complete* and eternal sentences to be *complete formulations* might lead one to suppose that when a non-eternal sentence is uttered, what is asserted can, in every case, be completely formulated by some eternal sentence. The idea here is that the information conveyed by the utterance of a non-eternal sentence depends not only on the sentence uttered but also on various features of the context of utterance. But this information can always be explicitly put into words; that is, it can be expressed by a sentence whose assertive utterance in any context, by anyone speaking the language in question, is the assertion of the proposition in question. Such a sentence is, of course, an eternal sentence.

Accordingly, W. V. O. Quine, in *Word and Object*, says that if we want to identify a proposition by explicit elaboration rather than by leaving the matter to circumstances of utterance, we can formulate an eternal sentence.[6] And although I shall not argue it here, Frege himself is committed to just such a view.[7] More recently Jerrold Katz, in his book *Semantic Theory*, endorses what he refers to as "Quine's idea"

> that a [non-eternal sentence] . . . can be expanded on the basis of the information in the context to provide another sentence that . . . always makes the statement in question, no matter what the context of utterance. The expansion consists of replacing each indexical element by an expression that has the same reference as the indexical element . . . but whose referent stays fixed with variations in time, place, speaker, etc. . . . Indexical . . . elements like 'I', 'he', [and] 'it' . . . will be replaced by precise specifications of the individuals or objects.[8]

Katz concludes that "the only alternative to [this view] is . . . a form of mysticism that claims that some things to which we can refer by the use of indexical elements are, in principle, beyond the range of unique description."[9]

Contrary to Frege, Quine, and Katz (among others), there are serious difficulties with this perhaps seemingly unproblematic view. In what follows I shall present two arguments to this effect.

First, it may be the case that someone asserts something by the utterance of a non-eternal sentence but is not in a position to replace the indexical elements and/or tensed verbs in his sentence with what Quine calls more "objective" terms. Consider a speaker who, although ignorant of the date (indeed, he is not certain even of the year), notices the snow falling and says, "It is snowing today." Now an eternal sentence counterpart for his uttered sentence would include, in place of the indexical 'today', an explicit indication of the date, say, "Tuesday, January 5, 1975." But in light of the speaker's ignorance of the date, is it at all plausible to maintain that what he asserted is fully captured or made explicit by some eternal sentence, for example, "It is snowing in Minneapolis on Tuesday, January 5, 1975"? Indeed, it would seem that one uttering this latter sentence would be asserting something different from what our speaker asserted, since this latter sentence makes information explicit which is not even known to our speaker. Accordingly, it would seem mistaken to claim that, in general, what is asserted by an utterance of a non-eternal sentence can be captured by some eternal sentence.

Now imagine a second speaker, talking to the first, who, unlike the first, knows the date. Imagine the second speaker to utter, by way of agreement, "It is snowing today." Does he assert a different proposition than the first speaker? It certainly does not seem obvious that he does. But if he asserts the same thing, then *even* in the case of a speaker who *can* replace all the indexical items in his sentence with "objective terms," it is questionable whether what he asserts can be precisely captured by some eternal sentence.

A second argument: how does one go about formulating an eternal sentence that "corresponds" to some utterance of a non-eternal sentence? Crucial is the replacement of indexical expressions. Now whatever item is picked out by an indexical expression can also be picked out by *various nonsynonymous* nonindexical expressions. Given some utterance of "It is covered with books," made in reference to some table, if we wish to obtain an eternal sentence, we can replace the indexical 'it' with any of several nonsynonymous descriptions, each of which denotes the table in question, for example, 'the table Jones is sitting at, at t_1'', 'the table in room 209 of Camden Hall at t_1'', and so on. Since these descriptions are not synonymous, it would seem that each of the resulting eternal sentences formulates a *different* proposition. The genuine eternal sentence counterpart will be the one that actually formulates the proposition the speaker asserted. But is there clearly one of these eternal sentences that, as opposed to the others, actually formulates what was asserted?

It might be supposed that we can decide by reference to the intention of the speaker which of these eternal sentences captures what was asserted. Surely the speaker, it might be supposed, knows which of these propositions he intended to express. This, however, will not do. In many cases, the speaker will have no such determinate intention. The speaker will often be aware of several descriptions, each of which uniquely picks out his referent, and will not be able to select one of these descriptions as *the correct one*, the one that captures what he meant by his utterance of 'it'. Accordingly, if asked which eternal sentence formulates the proposition he meant to assert, he will not be able to answer.

At this point two different routes might seem possible. First, we might insist that surely one of these eternal sentences formulates what he asserted despite the fact that there is (even for the speaker) no way of deciding which. Second, in light of the fact that there is absolutely no reason to think that any of these (as opposed to any other) is *the* formulation of what he asserts, we might deny that any one of them formulates precisely the proposition he asserted. The first of these alternatives seems to me clearly unacceptable. It is (to say the least) reasonable to suppose that if a single one of these nonequivalent sentences was the correct one, that is, if only it captured precisely what he asserted, there would be something about it which would give us a reason to select it over the others. It appears absurd to suppose that what the speaker asserted is in fact some unique proposition (made explicit by some single one of these eternal sentences) but that it is impossible to find out which proposition it is.[10]

We have noted two kinds of cases in which, it seems, no eternal sentence can plausibly be held to formulate what was asserted by an utterance of a non-eternal sentence. First, there are cases in which the speaker fails to have the requisite knowledge to eternalize his sentence, and second, there are cases in which the context and intentions of the speaker are such that no reason can be given as to why one of a group of *nonsynonymous* eternal sentences is the *genuine* corresponding eternal sentence.

The Fregean idea that what a person asserts is in every case a proposition which is *complete* and *determinate* now appears to be in trouble. With regard to the speaker who was ignorant of the date, our failure to eternalize his sentence with respect to date amounts to an admission that the temporal information was not part of what he asserted, although Frege's idea would seem to necessitate that it was. Similarly, in the case of the utterance of "It is covered with books," Frege's idea would seem to necessitate that one of those eternal sentences does formulate his thought. If every thought is a *complete* thought, if every assertion is the assertion of a fully determinate proposition, then it would seem to be the case that the speaker uttering "It is covered with books" must have expressed what is formulated by one of these eternal sentences.

I think, however, that we can still maintain a *version* of Frege's idea: propositions *are* complete and determinate, although not in the sense that Frege took them to be so. The fact that no eternal sentence counterpart can be found for an utterance of a given sentence is, I wish to argue, compatible with the fact that what was asserted is complete and determinate—complete and determinate in a way that guarantees, for example, eternal possession of truth-value.

Let us begin with the case of the speaker who was ignorant of the date. Granted that he did not assert what is formulated by, say, "It is snowing in Minneapolis on Tuesday, January 5, 1975," what he asserted still has the requisite determinateness. This is so because despite the fact that the speaker did not convey any *descriptive temporal information*, he nevertheless made a *temporal reference*. Thus what he asserted is *determinate* with respect to time.

The fact that what our speaker asserted *is* determinate with respect to time can be seen from the fact that someone uttering those same words at a different time would be asserting something different. But it is a mistake to think that the fact that such a proposition would be different must be accounted for by thinking of some temporally descriptive information as part of what was asserted.

Similar remarks apply to the utterance of "It is covered with books." Granted that there is no eternal sentence which is the genuine corresponding eternal sentence, what was asserted is nevertheless determinate; by the utterance of 'it' in the context in question, the speaker makes a definite reference. The fact that no descriptive phrase has priority over any other as a replacement for 'it' ought not to make us think that there is anything indefinite or indeterminate about what was asserted.

Earlier I quoted Frege to the effect that when uttering a non-eternal sentence, the speaker relies on the context of utterance to, so to speak, complete his thought. But how, precisely, are we to characterize the contribution of the context of utterance to the thought? The answer to this question implicit in the view I have been criticizing is that in using indexical expressions I communicate bits of descriptive identificatory information that are supplied, at least in part, by the context. The alternative I am proposing is that the circumstances of utterance do help to provide us with an identification of a referent, but not by providing some descriptive characterization of it.[11] When one says, "It is covered with books" (e.g. in the conspicuous presence of a table covered with books), the context fails to provide us with some unique characterization of the table; the context does reveal, however, *which item* is in question.

The position that I am criticizing seems natural, I think, given the perspective which views utterances of eternal sentences as *assertion* par excellence. Eternal sentences, it is often said, are the only kind needed for an adequate scientific account of the world. Thus Quine speaks of "purifying the language of science"[12] by banishing indicator words, tense, and so forth in favor of "objective" indication of persons, places, times, and so forth. And Bertrand Russell observes that "no egocentric particulars occur in the language of physics. Physics views space-time impartially, as God might be supposed to view it."[13] Of course, we do sometimes utter non-eternal sentences, for example, "It is covered with books." But in the case of such utterances, the context of utterance can be thought of as taking up the slack; we communicate information which cannot be gleaned from the sentence by relying on various features of the context of utterance.[14] Thus all utterances come to be thought of as amounting to utterances of eternal sentences, and it seems as if anything sayable is sayable via an eternal sentence.

It is undeniable that according to the view of indexicals suggested by this perspective, we can account for some facts that need accounting for. As Frege notes, "If someone wants to say the same today as he expressed yesterday using the word 'today', he must replace this word with 'yesterday'. Although the thought is the same its verbal expression must be different so that the sense, which would otherwise be affected by the differing times of utterance, is readjusted."[15] Now, on the theory of indexicals I have been criticizing, two such speakers assert the same thing just because the first speaker's 'today' and the second speaker's 'yesterday' are, given the different contexts of utterance, different ways of *specifying* the date. Similarly, when I say, "I am tired," and you say to me, "You are tired," the contexts of utterance supply the information not explicit in the sentences. In saying "I am tired," I specify who it is that is tired, just as I might have had I uttered some eternal sentence in which 'I' was replaced by an "objective indication" of my identity.

But whatever the merits of the view in question, if my arguments are correct it will not do as an account of indexical expressions. Moreover, the facts that this account of indexicals can accommodate *can* be accommodated on the view of indexicals that I am advocating. Indeed, I think those facts can be accommodated more naturally. When I say, "I am tired," and you say (to me), "You are tired," we assert the same thing *not* because by my using 'I' and your uttering 'you' we succeed in conveying the same descriptive identificatory information. We "say the same thing" because given the context of utterance, the reference of 'I' and 'you' is the same. We "say the same thing" because we have said (predicated) the same thing of the same item.

I will conclude by drawing attention to the similarity between my view of indexicals and some of Mill's remarks on proper names. Proper names like 'Socrates' are, according to Mill, "not connotative; they denote the individuals who are called by them, but they do not indicate or imply any attribute as belonging to those individuals."[16] Singular terms, as Mill recognized, are, however, often connotative.

Though we may give to an individual a name utterly unmeaning . . . which we call a proper name—a word which answers the purpose of *showing* what thing it is we are talking about, but not of telling anything about it; yet a [term] peculiar to an individual is not necessarily of this description. It may be significant of some attribute or some union of attributes which, being possessed by no object but one, determines the name exclusively to that individual.[17]

Mill contrasts subject-predicate propositions asserted by the use of connotative subject terms with those asserted by the use of nonconnotative subject terms. When the subject term is connotative, for example, a definite description, Mill thinks of the informational content of the subject term as part of what is asserted. "The assertion is . . . that whatever has the attributes connoted by the subject, has also those connoted by the predicate."[18] When the subject term is a proper name, that is, when the subject term has no descriptive content, then there is no descriptive characterization of the referent which *could* be part of what is asserted. Thus Mill says that when the subject term is a proper name "the meaning . . . is that the *individual thing* . . . has the attributes connoted by the predicate."[19] The function of a proper name (when it occurs in the subject position) is exhaustively characterized by noting what individual it is being used to pick out. Similarly, on my view of indexicals, to say "He is bald" of some man is to predicate baldness of some definite entity; the entity in question is picked out by my utterance of 'he', but by my use of this term I do not affirm anything of the referent; what I assert is not that *the thing having characteristics x, y, and z is bald*.

The analogy with Mill might suggest that on my view indexicals do not possess sense or meaning, that they have no informational content. But that is not quite right. I am not *fully* assimilating indexicals to Millian proper names. Indeed, indexicals (at least some indexicals) do have associated descriptive content. This "sense" is what makes a particular indexical an appropriate device for specifying the referent. I may assert of some man that *he* is bald; 'she', possessing a different sense, would not be an appropriate expression.[20] The analogy with Mill pertains rather to the propositional roles of the respective singular terms: indexicals (when they are used in the way under consideration here) are, like Millian proper names, used simply to make certain items subjects of discourse. Whatever sense, meaning, or informational content is possessed by an indexical does not figure in what someone asserts by its use.

THREE

Proper Names and Propositional Opacity

BERTRAND RUSSELL, as is well known, distinguishes between genuine (or logically) proper names and ordinary proper names. The use of a *genuine* proper name, in, for example, the subject position of a subject-predicate sentence, is, as we might say, purely referential; in using it the speaker simply makes some item the subject of discourse without attributing any properties to the item. The use of an ordinary proper name, on the other hand, involves the attribution of properties; ordinary proper names are, on Russell's view, abbreviated definite descriptions, and thus sentences containing them are to be analyzed in accordance with the theory of descriptions. Such analysis reveals, of course, the attributive character of ordinary names.

Hector-Neri Castañeda, in his paper "On the Philosophical Foundations of the Theory of Communication: Reference,"[1] appears to make a similar distinction:

In many of their ordinary uses proper names are abbreviations of definite descriptions.

Yet on some occasions [proper names] are used as genuine names, as means of referring to an entity without attributing to it any property whatsoever.... The point is that on the occasions under consideration, the name is being used without the intention of predicating any property.[2]

In this note, I wish to raise several questions with regard to Castañeda's account of communication via genuine names. Needless to say, one cannot do justice to the richness and complexity of Castañeda's views in a brief note. Nevertheless, I begin with a summary of his views on this matter which will be adequate for my purposes.

Consider an assertive utterance of a subject-predicate sentence. Castañeda holds, with Frege, that the *referent* of the subject term is not a constituent of the proposition expressed. And this is so for Castañeda (as well as, of course, for Frege) whether the subject term is a definite description or a proper name. The subject constituent of the proposition is, in every case, a *sense*, a "mode of presentation" of the referent, as Frege would say. Where, for example, the subject term is a definite description, the subject constituent of the proposition is the *sense* of that description; one who understands the descriptive phrase knows, as Castañeda puts it, what "identifying traits" of the referent are "before the consciousness of the speaker."[3]

If it were the case, as Frege apparently supposed, that an ordinary proper name had the sense of a definite description, then proper names would introduce no special complications into Castañeda's view. But, as noted above, Castañeda allows for a use of ordinary proper names as "genuine names," a use in which no "mode of presentation" of the referent, no information regarding "identifying traits," is conveyed. This raises the following difficulty: since in using a name as a genuine name, no mode of presentation is conveyed, how can such a mode of presentation be the subject constituent of the proposition expressed? Indeed, the thesis that names can be used in this way would seem to militate against a Fregean notion of proposition, for when a name is used and no mode of presentation is conveyed, it would seem natural to hold that what was asserted contains no such mode of presentation as a constituent. Following this line, we might be led to a kind of Russellian conception of a proposition, according to which the referent itself, and not some mode of presentation thereof, is, in some sense, a propositional constituent.[4]

Castañeda insists, however, on a Fregean notion of proposition. But how can such a "Fregean proposition" be expressed via an utterance of a sentence in which a name is used as a genuine name? Castañeda's answer is that indeed no such proposition is expressed when one uses a name in this way. "Communication by means of names does not consist of the revelation of the propositions in one's mind in full, but only of the structure of the propositions and just some of their constituents, for example, the predicated properties."[5] In other words, in assertively uttering a sentence such as "John was born on March 23, 1976" (let us assume that the name is being used as a genuine name), the speaker has such a Fregean proposition in mind but fails to fully reveal that proposition. He fails to fully reveal the proposition he has in mind because by his use of the name, he fails to reveal the *subject constituent* of the proposition; he fails to reveal, that is, the identifying traits of the referent that are "before his consciousness." Castañeda's idea here is that the speaker may characteristically think of the referent under a host of different identifying descriptions. The speaker's use of the name on a particular occasion does not reveal to the listener which identifying traits are the operative ones in the instance in question. As Castañeda puts it, the listener "can at most only guess as to what identifying traits of the [person] in question are before [the] consciousness [of the speaker]; the name does not reveal them to him. . . . The name . . . is propositionally opaque."[6]

If the name does not reveal the "identifying traits" in question, what is its semantic function? Castañeda's use of the term "genuine name," as well as some of the things he says about genuine names quoted earlier, suggest that his view is that the semantic function of the name is simply to refer, to make some item a subject of discourse without announcing the identifying traits under which it is being referred to; the name reveals merely the referent and not any "mode of presentation" thereof. This is quite clearly, however, not Castañeda's view of the matter. Indeed, he denies that the name *has* a semantic function. His idea is that *literally nothing* is revealed, *nothing* is communicated, by such a use of a name. The name merely marks or "signal[s] . . . the subject position of the proposition before [the] consciousness [of the speaker]."[7] This may, I think, be put as follows: a sentence containing a name is to be thought of on the analogy of an open sentence; the name is, from the point of view of its semantics, like a free variable—it merely marks the subject position.

How, then, is any communication via names possible? We certainly do communicate information via utterances of sentences like the one mentioned above. Castañeda's answer is that although a genuine name has no *semantic* role, it has a *causal* role. A speaker uses a name so as to cause his hearer to apprehend propositions about the person the speaker has in mind. The proposition that the hearer apprehends may, of course, be quite different from the one the speaker had in mind, since the traits under which the hearer identifies the referent may be quite different from those under which the speaker referred. Nevertheless, the communication is successful if the hearer apprehends a proposition about the right person.[8] The name, then, is to be thought of as a kind of triggering device; its utterance (in the right circumstances) causes the speaker to apprehend a proposition of the appropriate kind.

This is a rough sketch of Castañeda's view on the matter of communication via genuine names. In what follows I will raise two questions concerning this view. I will first discuss the bearing on Castañeda's view of the Donnellan-Kripke "causal theory of names," and second, offer an objection of my own.

1. From Castañeda's acknowledgment of a use of names as "genuine names," it might have appeared that he radically departs from the classical "sense" view of proper names, that is, the view that a proper name has the sense of a definite description. It now appears that there is no such radical departure—at least, there is a good deal in common. For the sort of proposition which, on the "sense view," gets asserted via an utterance of a proper name (a proposition which contains a "mode of presentation" of the referent as a subject constituent) is, for Castañeda, just the sort of proposition which is "before the consciousness" of the speaker when he uses a name as a genuine name.

Such "sense theories" have been criticized in recent years, most notably by Keith Donnellan and Saul Kripke. A main line of their argument has been that in using a proper name, successful reference is possible even when the speaker fails to possess any correct (uniquely) identifying characterization of the referent. Thus I can refer to α, assert and apprehend propositions about α, even though I do not possess a single, correct identifying description of α.

The Donnellan-Kripke account, if correct, is telling not only against a "sense theory" of proper names but also against Castañeda's view. On his view, as we have seen, the proposition in the mind of the speaker when he uses a proper name always contains a "mode of presentation" of the referent as a subject constituent, whereas if the Donnellan-Kripke account is correct, the speaker might not be in possession of any such identifying characterization which could be such a subject constituent.[9]

2. I will conclude by raising a further question about Castañeda's view of communication via genuine names. When using a name as a genuine name, the speaker, on Castañeda's view, fails to fully reveal the proposition he has in mind. Were he to fully reveal that proposition, he would use some other device in place of the name, one which would reveal the subject constituent of the proposition, for example, a definite description.[10] If Castañeda were correct, we would expect that if called upon to do so, the speaker could always tell us which proposition he had in mind. That is, he could produce a sentence which reveals precisely the (Fregean) proposition he was thinking. But this, or so it seems to me, is just what a speaker often cannot do. Consider an assertive utterance of "John was born on March 23, 1976." If the speaker knows enough about John, he will possess several (nonequivalent) unique characterizations of him. He may think of John as, for example, his best friend, his wife's brother, the best mathematician at Yale, and in countless other ways. For each replacement of the name 'John' in the uttered sentence by such a characterization (or by a conjunction of such characterizations) we obtain a sentence which formulates a different proposition.[11] This is so, of course, because the subject term in each of the resulting sentences picks out the referent via a different identifying trait (or set thereof). Now if the speaker is asked which of these sentences formulates the proposition he had in mind, he will often be unable to select some one sentence as *the* correct one. "Although I meant to refer to John," our speaker might well reply, "I don't think I meant to refer to him *as* my best friend, as opposed to, say, *as* my wife's brother. Nor did I intend to refer to him *as* my best friend *and* my wife's brother as opposed to, say, just *as* my best friend." If this response is one that we are likely to get, then we cannot suppose that the speaker had a Fregean proposition "before his consciousness."

Castañeda might at this point insist that the speaker *must have* thought of John under some characterization or other (otherwise, what makes his thought a thought about this person and not somebody else?). But whatever the merits of such a move, it would have the unfortunate consequence of making the proposition which is "before the consciousness" of the speaker unknown *even to the speaker*.

FOUR

Demonstrative Reference and Definite Descriptions

THE FREGEAN (or, more generally, descriptional) conception of singular reference, according to which an object is referred to in virtue of its unique possession of the properties associated with the referring expression, has, in the recent literature, been criticized by proponents of an opposing conception inspired by John Stuart Mill's remarks on proper names. Singular reference, on the Millian view, is thought of not on the model of *describing* but on the model of *pointing*.[1]

In "Indexical Reference and Propositional Content" (in this volume) I defended an account of reference by the use of indexical expressions, an account which sides with Mill against Gottlob Frege with regard to its model of singular reference. In this paper I shall extend the analysis to definite descriptions. I shall, in effect, be defending some theses of P. F. Strawson and Keith Donnellan as against Bertrand Russell's theory of descriptions. Indeed, my argument purports to establish a distinction between referential and attributive uses of definite descriptions, a distinction made famous by Donnellan.[2] The version of this distinction I wish to defend, and my argument in defense of it, differ, however, in crucial respects from Donnellan's. My account preserves the intuitive appeal of Donnellan's distinction, while it is, as I shall show, immune to a recent powerful objection.

Reprinted by permission from *Philosophical Studies* 40 (1981): 241–57. Copyright 1981 by D. Reidel Publishing Co.

An Amended Referential-Attributive Distinction

What is the distinction between referential and attributive uses of definite descriptions? Consider the referential use: there are contexts in which a speaker wishes to draw his audience's attention to an entity, perhaps one visually present to both speaker and audience, in order to go on and, for example, predicate something of it. It is irrelevant to the purposes of the speaker, in many such cases, how the attention of the audience is directed to the referent. Pointing with one's finger or uttering a demonstrative or proper name would do as well as some elaborate description. When a definite description is used in such a context, when it is used "referentially," it is, Donnellan says, "merely one tool for doing a certain job—calling attention to a person or thing—and in general any other device for doing the same job, another description or name, would do as well." By contrast, when a description is used attributively, "the definite description might be said to occur essentially, for the speaker wishes to speak about *whatever or whoever fits that description.*"[3]

To illustrate this distinction, in the case of a single sentence, consider the sentence, "Smith's murderer is insane." Suppose first that [a detective] come[s] upon poor Smith foully murdered. [He] might exclaim, "Smith's murderer is insane." I will assume . . . that . . . [he] does not know who murdered Smith (though this is not in the end essential to the case).[4] This, I shall say, is an attributive use of the definite description.

[By contrast, consider a situation] in which we expect and intend our audience to realize whom we have in mind when we speak of Smith's murderer and, most importantly, to know that it is this person about whom we are going to say something.

For example, suppose that Jones has been charged with Smith's murder and has been placed on trial. Imagine that there is a discussion of Jones's odd behavior at his trial. We might sum up our impression of his behavior by saying, "Smith's murderer is insane." If someone asks to whom we are referring by using this description, the answer here is "Jones." This, I shall say, is a referential use of the definite description.[5]

In the foregoing preliminary sketch of the distinction, I have, by design, failed to mention a supposed feature of referential use which is focal for both Donnellan and his critics. Donnellan maintains that the difference between the two uses of descriptions can be brought out by considering the consequences of the assumption that the definite description used fits nothing. Let us assume, then, that Smith was not murdered. If one says, "Smith's murderer is insane," using the description attributively (the detective case), then, depending on whether we adopt Russell's approach or Strawson's, we will say either that the statement made was false or that it has no truth-value.[6] If, however, we are using the description referentially (the courtroom case), then

> where the definite description is simply a means of identifying the person we want to talk about, it is quite possible for a correct identification to be made even though no one fits the description used. We were speaking about Jones even though he is not in fact Smith's murderer and, in the circumstances imagined, it was his behavior we were commenting upon. Jones might, for example, accuse us of saying false things of him in calling him insane, and it would be no defense, I should think, that our description, "the murderer of Smith," failed to fit him.[7]

Donnellan's view is that "using a definite description referentially, a speaker may *say something true* even though the description applies to nothing."[8]

Critics of Donnellan's distinction have often focused their attacks on the supposed feature of referential use just discussed. David Wiggins has argued that the distinction is flawed in that "Donnellan's [account] . . . depends on the, for me, incredible idea that if I say 'The man drinking champagne is F' and the man I mean, though drinking water, is F, then *what I say is true*. (To say that the idea is not credible is not to say that F is not true of the man I mean.)"[9] Essentially the same point is made by Michael Lockwood:

> The question here is whether a name or definite description is required actually to apply to an individual in order to serve as a means of making that individual a subject of assertion. Donnellan holds that it is not— that a speaker can be said to have made a statement about an object he has in mind, in uttering a referring expression, even if it fails to qualify as what Kripke calls "the semantic referent"[10] of the term in question. But it seems to me that Donnellan is here quite unnecessarily riding roughshod over the common-sense distinction between what a speaker means and what he actually succeeds in saying . . . genuine assertion (as opposed, say, to successful communication) calls, it seems to me, for a convergence between words and intention which, in the sort of case we are considering, is *ex hypothesi* lacking.[11]

My own inclination, at least for present purposes, is to sidestep this controversy, for it is clear that we need not decide this dispute in favor of Donnellan in order to preserve a referential-attributive distinction.[12]

There are two distinguishable issues here. First, can a description (or proper name, for that matter)[13] be used to refer to an item to which it does not apply? If I say, "Smith's murderer is insane," while observing Jones's odd behavior in the courtroom and if Jones is not Smith's murderer, have I succeeded in asserting the true proposition that Jones is insane? Donnellan thinks that I have succeeded in asserting this proposition, Lockwood and Wiggins hold that it is a necessary condition for referring to something that the expression used conventionally applies to the thing in question. A second question is this: is there a distinction to be drawn between referential and attributive uses of descriptions? Let us assume that Wiggins and Lockwood are correct: a description (or name) cannot be used to refer to an item to which it does not conventionally apply. This surely does not *preclude* a referential-attributive distinction, for we can still distinguish between cases in which a description, for example, 'Smith's murderer', is used to refer to some particular individual the speaker has in mind (in which case the speaker succeeds in so referring, according to Wiggins and Lockwood, *only if* the item is the murderer of Smith) and cases in which the description may be paraphrased as 'whoever murdered Smith'. Thus even if Wiggins and Lockwood are correct and Donnellan wrong, nothing follows about the existence of a referential-attributive distinction.

Donnellan does himself a disservice in claiming that the referential-attributive distinction can best be brought out by considering cases in which the description fits nothing. These cases are controversial, but to rule against Donnellan with respect to them is not to rule against the referential-attributive distinction. Donnellan's making such cases central has, I think, diverted attention away from the heart of his thesis. Thus Castañeda writes of the referential-attributive distinction:

> I think, to put it disrespectfully, that it is too much ado about practically nothing. The fact at the bottom of all that fuss has nothing to do with definite descriptions. It is the fact that one can succeed in making a hearer think of something α by means of expressions that do not in reality as the language goes correspond with α.[14]

The Semantic Significance of the Distinction

The view that there are two uses of descriptions is not, I think, likely to meet widespread opposition. It is not implausible to maintain that descriptions are sometimes used to call attention to some particular entity the speaker has in mind and sometimes used to speak of whatever it is that has certain properties.[15] What is controversial is Donnellan's view (which I share) that the propositional content of referential and attributive utterances, as well as their truth conditions (in a sense to be explained below), differ.[16] It is often urged, contrary to Donnellan, that although there are two *uses* of descriptions, there is a single *semantic* account applicable to both uses, a semantic treatment in accordance with Russell's theory of descriptions, for example. According to a proponent of such a view, when one utters, 'The F is G', *however* the description is used, the same proposition is asserted: there is one and only one F and it is G. To use Donnellan's example, whether our speaker who is present at Jones's trial says, "Smith's murderer is insane," in reaction to Jones's odd behavior (referential use) or whether he utters those words upon seeing Smith's brutally mutilated body, in which case he has no particular murderer in mind (attributive use), our speaker asserts the same thing—that there is one and only one murderer of Smith and he/she is insane. It is surely not obvious, it might be argued (against Donnellan), that what the speaker asserted (and the truth conditions thereof) should depend on whether he has Jones in mind (as Smith's murderer) or whether he has no idea who murdered Smith. Thus Kripke remarks, "I am tentatively inclined to believe, in opposition to Donnellan, that his remarks about reference have little to do with semantics or truth-conditions though they may be relevant to a theory of speech acts."[17] Kripke adds that in his view Donnellan's remarks require no modification of Russell's theory of descriptions.[18] Along similar lines, H. P. Grice, in "Vacuous Names," explicitly distinguishes "two . . . modes of employment" of descriptions, what he calls "the type (1) non-identificatory" (corresponding to attributive) and "the type (2) identificatory" (corresponding to referential). Grice goes on to say that "the truth conditions for a type (2) statement, no less for a type (1) statement, can be thought of as being given by a Russellian account of descriptions." He continues: "It is important to bear in mind that I am not suggesting that the difference between these . . . represents a difference in the meaning or sense which a descriptive phrase may have on different occasions; on the contrary, I am suggesting that descriptive phrases have no relevant systematic duplicity of meaning; their meaning is given by a Russellian account."[19]

I shall maintain, contrary to Kripke and Grice, that the distinction has significance at the level of propositional content and truth conditions. I shall introduce my positive account by means of an argument that Russell's theory of descriptions fails as an account of the use of descriptions in natural language.

An argument quite similar to the one I shall present was briefly noted by Donnellan some time ago.[20] Donnellan, however, never gave a central place to this argument (he merely sketches it in passing in a footnote), nor did he fully appreciate its force.[21] I shall begin by considering the applicability of Russell's theory to cases of referential use. Then I shall consider Russell's theory in connection with cases of attributive use.

The great majority of the definite descriptions we actually utilize in ordinary discourse are what Donnellan has called "indefinite definite descriptions," that is, they are not uniquely denoting. Examples are 'the table', 'the murderer', 'the man seated by the fire', 'the next President'. Consider an assertive utterance of a sentence containing such an indefinite definite description, for example, "The table is covered with books." The Russellian analysis of such an utterance would appear to be: one and only one thing is a table and it is covered with books. Strawson, in *Mind*,[22] argues that such utterances (some of which are undoubtedly true) present difficulties for Russell, since it is clear that it is not the case that *one and only one thing is a table* and is covered with books. In support of Russell, it might be argued that while Russell's account does require that there be a uniquely denoting description which figures in the speech act, it does not require that the description actually uttered be uniquely denoting. The description, for example, 'the table', as uttered in a particular context, may be elliptical for a uniquely denoting description, say, 'The (only) table in room 209 of Camden Hall at t_1'. In uttering "The table is covered with books," as in uttering any "noneternal sentence," the speaker, as Frege puts it, makes use of "certain accompanying conditions of utterance . . . as a means of expressing the thought."[23] In our example, the speaker relies on the context to indicate how his description is to be made uniquely denoting.

This defense of Russell, however, will not do. When one says, for example, "The table is covered with books," the table the speaker has in mind can be more fully described in any number of ways, by the use of any number of nonsynonymous, uniquely denoting descriptions (for example, 'the table in room 209 of Camden Hall at t_1', 'the table at which the author of *The Persistence of Objects* is sitting at t_1', etc.). Since these more complete descriptions are not synonymous, it follows that each time we replace the indefinite definite description 'the table' with a different one of these "Russellian" descriptions, it would seem that we obtain an expression for a *different proposition*, one that gets a different analysis via the theory of descriptions. For example, 'The table in room 209 of Camden Hall at t_1 is covered with books' receives a different Russellian expansion than does 'The table at which the author of *The Persistence of Objects* is sitting at t_1 is covered with books'. The question now arises, which of these more complete (or Russellian) descriptions (or conjunction of such descriptions) is *the correct one*, the one that actually captures what the speaker intended by his use of the indefinite definite description 'the table'? The question is important, for as noted, each of these nonequivalent descriptions determines a different Russellian analysis of the utterance.

With regard to this question, I wish to make two points. First, it is quite clearly wrong to suppose that, in many such cases, the circumstances of utterance put the listener in a position to select some one of these nonequivalent descriptions as the correct one, the one that actually captures what the speaker intended. Thus, even if one of these Russellian descriptions is *correct* (in the sense that only it captures what was intended), Russell's theory fails as an account of *what is communicated*.

Second, and more important, with regard to many such utterances none of these Russellian descriptions is *the correct one*. It is simply a mistake to view indefinite definite descriptions as elliptical for uniquely denoting descriptions. Let us begin with what appears to be an epistemological question: how are we to know *which* Russellian description is the correct one? Now it might be supposed that we could decide on one of these Russellian descriptions as the correct one by reference to the intentions of the speaker. In many cases, however, the speaker will have no such determinate intention. If the speaker is asked which Russellian description(s) was implicit in his utterance of 'the table', he will not ordinarily be able to answer. "Although I meant to refer to that table," our speaker might well reply, "I don't think I meant to refer to it *as* the table in room 209 of Camden Hall at t_1 as opposed to, say, *as* the table at which the author of *The Persistence of Objects* is sitting at t_1. Nor did I intend to refer to it *as* the table in 209 *and* the table at which the author is sitting as opposed to, say, just *as* the table in 209."

At this point our concern is no longer merely the epistemological one: how are we to know which of these Russellian descriptions is the correct one? It now becomes difficult to attach sense to the idea that one of these Russellian descriptions could be correct. Surely it is implausible in the extreme to suppose that in fact one of these descriptions captures what the speaker intended but that we cannot, even with the help of the speaker himself, come to know which description that is.[24]

Russell's theory fails as a *general* account of definite descriptions in natural language, since in so many cases (at least in many cases of referential use) the indefinite definite descriptions we actually utter are not elliptical for the uniquely denoting descriptions that Russell's theory requires. This raises the following question. Consider an assertive utterance of a sentence containing an indefinite definite description, for example, 'The table is covered with books'. Since the description actually uttered, 'the table', applies to many things and since there is no implicit Russellian description, that is, one that fits only the table in question, how are we to account for the fact that the speech act is not at all indefinite or indeterminate? Put differently, in uttering this sentence the speaker predicates the property (being covered with books) of not just any table but of the table in question. But it is hard to see how this can be so if the phrase 'the table' (which, after all, applies to many tables) is not a surrogate for a description which applies only to the table in question.

The same question arises with regard to indexical references, that is, references made by the use of 'I', 'he', 'she', 'it', and so forth. Consider an utterance of "It is covered with books" made in regard to some table. How is it that by my utterance of 'it', which applies to just about anything, I succeed in asserting a determinate proposition about this particular table? It might be tempting to answer this question by viewing the indexical 'it', as uttered in such a context, as a surrogate for some descriptive characterization of the table in question. If the indexical *were* a surrogate for, say, some Russellian description, we would certainly understand how a complete and determinate proposition gets asserted via an utterance of this sentence, which, from a semantic point of view, seems incomplete.

Indexicals, however, like indefinite definite descriptions, are not surrogates for Russellian descriptions. Indeed, the argument utilized above with regard to descriptions like 'the table' applies mutatis mutandis to the case of indexicals. Given some utterance of "It is covered with books," there will be any number of replacements for 'it' and no good reasons, at least in many cases, to choose one as the correct one.[25]

How, then, are we to account for the fact that in such cases a nondefective speech act is performed, a determinate assertion is made? Let us return to Frege's idea, mentioned above, that in uttering a non-eternal sentence, the speaker relies on the circumstances of utterance to supplement his words. The question is, how are we to characterize the circumstances of utterance? My answer is that the circumstances of utterance do help to provide us with an identification of the referent, but not by providing a more complete descriptive characterization of it. When one says, "The table is covered with books," for example, in the conspicuous presence of a single table, the context fails to reveal some Russellian description as lurking behind the utterance of 'the table'; the context does reveal, however, *which* item is in question.

Thus the speaker may use an indefinite definite description, that is, an expression which applies to many things, to make a *determinate reference*, indeed, a "demonstrative reference," to some particular thing. We are now in a position to understand how a fully determinate assertion is made by the utterance of this semantically indeterminate sentence: the proposition is determinate since the speaker makes a *determinate reference* and goes on to predicate a property of the thing to which he has referred.

The account just given departs not only from the Russellian perspective on definite descriptions but also, in several respects, from the Fregean semantical perspective. First, Frege does not allow for determinate reference in the absence of a sense which uniquely determines the reference. We have in effect seen, however, that determinate reference is possible in the absence of such a sense. A speaker may refer, for example, by means of an indefinite definite description, an expression which lacks such a complete sense. And as we have in effect seen, it is simply not true that in such cases the speaker relies on various features of the circumstances of utterance to supplement the sense of his words so as to yield such a complete sense. (Just as the context does not provide a Russellian description, it does not provide the sense of such a description.)

Second, Frege takes the "thought" (or, for our purposes, proposition) expressed by the utterance of a sentence to be a sentential sense, indeed a *complete sentential sense*. Whatever else the force of "complete" is here, it surely precludes having as a subject constituent of a subject-predicate proposition the sense of an indefinite definite description. Only the "complete" sense of a uniquely denoting description can be such a subject constituent. As we have in effect seen, however, there are cases in which there is no such complete sense which can plausibly be taken to play the role of subject constituent and yet something determinate is asserted.

Following David Kaplan,[26] I shall call the (non-Fregean) proposition asserted when a description is used referentially (e.g. in the subject position of a subject-predicate assertion) a "singular proposition."[27] In order to sharply distinguish referential and attributive uses, note the unique role played in such a singular proposition by the item demonstrated. Consider the proposition asserted by a referential utterance of "Smith's murderer is insane," in which Jones, on the witness stand, is demonstrated. Jones, we shall assume, is both guilty and crazy. The proposition in question is true then, since Jones, the item demonstrated, satisfies the predicate. Now consider a counterfactual situation in which (1) Jones is insane but (2) Jones is not Smith's murderer and indeed (3) Smith's murderer is quite sane. With respect to such a counterfactual situation, the proposition we have been considering, namely, the proposition that *that one, Jones, is insane*, is again true. That is, the proposition expressed by the actual-world utterance would have been true had things turned out as described by (1), (2), and (3).

The "demonstrative" analysis just given to cases of referential use is surely not applicable to cases of attributive use. Although we can speak of a "referent" even in attributive cases, that is, the "semantic referent" (that person who in fact murdered Smith), the semantic referent is surely not demonstrated by the speaker's attributive use of the description. What is asserted by an attributive utterance is not anything like "*That one*, Jones, is insane" but is rather "One and only one person murdered Smith and he/she is insane" (or some Strawsonian variant). There is therefore an important sense in which the truth or falsity of this proposition, unlike that of the referential case, does not depend upon Jones and his properties. We can see this by evaluating this proposition in the counterfactual situation described by (1), (2), and (3) above. The proposition we are considering, roughly that one and only one person murdered Smith and is insane— unlike the singular proposition of the referential case—would have been *false* had things turned out as described by (1), (2), and (3). This proposition would have been false because in the counterfactual situation, despite Jones's insanity, one and only one person murdered Smith and that person is quite sane.

It might seem plausible that Russell's theory of descriptions, even if incorrect with regard to referential cases, supplies the correct account in attributive cases.[28] There is, however, a difficulty with Russell's theory even when restricted to cases of attributive use, a difficulty which will further illuminate the role of demonstrative reference in our use of definite descriptions.[29] The difficulty is this: the argument I have advanced that Russell's theory gives an inadequate account of cases of referential use applies mutatis mutandis to cases of attributive use. Consider an attributive utterance of a sentence containing an indefinite definite description: the detective, upon seeing Smith's mutilated body, exclaims, "The murderer is insane!" In many such cases of attributive use, the description uttered is not uniquely denoting, nor is there any uniquely denoting description which is implicit. As in the cases of referential use discussed above, there will be any number of ways to fill out the description so as to yield a Russellian description (e.g. 'Harry Smith's murderer', 'the murderer of Joan Smith's husband', 'the murderer of the junior Senator from New Jersey in 1975'), and, in many cases, nothing about the circumstances of utterance or the intentions of the speaker which would indicate that any one of these Russellian descriptions is the correct one.[30]

If a speaker (attributively) utters such an indefinite definite description, which, after all, applies to many things, and if there is no implicit Russellian description, how are we to account for the fact that his speech act was not at all indeterminate or incomplete? We have already answered this question for referential uses of descriptions: what accounts for such determinateness in referential cases is that the description which applies to many items is used to make a determinate demonstrative reference to one particular thing.

What of attributive uses of descriptions? It appears that we cannot here account for propositional determinateness in the way just discussed, that is, by appeal to demonstrative reference, for, as noted above, in attributive cases there is no demonstration of the (semantic) referent of the description.[31] Moreover, were we to try to account for propositional determinateness in attributive cases by appeal to determinateness of semantic reference, were we to say that what was asserted was determinate because insanity was predicated of *this* item (i.e. the semantic referent), it would follow that *which* proposition is asserted depends upon *which* item it is that is the murderer (which item it is that is the semantic referent). But what was asserted by an attributive utterance of "The murderer is insane" does not, of course, depend on who the murderer is. One fully understands the proposition without having any idea who murdered Smith. Were we to mistakenly take the murderer to be Brown and later discover it to be Jones, we would not thereby correct a mistaken impression of what was asserted by the utterance. Indeed, if understanding such a proposition required knowledge of which item was the murderer, the speaker himself would, at least in many cases, not understand his own utterance, for in attributive cases the speaker often has no belief about who the murderer is.

We return to our problem, someone's saying, "The murderer is insane," and using the description attributively. We have seen that (1) 'the murderer' is not elliptical for some Russellian description and (2) no appeal to the referent of 'the murderer' will account for propositional determinancy. Nevertheless, we can account for such determinancy by resorting to the notion of demonstrative reference (and the accompanying idea of the contribution of the context of utterance). For in uttering "The murderer is insane" in the presence of the mutilated body, the speaker relies on the context to reveal *whose* murder is in question. The speaker, that is, makes an *implicit* reference to the victim.

That there is an implicit reference made in cases like the one under discussion may be seen by comparing utterances of

(1) The murderer is insane.
(2) His murderer is insane.

When a speaker utters (2), part of what accounts for the fact that he has asserted a determinate proposition is that he has made an *explicit* reference by using the possessive pronoun 'his', thus indicating which victim is in question. But this same indication can be accomplished, albeit implicitly, by simply uttering "The murderer is insane" in the presence of the body.

"Demonstrative" reference plays a role, then, even in some cases of the attributive use of descriptions. In this connection let us compare utterances of

(2) His murderer is insane.
(3) The murderer of the man on the couch is insane.
(4) The murderer of Smith is insane.

Examples (2), (3), and (4) reveal an important feature of the attributive use of descriptions which I will briefly explore. A description used attributively may contain indexical expressions, proper names, and finally other descriptions. Each of these kinds of singular term may be used *referentially* in the course of an attributive utterance of a description which contains them. Thus in uttering (2), the speaker uses the indexical 'his' referentially; that is, the semantic account of indexicals sketched above applies here. 'His', in this context, does not pick up new descriptive content; it is not a surrogate for the possessive form of some Russellian description. Similarly, in an attributive utterance of (3), the contained description 'the man on the couch' is used *referentially*. To see that these expressions *are* being used referentially, we need only to apply our by now familiar argument once again: there is no uniquely correct way (and therefore no correct way) to fill out the description 'the man on the couch' so as to make it uniquely denoting (and, similarly, no uniquely correct way to replace 'his' in 'his murderer' with [the possessive form of] some uniquely denoting description). Hence the description 'the man on the couch' is not elliptical for a Russellian description. Despite its being an indefinite definite description, we can appeal to its *referent* to account for the fact that a determinate proposition was asserted.

How General Is the Distinction?

We have seen the need for a semantically significant referential-attributive distinction in the case of utterances containing *indefinite* definite descriptions. Is the distinction more generally applicable, to uniquely denoting descriptions, for example? Specifically, is there a (semantically distinct) referential use of uniquely denoting descriptions? (Clearly there is such an attributive use; indeed, on Russell's theory all utterances containing descriptions receive what is in effect an attributive analysis.) I wish to maintain that there is a referential use of uniquely denoting descriptions. The problem is that the argument I used to establish referential use in the case of indefinite definite descriptions is not applicable to the case of uniquely denoting descriptions. In the case of an indefinite definite description, the notion of demonstrative reference is needed in order to explain how a determinate proposition can be asserted by means of an utterance containing a semantically indeterminate (i.e. not uniquely denoting) description. But in the case of a uniquely denoting description, the description itself is semantically determinate, and so there is no need to appeal to the notion of demonstrative reference to explain how a determinate proposition is asserted.

How, then, can we establish that uniquely denoting descriptions have a referential use? Imagine a speaker making a demonstrative reference via an utterance of 'the table' to a particular table in view, indeed the only table in view. Further imagine that he is speaking to someone who is confused and disoriented and who misunderstands him and either fails to have any idea which table he means or takes him to be speaking about a different table than the table in view. The speaker may try to make himself clear by adding further information to his description. Indeed, he may eventually add enough information so that his description is uniquely denoting. Since his sole interest is identifying for the listener the table he means, the speaker may very well not realize that the last description uniquely denotes, nor will he intend it to be taken in any radically different fashion than the earlier descriptions. We have then a continuum of descriptions, from 'the table' to more complete but still indefinite definite descriptions and finally to a uniquely denoting description. *Ex hypothesi*, all of the descriptions except the last are, in effect, demonstratives. The last description, however, is, at least from the point of view of the speaker, indistinguishable from the earlier ones (except for the addition of one further bit of information). It surely seems implausible to suppose that the last description receives an entirely different sort of analysis than do the earlier ones, one, say, in accordance with Russell's theory of descriptions. If the indefinite definite descriptions receive a demonstrative analysis, then so does the uniquely denoting description.

It seems plausible, if not absolutely forced by the preceding, to generalize further. Any definite description can, in appropriate circumstances, be used referentially—even a description which the speaker knows to be uniquely denoting. Whether a description is indeed being used referentially or attributively is a matter of the intentions of the speaker. Does he intend to demonstrate an individual, or does he intend to use the description attributively?

We have, then, a general referential-attributive distinction of semantic significance. It is not quite the distinction that Donnellan originally formulated, for I have put to one side Donnellan's controversial view about reference via a conventionally inapplicable expression.[32] My version of this distinction does, however, preserve and elucidate what was, to my mind at least, at the heart of that distinction, namely, the difference between the use of a description to *point* to an individual entity and the use of a description to speak of whatever it is that uniquely has certain properties.[33]

FIVE

The Semantic Significance of the Referential-Attributive Distinction

AT THE very heart of Keith Donnellan's distinction between referential and attributive uses of definite descriptions, at least as Donnellan wrote about the distinction in "Reference and Definite Descriptions,"[1] appeared to be the idea that a referentially used description refers to the item intended by the speaker even if the description fails to apply conventionally to that item. Donnellan, in so emphasizing this controversial idea, made it appear that the existence of a semantically significant referential-attributive distinction depends upon this controversial claim. The heart of the referential-attributive distinction lies elsewhere, or so I argued in "Demonstrative Reference and Definite Descriptions,"[2] the previous essay in this volume. The essential difference between referential and attributive occurrences of descriptions is the difference between the pointing use of a description, that is, the use of a description as a device of demonstrative reference, and the property-attributing use, that is, the use of a description to speak of whatever it is that has certain features.

Nathan U. Salmon contends in "Assertion and Incomplete Definite Descriptions"[3] that I have failed to establish that there is a semantically distinct referential use of definite descriptions. Salmon's criticism is twofold. He finds my view that there is a semantically distinct referential use unacceptable because it has, he argues, unacceptable consequences. My argument in favor of this view is, from his point of view, additionally defective; it rides roughshod over a Grice-inspired distinction Salmon introduces between the proposition the speaker asserts and the semantic content of the sentence he utters.

I shall first say a bit more about my positive view in "Demonstrative Reference and Definite Descriptions," specifically about the semantic significance of the referential-attributive distinction. I shall then review my argument in favor of this positive view. Finally, I shall discuss Salmon's criticisms.

What is the semantic significance of the referential-attributive distinction? A referentially used description functions semantically as a demonstrative; an attributively used one functions as a property-attributor.[4] Accordingly, referential and attributive utterances of "The murderer of Smith is insane" will express different propositions.[5] Consider the proposition asserted by a referential utterance in which Jones, on the witness stand, is demonstrated. Jones, we shall assume, is both guilty and crazy, and so this proposition is true. Now consider a counterfactual situation in which Jones is insane but in which no one has ever been murdered. *The sentence* "The murderer of Smith is insane" fails to describe such a possible world accurately. Were this sentence to be uttered in such a world, a false proposition (or one lacking in truth-value) would be asserted. Nevertheless, what is asserted by the actual-world referential utterance of this sentence, the proposition that *that one, Jones, is insane*, is true when we evaluate it with respect to such a world. Had things turned out as in the counterfactual circumstance, this proposition would have been true. This "singular proposition," so called following David Kaplan,[6] is thus true with respect to a possible world w just in case the very individual demonstrated in the actual world is insane in w.

What is asserted by an attributive utterance is not anything like the singular proposition that *that one, Jones, is insane*, but is rather the "general proposition" that (roughly) *one and only one person murdered Smith and that person is insane*. This general proposition will be true in the actual world, as was the singular proposition, since, *ex hypothesi*, one person, Jones, both murdered Smith and is crazy. Evaluated with respect to the ways things might have turned out, however, the truth-values of the singular proposition and the general proposition may diverge. The singular proposition that *that one, Jones, is insane* is, as we have seen, true with respect to the counterfactual situation described above, in which no one has been murdered but in which Jones is nevertheless insane. The general proposition that (roughly) *exactly one person murdered Smith and that person is insane* will be false (or lacking in truth-value) with respect to such a world. The general proposition is true with respect to a world w just in case Smith was murdered in w by exactly one person and that person is insane in w.

What was my argument for the thesis that referentially used definite descriptions require a different semantic treatment than do attributively used ones? First, I adduced a datum to be accounted for by any semantic account of definite descriptions. Next, I argued that the theories of Frege and Russell (Frege's sense-reference model and Russell's theory of descriptions), according to which all occurrences of definite descriptions are, in Donnellan's terms, attributive, could not accommodate this datum. Finally, I hypothesized that definite descriptions sometimes function as devices of demonstrative reference, and I argued that this hypothesis nicely accounts for the datum.

What is the datum? The great majority, if not virtually all, of the definite descriptions utilized by ordinary speakers are "incomplete" or "indefinite" definite descriptions; they fail to uniquely denote but rather apply to any number of items. When one says, "The murderer is insane," gesturing in the direction of Jones, the guilty party, one refers to Jones despite the fact that the uttered description, given its lexical meaning, fails to uniquely specify him.

The views of Frege and Russell, however, seem incompatible with this datum. Frege holds that reference is achieved only by means of a uniquely specifying sense. The impoverished sense of 'the murderer' fails to specify anything uniquely. How, then, does the speaker refer and assert a determinate proposition? Russell maintains that utterances of the form "The F is G" are to be analyzed as "There is one and only one thing that is F and it is G." This analysis also requires that the definite description uniquely denote. Otherwise the analysans will turn out *false*.

Somehow, however, speakers often manage to assert *truths* despite the fact that the descriptions they utter fail to uniquely denote.

There is a strategy that Frege employs in "The Thought: A Logical Inquiry"[7] that, if successful, would render my datum fully compatible with Frege's approach as well as Russell's.[8] The description actually uttered fails to uniquely specify a referent, but there is, it might be urged, a uniquely specifying description implicit in the utterance, and the speaker relies on the context to indicate this more complete description.

This Fregean strategy, however, will not do. The speaker and the auditor may be able to provide a number of more complete descriptions of the referent, but neither of them will, in general, be able to decide on one of these descriptions (or a single set) as the one that was implicit in the utterance. Nor are there any general sorts of considerations to which we can appeal to select *the* more complete description that was somehow implicit in the utterance. In the absence of any reason at all for selecting a unique description (or unique set) as the operative one, it seems reasonable to conclude that no such description was indeed operative.[9]

If this Fregean strategy does not work, if there is no uniquely specifying description implicit in the utterance, how are we to account for the fact that in such cases determinate references are made and determinate propositions asserted? My hypothesis was that the incomplete definite description functions semantically as a device of demonstrative reference. When one uses a demonstrative as in "That is a good book," one refers to a particular item despite the fact that one has not supplied anything like a uniquely specifying descriptive characterization of it. Nor is 'that' a surrogate, in such cases, for some such characterization.[10] The speaker relies on the context of the utterance not to reveal a uniquely specifying description of the referent but rather to reveal which item is in question. Expressions that function in this way, "demonstratively," as we might say, are not limited to the explicit demonstratives like 'this' and 'that', expressions that provide little or no descriptive information about their referents. The pronouns 'he' and 'she' provide examples of singular terms that have significant descriptive content but at the same time do not achieve reference by indicating, with the help of the context, some uniquely specifying descriptive characterization of the referent.[11] The definite description 'The murderer', just like 'he' and 'she', provides some descriptive information regarding the referent, but not nearly enough to secure reference. Reference is secured by the fact that the context makes clear which murderer is in question.[12]

What proposition is expressed by a referential utterance of "The murderer [or 'he', or 'that one'] is insane" in which Jones is demonstrated? It is surely not the Fregean proposition, the subject constituent of which is a sense that uniquely specifies the murderer in question, that is, Jones, for, as we have seen, there is no such uniquely specifying sense implicit in the utterance. Nor is the proposition the Russellian quantified version, for, again, there is no uniquely denoting description lurking behind the scenes. Since Jones was demonstrated and insanity predicated of him, what was asserted was that *that one, Jones, is insane*, a singular proposition, true with respect to a possible world w just in case Jones, the individual demonstrated in the actual world, is insane in w.

Now for Salmon's criticisms. Salmon grants that my argument against the Fregean strategy raises a pressing question for such an approach. He alludes to an answer on behalf of this strategy but stops short of actually providing such an answer. His detailed criticism is not directed at my claim that the sort of view he finds congenial cannot accommodate the data but rather at my positive hypothesis and its supporting argument. Salmon's claim that my positive view has unacceptable consequences raises issues of fundamental importance, and so I shall consider it first. I shall then turn to his claim that the argument I employ in defense of my positive view is defective.

Salmon writes:

A proponent of the semantic significance thesis, such as Wettstein, must maintain that the sentence "The murderer is insane," as used on this occasion [the speaker is looking at and, say, pointing to Jones, the actual murderer], is true with respect to any possible world in which Jones is insane, even if Smith [the actual victim] is alive and well, Jones is no murderer at all, and in fact, no murders are committed by anyone anywhere. It is clear, however that the sentence "The murderer is insane" is not true with respect to such a world, and indeed, it is clear that the phrase "the murderer" does not denote anyone, not even Jones, with respect to such a world.[13]

The Referential-Attributive Distinction 55

I believe that there is a confusion here concerning the key notion of truth conditions with respect to counterfactual circumstances. What exactly does Salmon take to be the items whose truth-values we evaluate with respect to counterfactual circumstances? Although Salmon sometimes speaks of *sentences* as the objects of evaluation, as he does in the last sentence cited, it is clear, I think, that his intention is better captured by the immediately preceding sentence, in which he takes the objects of evaluation to be *sentences as used on particular occasions*. Since the sentences under discussion are highly context-dependent, it is surely not the sentences, considered apart from any particular context, that are to be so evaluated. How might one even begin to evaluate a context-dependent sentence like "He is insane" (or "The murderer is insane") with respect to a possible world (or indeed even with respect to the actual world)? If we are not thinking about this sentence in connection with a particular context of utterance, how are we to tell whose insanity is at issue?

Salmon's idea, then, seems to be that we evaluate such sentences as used on a particular occasion with reference to particular individuals. That Salmon should suppose that *sentences as used on particular occasions* are the items to be evaluated is, however, puzzling for two reasons. First, as I shall explain below, it is not at all clear what it would be to evaluate a sentence, as used on an actual-world occasion, with respect to another possible world. Second, and even more puzzling, Salmon, throughout his paper, speaks of propositions as the objects of evaluation. His present contention that sentences, or sentences as used on particular actual-world occasions, are the objects of evaluation appears to represent an important but unannounced departure from the doctrine of the rest of the paper. Nor is this merely a notational difference. Salmon's criticism of my view depends crucially on the assumption that sentences (as used on particular occasions), rather than propositions, are what we are to evaluate with respect to counterfactual circumstances.

Consider an utterance of

(S) She used to be an ophthalmologist but has now become a professional tennis player

in a context which determines Renee Richards as the referent of 'she'. As a matter of actual fact, Richards, a man, gave up his medical practice and became a tennis professional after a transsexual operation in which he became a woman. Given my view that (deictic) pronouns function demonstratively, I am committed to the claim that (S) expresses, in the context, a singular proposition, true in any possible world in which Richards exists and has the same occupational history as in the actual world. Specifically, it is true in a world w_1 in which there are no women at all but in which Richards, having never had the operation and so being a male, has the right occupational history.

Am I, as Salmon supposes, committed to the claim that *the sentence (S), as used here and now*, is true with respect to w_1? To speak of (S) "as used here and now" is to speak of (S) cleansed of ambiguities and context-dependencies. Since (S) is unambiguous, the role of the context is to assign a reference to 'she'. We are, then, to evaluate (S), with the reference of 'she' fixed to be Richards, with respect to w_1. I find this puzzling, to say the least. *The sentence (S)* clearly fails to accurately describe w_1. On the other hand, the referent of 'she', Richards, does possess, in w_1, the property predicated of Richards in the sentence. How exactly are we to evaluate this entity, *the sentence as used on the actual-world occasion*?

That Salmon would evaluate (S), as used on the occasion in question, as untrue with respect to w_1 is clear. Since 'she' does not apply to anything in w_1, the sentence (S), as used in the actual-world occasion, cannot be true with respect to w_1.[14] Salmon would be forced to conclude that even a sentence like (S), the subject term of which is a deictic pronoun, does not determine a singular proposition, and he would need to search, in the spirit of what I called above the "Fregean strategy," for some more general proposition. Salmon's argument, then, if sound, is very powerful. It would show not only that I am wrong about referential definite descriptions but that Kaplan, John Perry,[15] I, and others are wrong about deictic pronouns.[16]

There is, however, no reason for someone who thinks that such "indexical"-containing sentences determine singular propositions to so conclude. What he needs to do is to point out that the question of whether *the sentence* (or the sentence as used on this occasion) is true with respect to counterfactual circumstances is just the wrong question. The object of evaluation with respect to counterfactual circumstances is what Salmon throughout his paper calls "the semantic content," the proposition expressed, and the proposition expressed in the context by 'S is S' is a singular proposition that is true in w_1.

Similarly, it is a mistake to ask whether the sentence "The murderer is insane," as used on the occasion in question, would be true or false in a world in which there were no murders. I am not committed to any answer whatever to that question in virtue of my view about referentially used descriptions. I am committed to the view that the *singular proposition* determined in the context in question is true in a possible world just in case Jones, the actual murderer, is insane in that world, whether or not he (or anyone else) committed a murder in that world. This, however, does not seem objectionable once we become clear that the object of such counterfactual evaluation is not a piece of language (as used on a certain occasion) but a content, in this case a singular proposition.

I turn now to Salmon's criticism of the argument I advanced in favor of the claim that there is a semantically distinct referential use of definite descriptions. It is a commonplace that speakers sometimes manage to convey a message that is quite different from the one formulated by the words they actually utter. Although I have doubts about Salmon's way of drawing the distinction between the message conveyed in such cases—Salmon's "speaker assertion"—and the proposition formulated by the sentence—Salmon's "semantic content"—I shall not pursue those doubts here, since Salmon's criticism of my argument does not depend upon the details of his analysis of the relevant distinction.[17]

Salmon and I agree that "the question of semantic significance of the referential use is concerned primarily with semantic content and not speaker assertion."[18] The issue is, not what the speaker who uses a description referentially manages to convey, but rather what proposition the semantic rules of the language assign to the utterance. Salmon seems to think, however, that I infer that the singular proposition is the one assigned by the semantic rules *from* the fact that the speaker manages to convey this proposition. Thus he writes:

Wettstein's discussion, like Donnellan's original paper and most other discussions of these and related issues, suffers from a failure to keep separate the notions of speaker's assertion and semantic content. Our main concern is with what the *words* express as their semantic content *with respect to* the relevant context of use. In order to establish the thesis of semantic significance of the referential use it will not do simply to show that in using a sentence referentially one thereby asserts the relevant singular proposition. For the speaker may also assert a relevant general proposition simultaneously. In any case, the relevant question is not what the speaker manages to assert, but what his or her words express.[19]

My problem here is that I fully agree that the inference in question would be fallacious. In fact, I said as much in my paper.[20] My argument for the semantic significance of the referential use was *not* that the speaker conveys the singular proposition in question so it must be that this proposition is the one he is committed to in virtue of the semantic rules of the language. My argument, as Salmon acknowledges both earlier and later in his paper, was that it seems implausible to suppose that the sort of general proposition required by Russellian or Fregean accounts was really expressed at all. Yet the sentence surely determines a proposition in the context. What proposition might this be? The case of indexical terms shows that sentences can determine propositions that are singular with respect to the subject constituent not only if the subject term is "connotationless" like a proper name but even if the subject term, say, 'she', embodies descriptive information about its referent. Could it be that definite descriptions, when they are used referentially, function in just the same way as indexicals? The hypothesis that referential descriptions do so function provides a plausible solution to our question of how a determinate proposition can be expressed by a sentence that is semantically indeterminate. My argument, then, was certainly not a species of what we might call "the pragmatic fallacy," the inference that since a speaker managed to convey a certain proposition, it must be that the semantic rules of the language assign that proposition to the utterance.[21]

SIX

Did the Greeks Really Worship Zeus?

Introduction: Reference Failure and
Reference to the Nonexistent

The week before final exams is a very busy time. Some student or other is always waiting to see me. One day during this hectic period, after an hour of seeing students, I mused, nodding toward the door, "This one probably wants an incomplete" (taking for granted that the individual in question was a graduate student). I was mistaken, however, for there was no student outside my door. Does the expression 'this one' refer in such a case? It is surely plausible to suppose that it does not. Who but a Meinongian would suppose otherwise? Terence Parsons has urged that not even a Meinongian need argue that I did refer.[1] Parsons, a defender of nonexistent objects, maintains that since my intention was to speak about a real thing, a flesh-and-blood student, and since there was no such object present, I simply failed to refer. Similarly, the faithful ancient Greek, when he tells his children, "Zeus sits on Mt. Olympus," fails to refer, for he intends to speak of an *existing* deity. Nonexistent objects, at least on Parson's version of Meinongianism, are not the booby prizes for intended but failed references to real things.

Unsuccessful attempts to refer to real things, argues Parsons, should be sharply distinguished from attempts to refer to non-

---

Reprinted by permission from *Synthese* 60 (1984): 439–49. Copyright 1984 by D. Reidel Publishing Co.

existent objects. While the ancient Greek's utterance of "Zeus sits on Mt. Olympus" was false or lacking in truth-value, since his 'Zeus' failed to refer, the contemporary historian appears to express a truth when he teaches that "Zeus sat on Mt. Olympus." His use of 'Zeus' thus appears to be quite different from that of the ancient Greek. Parsons explains this difference in terms of the respective speaker's referential intentions and the distinction between unsuccessful attempts to refer and reference to the nonexistent. The historian, as opposed to the ancient Greek, intends to refer to a *nonexistent* object, the mythological Zeus, and in this he succeeds. His remark is true in the straightforward sense that the object to which he refers possesses the property he predicates of it.[2]

Parsons believes that the distinction between failing to refer and referring to the nonexistent is one that ordinary speakers make without difficulty, that people react quite differently to failures of reference than to references to the nonexistent. I shall quote two dialogues formulated by Parsons to illustrate his point. We are supposed to find speaker *A*'s reactions normal.[3]

Dialogue 1: Reference failure
A. The man in the doorway over there looks pretty silly.
B. But there is no man in the doorway over there.
A. [Looks again.] Oh! I thought there was; I was wrong.
B. Does he look anything like your department chairman?
A. Who?
B. The man in the doorway over there.
A. There isn't any man there; I was mistaken about that.
B. Well, he doesn't exist, but he's there, isn't he?
A. [Exasperated.] Look, I was talking about a guy who exists; that is, I thought I was, but I was wrong, I wasn't talking about anybody. I can't tell you what he looks like because there's no "he" to look like anything.

Speaker *A*, in this dialogue, was "trying to refer to someone, but he just made a mistake and failed to do so. . . . When confronted with questions about the object he was referring to, he treats those questions as spurious (. . . once he has realized his mistake)."[4]

Dialogue 2: Reference to a nonexistent object
A. The unicorn I dreamed about last night looked pretty silly.
C. But there are no unicorns.
A. So what?

C. Well, there aren't any unicorns, so there couldn't be any such thing as the unicorn you dreamed about last night. So "it" couldn't possibly have looked silly.
A. Come on, it's not a real unicorn, it's one I dreamed about.
B. Did it look anything like your department chairman?
A. No, actually it looked a little bit like my hairdresser.

Here A "rejects the contention that he has failed to refer to anything, though he grants that what he is referring to doesn't exist. And he treats questions about it as perfectly reasonable and straightforward."[5]

Parsons's distinction between failing to refer and referring to the nonexistent is both independently interesting and important for his defense of the Meinongian view that there are nonexistent objects. I agree, moreover, that people do react quite differently in the two sorts of cases, as Parsons's dialogues bring out. I shall argue, nevertheless, that this crucial distinction fails to do the work required of it in Parsons's system. Moreover, the ways in which Parsons's apparatus turns out to be inadequate will point the way to a non-Meinongian approach to understanding our discourse about fiction, mythology, and related realms.

First Problem: Anaphora

Consider the following dialogue:

Jones. [Hallucinating.] Look at that beautiful woman.
Dr. Himmelfarb [his psychotherapist]. What does she look like?

Jones uses a singular term, 'that beautiful woman', intending to refer to what he thinks he sees across the room. Dr. Himmelfarb recognizes that there is no such woman and so does not utter his singular term, 'she', with the same sort of intention. Since no woman is there, Jones's referential intention is thwarted. The lack of a real woman, however, presents no problem for the fulfillment of Himmelfarb's intention.

Parsons's distinction between failing to refer and referring to the nonexistent seems straightforwardly applicable here. Jones failed to refer, since he intended to refer to a real woman and this intention was thwarted. His therapist, on the other hand, succeeded in referring, albeit to Jones's hallucinatory and therefore nonexistent woman.[6]

The application of Parsons's distinction to cases like that of Jones and Himmelfarb, however, presents a serious difficulty. The source of the difficulty is the fact that Himmelfarb's utterance of "she" is *anaphorically* related to Jones's utterance of "that beautiful woman." Himmelfarb's "she," since it is anaphoric, refers only if its antecedent, Jones's "that beautiful woman," refers, and so, contrary to what Parsons maintains, it cannot be that only Himmelfarb successfully refers.

I have applied Parsons's distinctions to an example about hallucination. While Parsons has not written about hallucinatory objects as examples of nonexistent objects, he does take dream objects to be nonexistent entities, and it would appear that many of Parsons's arguments concerning dream objects apply to hallucinatory objects as well.[7] In any case, Parsons does take mythological objects to be nonexistent entities, and it is easy to generate the same problem in terms of mythological objects.

Parsons writes: "There is often an early time at which the myth is generally believed to be a true account. At such a stage in history, apparent references to the participants of the recounted happenings should be treated as genuine failures of reference to real objects rather than as successful references to unreal ones."[8] Imagine a dialogue between an anthropologist and one who believes in a form of religion that is primitive from the point of view of the anthropologist. The native is reporting on the requirements established by some deity and the anthropologist queries, "Does he demand human sacrifices?" Clearly, the same problems arise. The native intends to (but fails to) refer to an existing thing, the anthropologist—according to Parsons—intends to refer to a nonexisting thing and succeeds in so referring, and yet the anthropologist's singular term certainly appears to be anaphorically connected to the native's.

These dialogues are puzzling, however, quite independently of any special problems they create for Parsons. The first speaker in each dialogue intends to refer to an existing entity. The second speaker's pronoun is anaphoric. Yet the second speaker does not intend to speak of an existing thing. How can this be? If the pronoun is anaphoric, moreover, and its antecedent fails to refer, the anaphoric pronoun itself must fail to refer. How, then, can we account for the second speaker's evident success?

Let us begin with the question of the second speaker's success. The second speaker utters an anaphoric pronoun, and since its antecedent fails to refer, his success, contra Parsons, cannot consist in a successful *reference*. He, at the same time, does not "fail to refer," at least not in the same sense as does the first speaker, since he does not even try to refer. Rather, he uses a singular term *as if* he intended to refer to the first speaker's intended referent. His use of the pronoun is a form of pretense. He mimics the first speaker's use of language in order to obtain whatever information he is after. He succeeds, then, not in referring but rather in doing what he set out to do, that is, speaking as if he were referring. His pronoun can be anaphoric, despite the discrepancy between his intentions and those of the first speaker, because anaphora does not require a match of referential intentions. What it does require is that the pronoun uttered by the second speaker refer to the same thing as does its antecedent, if it refers at all. This relationship between the singular terms obtains in the cases we are considering. Indeed, the second speaker intends that his pronoun is related in just that way to the first speaker's singular term. He intends to be using his pronoun in such a way that *if* the first speaker has indeed referred, then he, the second speaker, *is referring* to the first speaker's referent.

To fully explore and defend this idea of pretended reference would, of course, be a major undertaking.[9] It promises, however, to supply a coherent account of the puzzle I have been discussing. First, it makes understandable the anaphoric connection between the utterances. Dr. Himmelfarb, for example, is "talking about" the same object as is his patient, Jones. At the same time, Himmelfarb does not intend to refer to an existing thing or, for that matter, to anything at all. For all this, we can still preserve the important distinction between Jones's failure and Himmelfarb's success: they intended to do quite different things.

Is such an approach available to Parsons? Perhaps Parsons could modify his view to cover such cases of discourse between, in general terms, the believer and the critic. He would thus maintain that although, in general, the critic's remarks about Zeus, the hallucinatory woman, the god of the native, and so on are remarks about—genuine references to—nonexistent objects, the critic *sometimes*, for particular purposes, feigns reference and speaks as if there really are Greek gods and so forth. When the anthropologist needs information from his informant, for example, he mimics the latter's use of language and merely pretends to refer. When he lectures or writes about mythological entities, he really refers, albeit to nonexistent objects.

Consider, however, the following notes that the anthropologist makes concerning his conversation with the native:

Native. [Remarks on the god's attributes.]
Me. Does he demand human sacrifices?
Native. [Responds.]

The anthropologist continues his notes as follows: "I later learned that he is omnipotent and, at the same time, capricious." This last remark is obviously not aimed at obtaining information from the native but rather is aimed at the anthropologist himself, or perhaps his co-workers or students. If the anthropologist ever makes a genuine reference to a nonexistent entity (as opposed to a feigned reference to a real thing), this would presumably be such a case. The anthropologist's use of 'he' in this last entry in his notebook, however, does not appear to be any different in the relevant respect from his use of 'he' in his preceding question. If the first is not a genuine reference to a nonexistent object, then neither is the second. If the first is a pretended reference, then so is the second. There will, of course, be differences. The point of the pretense in the first case is to obtain information from the native by speaking *as if* the anthropologist shared the latter's beliefs.[10] The point of the pretense in the case of the anthropologist's later notes is rather that it allows the anthropologist to convey information about the native's beliefs. Nevertheless, the two utterances[11] exemplify, as they indeed appear to, a single sort of use of singular terms. The second, moreover, appears to be a fairly typical use of a singular term in discourse about mythology, and so it is certainly tempting to give a unified account, in terms of the notion of pretended reference, of all talk of mythological entities, fictional entities, and so on and thus do without nonexistent entities.

Second Problem: Attitude Reports

I have argued that Parsons's distinction between failing to refer and referring to the nonexistent is not adequate to the dialogues between the believer and the critic. There are further difficulties when we consider the critic's reports of the believer's attitudes.

Parsons states that an utterance of "Several of the Greek gods were also worshipped by the Romans, though they called them by different names" involves a reference to, and thus expresses a claim about, nonexistent objects, the claim that certain nonexistent objects, namely, the Greek gods, were also worshipped—under different names—by the Romans.[12] It would surely seem, however, that neither the Greeks nor the Romans worshipped nonexistent objects. Perhaps it is possible to worship a nonexistent being. Parsons suggests that just as "there are people who venerate Jesus without taking him to be divine," one might worship God without believing that there really is such a being.[13] Surely, however, when a faithful Greek prayed, he was not praying to such a being. His worship, no less than his referential utterance of "Zeus," is aimed at what he takes to be an existent, and we ought not to think of him as hitting on a nonexistent by default. My point is that just as Parsons distinguishes reference to the nonexistent from attempted but failed reference to what one mistakenly takes to exist, he ought to distinguish genuine worship of a nonexistent from attempts to worship what one mistakenly takes to be existent. If Parsons makes the latter distinction, then the uncontroversial truth that several Greek gods were worshipped by the Romans under different names turns out false, for the Greek gods, that is, the nonexistent objects *we* refer to as "the Greek gods," were worshipped by neither the Greeks nor the Romans.

Parsons would no doubt maintain that an utterance of "Several of the Greek gods were also believed by the Romans to have superhuman powers, though the Romans called them by different names" also expresses a claim about nonexistent objects.[14] Let us again ask, did the Greeks have such a belief about a nonexistent object, or rather were they aiming, without success, at an existent god? Again, an uncontroversial truth turns out false on Parsons's analysis, since neither the Greeks nor the Romans had such beliefs about the relevant nonexistent objects.

Why might Parsons suppose that the Greeks worshipped and had beliefs about the nonexistent object that we refer to as "Zeus"? Objects, on Parsons's view, are individuated by their "nuclear properties," properties expressed by predicates like 'is tall', 'is blue', 'kicked Socrates', 'is a mountain', and so on. Then there are "extranuclear properties" that do not figure in the individuation of objects, properties expressed by ontological predicates like 'exists', modal predicates like 'is possible', and intentional predicates like 'is thought about by Meinong'. The nonexistent Zeus that the historian writes about presumably possesses all and only those properties that the Greeks believed their Zeus to possess, except that the Greeks took Zeus to exist. Existence, however, is not a nuclear property, and so the Zeus of the historian and the Zeus of the ancient Greek share all their nuclear properties. Since objects are individuated by their nuclear properties, or as Parsons puts it, "If x and y have exactly the same nuclear properties, then $x = y$,"[15] it follows that the Zeus of the ancient Greek and the Zeus of the historian are one and the same.

I urged above that on Parsons's view it should turn out false that the ancient Greeks worshipped or had beliefs about "our" Zeus. When they prayed to Zeus, for example, they certainly did not intend to be worshipping a nonexistent object. A natural response, given Parsons's account of individuation, is that the ancient Greeks really did worship Zeus, that is, the nonexistent object referred to by my use of 'Zeus'. The Greeks, of course, would not have characterized *him* in the way we do, that is, as nonexistent. Indeed, they mistakenly attributed to him a characteristic he lacked, existence. Nevertheless, it was *he* they worshipped (and had beliefs about). It is not, then, that in aiming at an existent and failing to make contact, one gets a nonexistent as a booby prize. It is rather that, since existence is not an individuating property, when one aims at what one takes to be an existing object, F, one necessarily aims at and makes contact with F, even if one is wrong about its existence.

The view that the ancient Greeks worshipped and had beliefs about the nonexistent Zeus is, then, certainly not without support in Parsons's system. The problem remains, however, as to how this line is consonant with Parsons's insistence on the distinction between failing to refer and referring to a nonexistent, with the idea that when one unsuccessfully attempts to refer to a real thing, one does not thereby hit upon an unreal thing. Indeed, these two strands in Parsons's system seem to be in tension with one another. One might, I suppose, try to draw the relevant distinction for the case of reference, but not draw the parallel distinction for worship, belief, and so on. This seems implausible. Suppose that the ancient Greek thinks to himself that no doubt Zeus is still on Mt. Olympus. Such a thought, according to the defense of Parsons that we are considering, is genuinely about Zeus, that is, about the nonexistent Zeus. This is so since, on Parsons's view, the Greek's mistaken belief in the existence of Zeus does not prevent him from having beliefs about, or thinking thoughts about, the nonexistent Zeus. If so, it is very hard to see why his verbalization of what he believes, his utterance of "No doubt Zeus is still on Mt. Olympus," fails to make reference to the object of his belief. Parsons, at the very least, would owe us an account of why belief and worship ought to be treated so differently from reference.

Parsons's remarks on belief and worship and the apparent basis of those remarks in his views about individuation thus threaten his distinction between failing to refer and referring to the nonexistent. A related point is that the substantial intuition to which Parsons appeals to support his view that there are cases of genuine reference failure militates against the view that the Greeks really worshipped and had beliefs about the nonexistent entity that we refer to as "Zeus." Parsons formulates a dialogue between ordinary speakers, quoted above, that emphasizes their familiarity with the idea of reference failure and their great impatience, in cases of reference failure, with the suggestion that there really was some nonexistent thing that they succeeded in referring to. Adapting Parsons's dialogue to my own case, when I said, "This one probably wants an incomplete," I soon found out that I was mistaken and that there was no student outside my door. Had a colleague proceeded to ask (as does speaker B in Parsons's dialogue), "Well, he doesn't exist, but he's there, isn't he?" I would not have been very patient—as Parsons emphasizes. Nor would I have been patient with the suggestion that although I undoubtedly failed to refer to anything at all, no doubt I had a belief about a nonexistent student, that is, that there was some nonexistent object that I mistakenly took to be existent and to have the properties of standing outside my door and probably wanting an incomplete. Indeed, Parsons's dialogue strongly suggests this latter impatience as well. As Parsons's speaker A says, "Look, I was talking about a guy who exists; that is, I thought I was, but I was wrong, I wasn't talking about anybody. I can't tell you what he looks like because there's no 'he' to look like anything."

Parsons rightly stresses that it is one thing to posit nonexistents as referents of discourse about fiction or mythology and quite another to have them as booby prizes for intended but failed references to real things. It would be equally unintuitive, however, to insist that such failed references involve beliefs about nonexistent objects. This is implausible in the case of my unsuccessful reference to my imagined student and equally implausible in the case of the faithful Greek's unsuccessful attempts to refer to a real Zeus.

One of the contributions of Parsons's approach is a sharp distinction between two questions that are often run together. First, are there nonexistent objects? Second, when one unsuccessfully attempts to refer to some real thing, has one thereby referred to a nonexistent? Answering the first question in the affirmative does not entail so answering the second. Having distinguished the two questions, Parsons proceeds to defend both nonexistent objects *and* the highly intuitive thesis that failures of reference to real things are just that, failures of reference.

I have argued that Parsons's attempt to coordinate a theory of nonexistent objects with the highly intuitive thesis about reference failure raises unanswered questions. Some of the difficulties raised, those involving anaphoric connections between the remarks of the critic and those of the believer, seem to suggest a perspective on the question of how to understand apparent reference to the nonexistent that is at odds with Parsons's perspective. According to the suggested perspective such apparent reference is to be thought of as pretended reference to real things. Needless to say, working out this idea is quite another matter.[16]

SEVEN

How to Bridge the Gap Between Meaning and Reference

Introduction

There is a temptation during a revolution to minimize the significant differences among the revolutionary parties. The activists themselves, because of their deep and unanimous opposition to the old regime and their exhilaration at recent successes, often find it difficult to overcome the illusion of general agreement on fundamentals. The past quarter of a century has been a period of revolutionary activity in the philosophy of language. The members of the old regime are, as it were, the proponents of the Fregean picture of how words hook up with the world, the idea that singular terms express descriptive concepts and refer to those items that satisfy the concepts. Gottlob Frege's perspective has been vigorously attacked by those recently called by one anthologist "the new theorists of reference," originally Keith Donnellan, David Kaplan, Saul Kripke, and Hilary Putnam. Singular terms refer, according to these theorists, not by expressing concepts but in some much more immediate and direct way. The definite description, Frege's paradigm, has been replaced by a new paradigm or two, the demonstrative expression and/or the Millian proper name that merely tags but does describe its bearer.

Reprinted by permission from *Synthese* 58 (1984): 63–84. Copyright 1984 by D. Reidel Publishing Co.

I plead guilty, as one of the advocates of the newer approach, to the charge of laboring under the delusion of agreement on fundamentals. I became suspicious, however, when I was accused of advocating the causal theory of reference, a view that seemed foreign to my thinking but was supposedly central to, or even definitive of, the new approach. The question I shall address, the question mentioned in the title of this essay, will highlight profound disagreements among the new theorists and will provide an opportunity to further develop the direct reference approach. I shall restrict my discussion to indexical reference, specifically to reference by means of pronouns and demonstratives.

That there is a gap between meaning and reference in the case of indexical expressions has been a cornerstone of the new approach. Consider the first-person pronoun. Each of us can use it to refer to ourselves, yet it is not ambiguous. Its lexical meaning remains constant from your use of it to mine. I am not, then, the referent of my use of 'I' simply in virtue of its lexical meaning. There is, so to speak, not enough to this meaning, as opposed to the meaning of, say, 'the first President of the United States', to determine one individual rather than another. The same is true for the demonstrative 'that'. 'That' can be used to refer to anything at all. Its lexical meaning does not vary, however, from use to use. The reference of an utterance of 'that' is thus not determined solely by its meager lexical meaning. Exactly what bridges the gap between the *meager* lexical meaning of such an indexical expression and its *determinate* reference? What factor(s) enter into the determination of the reference of an indexical over and above its meaning?[1]

The answer I shall give, as a first approximation, is that the gap is to be bridged by features of the context of utterance. My idea is that the reference is determined by the very features which make the reference available to the auditor.[2] I shall argue for this idea by way of criticizing its two main opponents:

1. *The causal theory of reference*. Although this title is often used sloppily to characterize the view of virtually any opponent of the Fregean description paradigm, it more accurately refers to a view about reference that parallels other causal theories in philosophy, the causal theories of perception, knowledge, and so

on. The causal theorist maintains that the gap is to be bridged by the existence of a causal connection between the utterance of the indexical and the referent. Specifically, the referent of a token of 'that' is the unique item that stands in the appropriate causal relation to the production of that token.[3]

2. *The intentional theory.* Causal theories are often championed by physicalists who see such theories as offering hope for a reduction of apparently intentional, mental phenomena in terms of physical causation. A philosopher who is disinclined to pursue such a reductionist program might insist that reference is irreducibly intentional. One form such a proposal may take yields another answer to our question. The gap between meaning and reference is bridged, on this view, by the fact that the speaker utters the indexical with the intention of communicating about a particular item he has in mind. What makes some particular book the referent of "That is an interesting book" is not, on this view, anything about the causal history of the utterance but rather something about the mental state of the speaker, specifically his intention to refer to the item he has in mind.[4]

One of the recurrent themes in the new theory of reference, one that it shares with the approach of Wittgenstein, is that an individualistic or agent-centered picture of language and thought is inadequate and needs to be replaced or at least supplemented by a picture that sees language as a social institution.[5] To maintain that the reference of an indexical expression is determined by the causal history of the utterance or by the referential intentions of the speaker is to maintain an individualistic view, at least by comparison with my approach. The reference of a token of 'that' is determined, on these views, by considerations *about the speaker*, specifically his causal history or intentional states. Features of the context of utterance, for example, interactions between the speaker and addressee like pointing gestures, by means of which the addressee interprets the demonstrative utterance, play no semantic role. Such contextual cues may facilitate communication, but they do not make it the case that one thing rather than another is the referent. My view, however, is that such contextual cues and indeed a whole range of extra-contextual cues, provided, for example, by the social and cultural environment, have semantic significance. It is by means of such cues that the gap between meaning and reference is to be bridged.

Not only are natural languages *social* institutions but they are social *institutions*. I shall emphasize the institutional character of natural language in the following respect. The (or at least a) primary purpose of natural language is to allow for communication concerning the items speakers have in mind and about which they wish to inform others, ask questions, and so on.[6] Natural languages, however, like other *institutions*, the law, for instance, provide for the fulfillment of the institution's primary functions by means of a complex system of rules and conventions. The institutional rules and conventions, although their *point* is to facilitate communication, attain a life of their own once instituted. It is thus important for a person who wishes to communicate his beliefs by means of English sentences to find institutionally acceptable means for doing so. Failing to find such means, he may find himself having "said," in an institutional sense, something other than what he meant, even something other than what he succeeded in conveying. His auditor, that is, may be able to tell what he is getting at despite his having said, strictly speaking, something quite different. A frequently noted example involves a speaker's using a term and meaning by it something other than what it means in the language. Final exams in introductory philosophy courses provide many examples. I shall discuss below a less frequently noted example of the distinction between what was said, strictly speaking, and what was meant or intended. This sort of example will play a crucial role in my arguments against the intentional theory.

Pure Indexicals

Kaplan introduces a useful distinction within the class of indexical expressions.[7] I begin by considering those expressions which Kaplan classifies as "pure indexicals," such as 'I', 'now', 'here', and 'today'. In the next section I turn to Kaplan's "demonstratives," such as 'this', 'that', 'he', and 'she'. Pure indexicals and demonstratives are similar in that both are "context sensitive," as opposed to, say, "the first President of the United States," the reference of which does not vary with the context of utterance. Indexicals are unlike demonstratives, however, in that the reference of a given indexical varies from context to context in a very regular way. 'I' always refers to what Kaplan calls the "agent" of the context, the speaker or writer. Demonstratives like 'that' exhibit no such regular variation of reference. What can be said of the reference of 'that' in every context?[8]

Let us begin with 'now'. Waiting for the baby-sitter to arrive, I say, "The movie is starting now." 'Now' picks out a certain time.[9] How does that happen? How does the reference of 'now' get determined? Is it a matter of the right sort of causal relation holding between the referent and the utterance? Implausible. It is hard enough to think of times as *referents*, let alone to think of them as standing in causal relations. Perhaps some account can be given according to which a time can stand in some (indeed in *the* appropriate) causal relation to an utterance of "now." Causal relations between times and utterances are, in any case, a far cry from the standard examples causal theorists give to motivate their view, and it is not clear how references to times are to be accommodated. Another example is "Here I sit." Think about 'I'. What determines its reference? A causal relation? What are the terms of this relation? Michael Devitt states that first-person references are to be accounted for by the causal relations in which one stands to oneself. Devitt mentions introspection as the relevant causal process.[10] It is far from clear, however, that first-person references are always, or even typically, related to introspection. Devitt's view here certainly requires detailed development and defense. Devitt, though, mentions it only in passing.

There is, in any case, a much simpler and more natural account of how the reference of a pure indexical, 'I', for example, gets determined.[11] It is a rule of our language, internalized by every competent speaker, that 'I' refers to the agent of the context.[12] Thus I am the referent of some appropriate utterance of the first-person pronoun, not because I stand in some causal relation to myself, but rather because *I uttered it*. It is, then, a fact about the context which bridges the gap between meaning and reference.

Am I the referent of 'I' because I uttered it, or rather because, as the intentional theorist would have it, I intended to communicate about myself, I had myself in mind?[13] My strategy against the intentional theory will be to show that a speaker who refers using 'I' refers to himself, even if he has someone other than himself in mind. Examples involving mistaken-identity beliefs seem like promising terrain, examples in which a speaker believes he is someone else and intends to speak of this other person. Consider Ahern, an insane historian who believes he is de Gaulle. If we are to generate an example in which Ahern has de Gaulle in mind when he uses 'I', we need to proceed carefully, for despite Ahern's crazy belief, he, like the rest of us, intends to speak of himself when he uses 'I'—at least most of the time. If someone feels uncomfortable because he has not eaten for hours and says, "I am hungry," he presumably has himself in mind even if he is suffering from amnesia and thus "does not know who he is" and even if, like Ahern, he takes himself to be de Gaulle.[14]

Imagine, however, that Ahern is lecturing on modern European history, and in the course of speaking about de Gaulle's accomplishments, he says, " . . . and then I marched triumphantly into Paris." Such a remark may be motivated by different factors. Ahern may be bragging. The point of his remark may be that *he* did it. Alternatively, his interest may be in the history of the period. His point may be that *de Gaulle* did it, and he, Ahern, said "I" only because 'I', given his mistaken beliefs, seemed the contextually appropriate expression for referring to de Gaulle. We might even imagine that he was trying to keep his belief about de Gaulle's identity a secret but that he slipped and said "I," thus revealing his secret to the class. Perhaps the lecture is accompanied by a silent film of de Gaulle's return. Just as Ahern makes his remark, he points to de Gaulle. It is this history-lecture case, as opposed to the bragging case, that we are after. Here Ahern has de Gaulle rather than himself in mind.[15]

What conclusions can we draw from this example? Ahern's remark, "I marched triumphantly into Paris," is, strictly speaking, false. This is not, however, to say that everything he meant was false or that everything he succeeded in communicating to his audience was false. After all, he intended to communicate that de Gaulle marched triumphantly into Paris, and he may very well have communicated this if, for example, his students were aware of his delusion. Nevertheless, he utilized the institutional apparatus of English to convey his beliefs and, in doing

The Gap Between Meaning and Reference 75

so, asserted a false proposition. What he said, strictly speaking, was false. Two conclusions follow, both of which are damaging to the intentional theory. First, the speaker's uttering a singular term and intending to communicate about something, his having it in mind, is not a sufficient condition for reference to it. Ahern had de Gaulle in mind but nevertheless failed to refer to him.[16] Second, having oneself in mind is not even necessary for first-person pronomial reference. Ahern referred to himself despite his failure to have himself in mind.[17]

The intentional theorist may at this point resist the idea that a speaker can use the first-person pronoun competently and have someone else in mind. Ahern, since he believes he *is* de Gaulle, it may be urged, does have himself in mind.[18] Such resistance is, however, misplaced. A person who wishes to speak about a particular item he has in mind but has mistaken for a different item will often use a singular term that conventionally applies, not to his intended referent, but to the item he has confused it with. Someone says, "What is that man doing out there?" Another responds, mistaking the man they see for Jones, "It looks like Jones. Jones appears to be raking leaves." The second speaker wishes to answer a question about "the man out there." Yet because of his mistaken belief, he uses a term which fails to conventionally apply to that man.[19] Similarly, if I mistakenly take myself to be de Gaulle, I may use his name when I really want to convey information about myself, as in "De Gaulle is hungry." Given that same mistaken belief, I may use a term that applies to me, such as 'I', when I really want to communicate about de Gaulle. Surely the first-person pronoun is not immune to this intended reference versus conventional application phenomenon.

Nevertheless the claim that the deranged teacher has de Gaulle in mind, that de Gaulle is *the* intended referent, needs to be qualified.[20] There is surely a sense in which he also intends to communicate about himself.[21] After all, he thinks he *is* de Gaulle; he said, "*I* marched triumphantly . . ." Why not say that the speaker, in such cases, has both individuals in mind? Indeed, I think we should say this—with one qualification: the speaker does not have them in mind equally. This may be brought out by noting that the history lecturer, who genuinely intends to be teaching about de Gaulle and is not interested in bragging, intends to communicate about himself only insofar as he takes himself to be de Gaulle. Were he to learn about his mistake (and somehow not become catatonic), he could still accomplish his communicative goal by simply substituting 'de Gaulle' for 'I'. His intending to communicate information about himself is thus a *subsidiary* intention.[22]

Cases of divergence of intended reference and conventional application often involve two havings-in-mind, one primary and one subsidiary.[23] Furthermore, when a speaker refers by using 'I', since he knows that 'I' always refers to the utterer, he will surely have himself in mind at least in the subsidiary sense. This does not, however, provide any support for the intentional theorist. The intentional theorist maintained that when the point of the historian's utterance was not to brag about himself but to convey information about de Gaulle, then de Gaulle was the referent of 'I', that the referent was what the individual had *primarily* in mind. This thesis is just what the Ahern example shows to be false.[24]

I conclude that the intentional theorist is mistaken, at least with regard to first-person pronomial reference, and indeed, he is mistaken with regard to references by the other expressions Kaplan classifies as pure indexicals, 'here' and 'now', for example, for my argument is applicable to them as well. The gap between the meaning and reference of a pure indexical is to be bridged neither by the speaker's causal connections nor by his mental states but rather by publicly available features of the context of utterance.[25]

Demonstratives: Critical Remarks

The linguistic rule that governs 'I' specifies its reference in terms of a simple, noncausal, nonintentional property of the context. The singular terms which Kaplan calls "demonstratives" are quite a different matter, or so it seems. It appears to be difficult to specify the references of 'this', 'that', 'he', or 'she' in terms of some such property. How, then, does the reference of 'that', for instance, get determined?

The causal theory of reference, while it seemed so highly counterintuitive for the pure indexicals, does not seem so here. One who finds the causal-theoretic approach generally appealing in philosophy might readily suppose that the referent of "He is a nice man" is the unique man who occupies just the right place in the causal history of the utterance. Even here, however, the causal theory will not do. A speaker who is causally isolated from an entity can still refer to it by uttering a demonstrative while pointing to it. Even blindfolded and thus visually cut off from one's surroundings, one can point and say things like "That is a tree," "That is a cow," and so on. (Imagine this occurring on a picnic with one's children.) Such guesses would be either true or false, and so one would have referred despite a lack of causal connection with the items pointed to. Colin McGinn gives an example of a factory inspector who is supposed to approve or disapprove of each car that comes off the assembly line. "That one is roadworthy," he typically says. The inspector momentarily looks away as a new car appears. He nevertheless makes the same remark with his usual gesture in the direction of the assembly line. He is not causally connected with the new car in any appropriate way, but he surely refers to it. If the car is defective, he can be accused of having said something false.[26]

How about an intentional theory of demonstratives? Suppose someone in a room full of people says, "He is a nice man," referring to some man across the room. It is not implausible to suppose that what makes one of the men in the room the referent of 'he' is that the speaker had him in mind. Nevertheless, the intentional account is no more adequate here than it was in the case of the pure indexicals.

. A variation on the theme of intended reference/conventional application will provide an example. A speaker wishes to say something about a certain man, Jones, whom he mistakenly thinks he sees in the distance. Jones recently had open-heart surgery, and the speaker has heard that Jones has foolishly been exerting himself raking leaves. He says, pointing to the man whom he takes to be Jones but who is actually Smith, "That is a self-destructive man. He has been raking leaves against his doctor's orders." Here the speaker actually has Jones, rather than the man he sees, primarily in mind. He intends to refer to "that man over there" only insofar as he takes him to be Jones. Were he to learn of his mistake, he could still accomplish his communicative end by substituting 'Jones' for 'that'.

Jones, then, is the individual he has in mind in the primary sense. Nevertheless, when he says, "That is a self-destructive man," he speaks falsely, for the man he points out, Smith, is, we may assume, in excellent physical and mental health. Primary havings-in-mind, just like the pure indexicals, are not sufficient for determining the reference of demonstratives (since the really self-destructive Jones was not referred to), nor are such havings-in-mind necessary (since Smith, the man pointed out but not primarily intended *was* referred to).[27]

Demonstratives: Positive Remarks

Reference is socially determined in a deeper way than has been allowed for even by the new theorists of reference.[28] The causal and intentional views fall short precisely because they fail to recognize the semantic significance of, say, the speaker's communicational interactions. The very examples which show the inadequacy of causal/intentional views, cases of "blind pointing" (the picnic example) and the recent Smith-Jones case, strongly suggest that pointing gestures not only provide cues as to the reference but actually determine the reference.[29]

Pointing, however, is not unique in playing both roles. The reference to Smith, the man in the distance, would remain unchanged if the speaker did not point but rather took advantage of the fact that Smith was the only individual in view. The reference would remain unchanged if there were a number of people in view but Smith was somehow prominent, he was, say, walking toward the speaker and the auditor and waving in their direction. There are a host of such contextual features that provide cues to the auditor and, at the same time, enter into the determination of reference.[30]

The semantically significant cues, moreover, are not limited to those provided by the context of utterance. Just as the fact that some individual is walking toward the speaker and the auditor and waving can, in the right circumstances, both indicate and determine that he is the referent, so too can the fact that the speaker and the auditor were just talking about someone, or that when they last spoke, their conversation was dominated by a discussion of something, or that something has dominated their attention recently even if they have not spoken about it. "I've been thinking about it, and I can actually prove that he is wrong," might open a conversation with a colleague. Jimmy Carter might wake up in the middle of the night after his debate with Reagan and say to Rosalyn, "He really beat me. I could have done much better than that." Relevant cues, then, can be provided by what the addressee knows about the speaker's interests, desires, history, and so on.[31]

Semantically significant cues *can be* provided by an extremely wide range of contextual and extra-contextual factors. This is not to say, however, that every bit of information that the addressee finds helpful in interpreting the utterance is semantically significant. The auditor in the Smith-Jones case, if he knows enough, might infer that the speaker, despite pointing to Smith, really had Jones in mind. The auditor might know that the speaker had been very upset at his sick friend Jones's behavior, that the man in the distance looks like Jones but is really Smith, and so on. These cues have a bearing on the utterance's "interpretation" in some broad sense, but they do not affect the determination of what was, strictly speaking, said. Jones, although he was indicated by these cues, is not the referent but is merely the intended referent.

What distinguishes the semantically significant cues? Notice that the cues just mentioned, the ones that might have identified Jones as the *intended* referent, were clearly not the cues that the speaker was relying on to convey his intended reference. The cue that the speaker clearly relied upon was the pointing gesture, a cue that indicated Smith and not Jones, his intended referent. This suggests that the semantically significant cues are those that the speaker relied upon. The referent is the individual *these* cues identify, whether or not he was the intended referent, the individual these cues were intended to identify.[32]

This is not quite right, however, for a speaker is sometimes responsible for unintended cues. Suppose that our speaker walks up to Smith, stares straight at him, extends his finger right in Smith's face, and says, "That is a self-destructive man." No one, as I imagine the scene, could have any doubt that the speaker intends to ostensively indicate Smith. Unfortunately for all concerned, however, our speaker was merely stretching, his mind was elsewhere, and he intended to convey his reference by more subtle background cues, cues that indeed identify Jones, his intended referent. In such a case, I am strongly inclined to suppose that the speaker is responsible for his apparent pointing gesture and that Smith, the individual apparently pointed to, is the referent. If Smith is not self-destructive, then what the speaker has said, strictly speaking, is false.[33] Someone who utters a demonstrative is responsible, from the point of view of the natural language institution, for making his intended reference available to his addressee, and so he is responsible for the cues that a competent and attentive addressee would take him to be exploiting. The cues for which he is responsible, those that he, to all appearances, exploits, are the cues that determine the reference.[34]

The gap between meaning and reference is to be bridged by the cues that the competent and attentive addressee will reasonably take the speaker to be exploiting. My account, although it denies that intentions determine reference, does not deny the importance of speakers' intentions. Indeed, the *point* of the institutionalized conventions I have been discussing is to facilitate communication concerning the items speakers have in mind and about which they intend to inform others, ask questions, and so on. In the most usual, everyday cases, moreover, people refer to the items they intend, the items they have in mind in the primary sense, and in such cases the referent is just the intended referent. It is in the unusual cases involving misidentification in which reference and intended reference can diverge.

Playing an important role, on my view, are intentions other than referential intentions: the speaker's reliance on certain cues, that is, his intention to utilize certain cues, discussed above, as well as the intention to address a particular audience. A competent and attentive *bystander* might reasonably interpret an utterance very differently than does the *addressee*, because of, for example, different visual perspectives on the speaker's pointing gesture or different bits of background knowledge that they would reasonably assume the speaker to be exploiting. What the speaker says, strictly speaking, and thus his reference, is determined by the cues available to the addressee. The bystander is irrelevant. What makes a particular individual "the addressee"? Here the speaker's intention to address a particular audience comes into play. This intention does not straightforwardly determine the addressee, however, any more than the intention to utilize certain cues straightforwardly determined the semantically significant cues. If a speaker gives every indication that he is speaking to a particular person, then the latter is the addressee even if the speaker actually intends to be speaking to someone else. The addressee is the individual whom it is reasonable to take the speaker to be addressing.

We have, then, a noncausal, nonintentional account of the reference of demonstratives. Referential intentions, however, seem to be particularly resistant to being banished as semantic determinants; they crop up in unexpected places. Kaplan notes that

> whenever I point at something, from the surveyor's point of view I point at many things. When I point at my son (and say "I love [that]"), I may also be pointing at a book he is holding, his jacket, a button on his jacket, his skin, his heart, and his dog standing behind him—from a surveyor's point of view.[35]

Kaplan's emphasis on the surveyor's point of view encourages a misconception of our practice of pointing. One can certainly indicate an object by a pointing gesture even though the object is not geometrically along a line projected from the pointing finger. Surely it is enough that the referent be in a vaguely defined neighborhood of such a line. Thus one can refer to a man via an utterance of 'he' and a pointing gesture even if the gesture misses his right ear by half an inch—from the surveyor's point of view.[36] But now Kaplan's indeterminacy is multiplied. Not only is pointing indeterminate along the line of the pointing finger; it is indeterminate *around* that line. One can gesture with one's head, moreover, in such a fashion that there is not even a clear line of pointing, thus complicating matters even further.

I have argued that the reference of a demonstrative utterance accompanied by a pointing gesture depends not on what the speaker has in mind but rather on what his pointing gesture indicates. The gesture, we now see, fails to indicate a unique item. How, then, are we to account for the determinate reference if not by appeal to the speaker's referential intention? The intentional theorist would still not be vindicated, for as the Smith-Jones case of the previous section showed, the reference of a demonstrative is not determined by what the speaker has in mind. Nevertheless, such intentions would play an important role, that of resolving the indeterminacy of pointing gestures.[37]

The indeterminacy of pointing, however, does not necessitate such an appeal to referential intentions. I agree that ostension is indeterminate. Indeed, it is irremediably indeterminate. This indeterminacy is not an illusion to be overcome by finding some factor which shows us that the ostension was determinate all along, the speaker's intention, for example, or some subtle and sophisticated rules of pointing. Still, the indeterminacy creates no problem. Imagine that I point to one of several women in the room and say, "She is the author of an important paper in decision theory." My pointing gesture, we may suppose, takes us to her, to a book she is holding, to her sweater, her kidney, and so on. Nevertheless, I have referred to her. Although the pointing gesture is indeterminate, it surely provides enough of a cue *given* that the demonstrative used was 'she' and that there are no other females in the range of the pointing. Imagine an utterance of "That one is the author of an important paper in decision theory" accompanied by a gesture toward the same woman. Again the gesture, considered in isolation, is indeterminate. It is a sufficient indication, however, in the presence of additional cues, for example, the fact that the predicate indicates that the speaker intends to talk about a person and there is no other person in the range of the pointing. Other examples we might construct would have all sorts of cues contributing to the indicated-individual calculation.

Let us consider another problem with respect to which referential intentions threaten to intrude. What if the addressee, through no fault of his own, cannot ascertain the reference? When Kaplan points in his son's direction and says, "I love that," his auditor might not be able to tell whether Kaplan means that he loves his son or whether Kaplan—exploiting the fact that he has spent a good part of the day praising the book that his son is carrying, *The Phenomenology of Spirit*—means that he loves the book. Even where there is no puzzle about which cues are intended, the available cues may fail to determine a unique individual. An inadvertent speaker may try to indicate an individual by an utterance of "he" accompanied by a vague gesture of his head, but may fail to do so because of the presence, unnoticed by the speaker, of two men in the range of the vague gesture. Should we allow that, at least in such cases, what is referred to depends upon what the speaker had in mind? After all, the addressee will typically ask such a speaker which item he was speaking about.

It is far from obvious, however, that we should take the speaker's response to settle the question of what it was that he, strictly speaking, said. The question posed to him did not concern such institutional matters. The addressee's interest, in such conversational contexts, is in which item the speaker meant, which he had in mind, and his answer should be interpreted in this light. If the speaker fails to make his reference available, his speech act is defective, and not even the best intentions can repair the defect. The speaker, strictly speaking, has not asserted anything determinate, that is, anything at all. The defect is, of course, negligible for the practical purposes of ordinary communication, since the speaker, when questioned, easily supplies the information about which thing he meant. Here, as in the de Gaulle case, the speaker may be able to convey his message without having said it. Cases in which the speaker fails to make the reference available to the addressee do not require us to introduce intentions as semantic determinants.

Conclusion

I shall conclude by discussing a recent proposal by Colin McGinn, in "The Mechanism of Reference," a proposal that, like my own, gives great weight to the context of utterance in the determination of reference. Unlike my view, however, McGinn holds that the reference of indexicals and demonstratives is always determined by features of the immediate context of utterance and never by what I have called "extra-contextual cues." Even in cases in which McGinn and I agree that the semantic determinants are features of the immediate context, our accounts of precisely how the context contributes to the determination of reference greatly differ. What is crucial, holds McGinn, are the spatio-temporal relations between "the speaker's actions and the things around him."[38] Thus, in the case of demonstratives, the pointing gesture is, for McGinn, not merely one way among many in which the context can contribute to the determination of reference, as it is for me. Indeed, McGinn proposes that the semantic rule governing demonstratives in English runs as follows: "the referent of a token of 'that F' is to be the first F to intersect the line projected from the pointing finger, i.e. the F at the place indicated—one might almost say geometrically—by the accompanying gesture."[39]

Although I agree with much in McGinn's interesting paper, I find his account of the contribution of the context implausible. I shall restrict myself to a few comments, since a full discussion is not possible here. First, McGinn formulates a rule of reference, not for demonstratives like 'this' and 'that', but rather for demonstrative phrases like 'that man'. Were one to try to formulate a McGinn-like rule for 'that' *simpliciter*, for example, "the referent of a token of 'that' is the first thing to intersect the line projected from the pointing finger," one would encounter problems. Why, for example, is the line projected from the pointing finger not stopped by the first speck of dust it hits, or the first air molecule, and so on? McGinn, as he explained in conversation, assumes that utterances of "this" and "that" are always elliptical for expressions of the form "this F," and so the problem just mentioned is avoided, but it is avoided at a cost. The thesis that demonstratives like 'this' and 'that' are elliptical surely stands in need of argument and is, to my mind at least, highly implausible.[40]

Second, as I maintain above[41] and as McGinn himself notes, pointing is quite inessential to the use of demonstratives. McGinn tries to account for this with the remark that where there is only one F around, it is not important that the speaker point. "The location of the speaker's body is what serves as the paralinguistic determinant of such reference when no other or finer spatio-temporal directions are required by the hearer."[42] The inessentiality of pointing goes much deeper, however, than McGinn can allow for. Even when there are thirty men around, I may say, "That one is a outrageous," or (to accommodate McGinn's view that 'that' always requires a sortal) "That man is outrageous," without any finger-pointing gesture, nod of the head, or anything similar. I nevertheless refer to a particular man just in case something about the communicational interaction makes it perfectly clear who is in question. Imagine that you are my addressee, that we speak often about how outrageous James Watt, the U.S. Secretary of the Interior, is, and that we are at a reception for the Queen of England at which Watt is present. Further imagine that Watt is speaking into a microphone while moving around the room, so that we can hear him but have no idea where he is at the moment. After some particularly outrageous remark of Watt's, I say, "That man is outrageous." Clearly, Watt is the referent, the reference certainly seems to be a straightforward demonstrative reference, and yet nothing like a spatial relation determines the reference. Watt is the referent in virtue of the cues available to the addressee, considerations that include the facts that his voice was, so to speak, perceptually salient, that you—the addressee—know that I often express this view about Watt, and so on.

Finally, a consequence of McGinn's view that I find dubious is the thesis, certainly not unique to McGinn, that one can demonstratively refer only to items to which one is in a position to point. With respect to the last example, imagine that immediately after Watt's speech Watt leaves the room. Further imagine that, unlike the last case, I suppress my anger for the duration of his speech but can hardly contain myself. Immediately after his departure I say, "That man is outrageous." Again, I take it that I have demonstratively referred to Watt and that what makes Watt the referent is the fact that he is the individual indicated by the cues. Nor is it crucial that my remark be made immediately after the speech. You and I may be on our way home after the speech, or we may meet days later and it may be obvious to you that I am still fuming about the speech. I may say, "That man is outrageous," realizing that it will be obvious that Watt is in question. It is plausible to suppose that we can refer demonstratively to individuals far removed from us in space and time.[43]

I have advanced what we might call a contextual account of indexical reference, now using 'contextual' in the broad sense in which we speak not only of linguistic contexts but also of social and cultural ones, and using 'indexical' for the class that includes both the pure indexicals and the demonstratives. The simplest and cleanest case is that of the pure indexicals. The reference of 'I', for example, is determined by a quite pedestrian feature of the context, namely, who is speaking. The reference of demonstratives, a much messier business, is determined by a much messier collection of contextual features. Reference is determined in both cases, however, by those very features of communicational interactions that make the reference available.[44]

EIGHT

Frege-Russell Semantics?

CONTEMPORARY semantical discussions make mention of the traditional approach to semantics represented by Frege and/or Russell—even sometimes by Frege-Russell. Is there a Frege-Russell view in the philosophy of language? How much of a common semantical perspective did Gottlob Frege and Bertrand Russell share? The matter bears exploration. I begin with Frege and Russell on propositions.

Introduction: Propositions, Acquaintance, and Direct Reference

Russell was not shy about the difference between his account of propositions and Frege's.

I believe that in spite of all its snowfields, Mont Blanc is itself a component part of what is actually asserted in the proposition 'Mont Blanc is more than 4000 metres high.' We do not assert the thought, for this is a private psychological matter. We assert the object of the thought, and this is, to my mind, a certain complex (an objective proposition, one might say) in which Mont Blanc is itself a component part.[1]

Russell, in this letter to Frege, is not being altogether fair to Frege, for Frege surely never suggested that thoughts, in the sense of private psychological entities, are the items that we assert. What Frege calls "thoughts" are what we call propositions. Frege takes propositions to be apprehended by the mind but insists that they do not reside in the mind. Nevertheless, the substantial disagreement between the two is clear enough. Fregean thoughts are thoroughly conceptual; they are the senses of sentences, and their constituents are the senses of the sentential components. Russell, on the contrary, thinks that there are nonconceptual constituents of propositions, that, contra Frege, the *references* of expressions, things like you and me, can "occur in what is asserted."

Frege's views on propositional constituency are intimately related to his basic semantic picture. Fregean senses are at once the ingredients in propositions and the items in terms of which the word-world relation is to be understood. Russell's idea that the references of expressions can be constituents of propositions, an idea that sounds bizarre to those of us brought up on Frege, is very much connected to his rejection of Frege's sense-reference view and his substitution of a very different basic semantic perspective.[2]

There is another aspect of Russell's view about propositional constituents worth noting here. Focusing upon this aspect will set the stage for a discussion of just how different Russell's basic semantic picture is from Frege's. It will illustrate, moreover, the intimate connection between Russell's semantic views and his epistemological outlook. Russell announces a "fundamental epistemological principle": "Every proposition which we can understand must be composed wholly of constituents with which we are acquainted."[3]

Russell goes on to explain that "we have acquaintance with sense-data, with many universals, and possibly with ourselves [Russell here has Humean worries about the self as a possible object of acquaintance], but not with physical objects, or other minds."[4] Russell's fundamental principle does not quite limit the constituents of propositions to objects of direct acquaintance. There may be propositions that contain things with which we are not acquainted. These, however, are not propositions that we can understand or, presumably, assert. The propositions that we can understand or assert, then, may contain only sense data, universals, and (perhaps) ourselves.[5]

The dispute between Frege and Russell concerning the constituents of propositions, I have said, betokens a fundamental difference in semantic perspective. Russell maintains that when one is acquainted with something, a present sense datum, say, or oneself, one can refer to it without the mediation of anything like a Fregean sense. One can refer to it, as we might say, *directly*.[6] Indeed, Russell invents a new linguistic category, the "genuine" or "logically proper" name, that subsumes expressions that function in this most un-Fregean way. A logically proper name—Russell's examples of logically proper names of particulars are 'I' (if indeed we are acquainted with the self) and 'this' (when the latter is used to refer to a present sense datum)—is a "mere noise or shape conventionally used to designate a certain [thing]; it gives us no information about that [thing], and has nothing that can be called its meaning as opposed to denotation."[7]

I have so far called attention to two Russellian notions that depart radically from the Fregean outlook: nonconceptual constituents of propositions and conceptually unmediated reference. Acquaintance, as we have seen, furnishes a link between them. One can refer directly, by means of a genuine name, only to an object of acquaintance, and when one does so, the referent itself will be a constituent of the proposition expressed.

Frege's Rejection of Sinnless Reference: The Representative Theory of Conception

Russell's idea of direct, *Sinn*less reference is one that Frege does not ever explicitly consider, and one that he surely would have rejected, both early and late. In the *Begriffsschrift*, however, Frege seems to have advanced a closely related idea. Frege appears to have held that while names have associated modes of presentation—he calls them "ways of determining the content"—the semantic function of a name is not to introduce its associated mode of presentation into the proposition expressed. The semantic function of a name is rather merely to make its referent a subject of discourse.[8] The early Frege thus shares with Russell the idea that nothing senselike gets into the proposition. Russell's proposal, however, goes far beyond Frege's early view. Russell, unlike Frege, gives no role at all to modes of presentation. The connection between linguistic expression and referent, for Russell, is not to be explained by the referent's fitting the term's associated mode of presentation, the referent's having the property associated with the term, for there is no such mode of presentation, or property, associated with the expression.

What was so unthinkable to Frege about *Sinn*less reference? It is sometimes suggested that Frege rejects the possibility of direct reference because of his puzzle about informative identity. This seems unlikely. The Frege of the *Begriffsschrift*, I have suggested, had modes of presentation in his intellectual repertoire. The early Frege did not suppose, though, that this solved the problem of informativeness. Still, one might think, senses were at least necessary (if not sufficient) for a solution. I do not believe that even this much is correct. Frege's *Begriffsschrift* metalinguistic account of identity sentences works just as well for senseless, directly referential names as it does for names that have associated modes of presentation. Let 'Hesperus' and 'Phosphorus' be directly referential, mere "noises or shapes conventionally used to designate," that give no information about their referents.[9] Given Frege's metalinguistic account of identity, the proposition expressed by 'Hesperus = Phosphorus' will be the nontrivial proposition that the referent of the one name is identical to the referent of the other, quite different name. Thus Frege's puzzle is not, at least to the early Frege, solved by the introduction of senses, and his proposed solution would work as well for *Sinn*less names. All of this suggests that the informativeness puzzle was not the key to Frege's adoption of his fundamental thesis that reference requires an associated mode of presentation.

One gets the feeling from reading and rereading Frege, moreover, that his implicit denial of the possibility of conceptually unmediated reference plays a role much more fundamental than is allowed for by the prior suggestion. It is not merely that the reference-without-sense picture is not adequate to certain puzzles. It is that the very idea of *Sinn*less reference is somehow incoherent. In some strong sense, there could not be reference without sense. Whether or not Frege held this strong view, and I bet that he did, it is certainly consonant with the things that he does say. It is, moreover, a view worth exploring, if for no other reason than because it is the sort of thing one often hears in discussions with philosophers of broadly Fregean orientation. Why might Frege, or anyone else for that matter, think that Russell's idea is thus incoherent, or impossible, or something of the like?

My speculation is that something very deep inclined Frege to suppose that reference without sense was impossible: Frege's philosophical picture of thought and of the contents of thought. Here is an analogy. A view sometimes called "the representative theory of perception" maintains that the perception of a physical object requires, perhaps consists in, the apprehension of sense data that represent the physical object. Direct perceptual apprehension of physical objects, on such a view, is impossible, perhaps even incoherent. My proposal is that Frege held an analogous view about *thought*, a "representative theory of *conception*." The idea here is that thought about an object requires, and perhaps consists in, the apprehension of a concept that represents the object. Frege, I want to suggest, was drawn, even early on, to the idea that thinking of an object requires—maybe even consists in—the direct apprehension of a sense, of a mode of presentation of the object.

This traditional idea has had considerable appeal. Indeed, what is taken to be the alternative might seem almost magical: the direct apprehension in thought of things thought about. When you think about me, to give an example, don't you have to think about me *in a certain way*, as, for example, the author of this paper? What would it mean to *just think about me*, to think about me without, so to speak, bringing me under a concept? Such considerations, whether or not they are in the end conclusive, have certainly made the representative theory tempting, prima facie plausible.

If Frege, even at the time of the *Begriffsschrift*, indeed accepted the representative theory of conception, this would explain why reference without sense would seem incoherent. Notice that to accept the representative theory, one need not accept Frege's later view that the representations constitute the content of the proposition expressed. The propositional content might even include—as Russell maintained, and as Frege's remarks in the *Begriffsschrift* suggest—the object thought about. There is, of course, a certain tension between this Russellian conception of propositional content and the idea that to be thinking of Hesperus is just to be entertaining a concept. It is this tension, I want to suggest, that gets resolved with Frege's "On Sense and Reference" conception of propositional content.

Was Russell a Representationalist?

According to Russell, when one stands in direct epistemic contact with something, one needs no representational intermediaries in order to think about, or refer to, it. Russell was, in this respect, an arch-anti-representationalist. Notice, however, the role of the epistemic immediacy. *It* is what precludes the need for any representational intermediary. What about examples in which someone speaks or thinks about something with which he is not acquainted? Here Russell's representationalism comes to the fore. I cannot, held Russell, directly apprehend external objects, the pen I am now using, for example. The only way I can make cognitive contact with such things, albeit a kind of inferior contact, is (roughly) by apprehending concepts that represent the things. I say "roughly" because Russell's representationalism is so different from Frege's that talk of Russellian "mediating concepts" needs substantial qualification—to be provided in the last section below, "Concluding Remarks." Russell endorses a *kind* of conceptually mediated reference, but he never made it ubiquitous, as did Frege. We revert to "mediating concepts" only when we wish to speak of something with which we lack epistemic intimacy, according to Russell.

This is not to say, however, that Russell took conceptually mediated reference to be a kind of unusual exception. The overwhelming majority of the things about which people ordinarily speak, Russell is the first to admit, are not objects of acquaintance. Ordinary names of other people, since they refer to things with which I cannot be acquainted, surely do not function for me as genuine names, but rather as concept introducers. Ordinary proper names, that is, function as definite descriptions. Even demonstratives like 'this' and 'that', expressions that intuitively perhaps come as close as any to being pointing devices that do not refer by conceptually characterizing the referent, are ordinarily used, not to refer to sense data, but to refer to external physical objects. Most ordinary singular terms, according to Russell, are surrogates for definite descriptions. Logically proper names, despite their theoretical interest, do not seem to have much to do with ordinary linguistic practice.

> Common words, even proper names, are usually really descriptions. That is to say, the thought in the mind of a person using a proper name correctly can generally be expressed explicitly if we replace the proper name by a description. Moreover, the description required to express the thought will vary for different people, or for the same person at different times. The only thing constant (so long as the name is rightly used) is the object to which the name applies. But so long as this remains constant, the particular description involved usually makes no difference to the truth or falsehood of the proposition in which the name appears.[10]

Sounds just like Frege, no?

> In the case of an actual proper name such as 'Aristotle' opinions as to the sense may differ. It might, for instance, be taken to be the following: the pupil of Plato and teacher of Alexander the Great. Anybody who does this will attach another sense to the sentence 'Aristotle was born in Stagira' than will a man who takes as the sense of the name: the teacher of Alexander the Great who was born in Stagira. So long as the reference remains the same, such variations of sense may be tolerated, although they are to be avoided in the theoretical structure of a demonstrative science and ought not to occur in a perfect language.[11]

We seem to have arrived at a Frege-Russell consensus. Ordinary singular terms, at least the great majority of them, are not directly referential. They refer by expressing concepts. This is not, of course, to say that Frege and Russell agree on all the essentials. Russell, but not Frege, thinks that at least some singular terms are directly referential. Russell's reason, moreover, for thinking that the great majority of singular terms express concepts is that the great majority of the things about which we wish to speak are not objects of acquaintance. Frege certainly never suggests that epistemic immediacy with an object would somehow make possible *Sinn*less reference to it. Finally, as noted above, talk of Russellian "mediating concepts" needs serious qualification.

Nevertheless, Frege and Russell seem to share something of a common perspective. Ordinary singular terms make mediated semantic contact with things. The propositional constituents that correspond to ordinary singular terms, are, moreover, for both Frege and Russell, the mediating representation, not the reference. Russell, one might suppose, was the first in a long line of neo-Fregeans.

Why Russell Was Not a Neo-Fregean

Russell, however, seems to take pains to distance himself from Fregean representationalism. His view, contrary to the suggestion of the last paragraph, was not that Frege's approach, or something much like it, successfully accounts, at least in general, for linguistic phenomena, that such an approach misfires only with regard to the theoretically interesting, although rarely occurring, phenomenon of logically proper names. Russell believed, on the contrary, that the sense-reference picture was fundamentally mistaken.[12] How, then, shall we construe *his* representationalism? How, specifically, does it differ from Frege's?

Let us begin by drawing a distinction, crucial from Russell's point of view, between two sorts of definite descriptions, ones like 'the most long-lived of men', as opposed to ones like 'the material object causally responsible for this' (where 'this' refers to a present sense datum).[13] The relevant difference is that only the first is, as we might say, "purely qualitative," or "purely descriptional."[14] The second, insofar as it contains what Russell would consider a genuine name, is a sort of hybrid. Russell held that the definite descriptions our ordinary singular terms conceal are not purely descriptional.

A description known to be applicable to a particular must involve some reference to a particular with which we are acquainted, if our knowledge about the thing described is not to be merely what follows logically from the description. All names of places—London, England, Europe, the Earth, the Solar System— . . . involve, when used, descriptions which start from some one or more particulars with which we are acquainted.[15] I suspect that even the Universe, as considered by metaphysics, involves such a connection with particulars. In logic, on the contrary, where we are concerned not merely with what does exist, but with whatever might or could exist or be, no reference to actual particulars is involved.[16]

When I say, "London is ugly," or, to use an indexical phrase instead of a name, "This pen ran out of ink," the respective singular terms, 'London' and 'this pen', purport to refer to things that are not possible objects of acquaintance, and so, thinks Russell, those terms must be surrogates for definite descriptions. 'London' and 'this pen' are, at the same time, terms that I "know to be applicable to particulars," and so the descriptions that each of these terms conceals must involve reference to things with which I am acquainted. The description concealed by 'this pen' might be, for example, 'the pen causally responsible for this' (where the demonstrative refers to some relevant sense datum).

Russell's notion of genuine name thus plays a role much more central than we had supposed. It is not merely that Russell makes theoretical room for direct reference even as he admits that, in practice, ordinary singular terms are, by and large, descriptional. Direct reference is involved even in our conceptually mediated references to ordinary things. Russell's representationalism is thus a far cry from Frege's.

What led Russell to make hybrid description the effective paradigm, to reject the Fregean purely qualitative paradigm? As noted above, Russell tells us that "a description known to be applicable to a particular must involve some reference to a particular with which we are acquainted, if our knowledge about the thing described is not to be merely what follows logically from the description." There is, Russell seems to be saying, a certain sort of knowledge about the denotation of a purely qualitative description that is, in principle, unattainable. So if ordinary names abbreviated such descriptions, we could not have this sort of knowledge of their denotations. Russell holds, however, that, in the case of ordinary names, we surely do have this kind of knowledge.

One thing that is confusing about Russell's discussion is that he has characterized the impossible-to-attain knowledge in two ways that do not sound as though they come to the same thing. We cannot know, he tells us, that a purely qualitative description is "applicable to a particular." And we cannot know "anything that does not follow from the description itself."

Let us begin with the second, and more tractable, formulation. One can know, perhaps one automatically knows, that the denotation of 'the most long-lived of men', if such exists, must be a man, and must have lived longer than any other man. This much presumably "follows from the description." One cannot go beyond such knowledge, however, and come to know that the denotation of this description is, say, Chinese, or is the man standing before me now. (Why not? I shall return to this below.)

What about Russell's other characterization of the unattainable sort of knowledge, "knowledge that the description is applicable to a particular"? Russell apparently does not here intend to rule out the possibility of coming to know that a purely qualitative description has a denotation, that something or other satisfies the description. He tells us, for example, that "'the most long-lived of men' is a description which must apply to some man, but we can make no judgments about this man which involve knowledge about him beyond what the description gives."[17] The knowledge Russell apparently means to exclude as "knowledge that the description is applicable to a particular" is knowledge that, as Russell sometimes says, the description applies to a "particular particular." One cannot come to know, that is, to *which thing it is* that the description applies. One cannot, for example, come to know who was the most long-lived man.[18]

The case is quite different, according to Russell, for hybrid descriptions, or for names that abbreviate them. I can know not only that the name 'Jonathan Wettstein', the name of my son, has a denotation. I can also know which thing it is to which the name applies. It applies to my son, the very person sitting across the table from me now, and so on.[19]

Putting aside the differences in the two formulations, Russell certainly seems to be saying that we cannot, in principle, come to know anything substantive about the denotation of descriptions like 'the most long-lived of men'. It is time that we asked, why in the world not? Why, in principle, couldn't we conduct a study and come to learn that there is a uniquely most long-lived person, that she is Chinese, that her name is such-and-such, and so on? Indeed, allowing ourselves Russell's intuitive talk of *knowing who*, we could presumably meet the relevant person and thus come to know who she is, that she is, for example, the person standing before me now. Why should, and how could, the fact that our initial specification was in purely qualitative terms preclude such knowledge?

I suspect that Russell has not expressed himself well, that he would have agreed that we can have knowledge of the denotation of a purely qualitative description that goes beyond the information contained in the description. Russell's motivation for the thesis that ordinary names are descriptional, but not purely descriptional, is not, I want to suggest, quite what it appears to be.

Russell tells us in *The Problems of Philosophy* that

> there are various stages in the removal from acquaintance with particulars: there is Bismarck to people who knew him; Bismarck to those who only know of him through history; the man with the iron mask; the most long-lived of men. These are progressively removed from acquaintance with particulars; the first comes as near to acquaintance as is possible in regard to another person; in the second, we shall still be said to know "who Bismarck was"; in the third, we do not know who was the man with the iron mask, though we know many propositions about him which are not logically deducible from the fact that he wore an iron mask;[20] in the fourth, finally, we know nothing beyond what is logically deducible from the definition of the man.[21]

Let us distinguish, along Russellian lines, three ways of making epistemic contact with particulars. At one extreme, one makes the most direct sort of epistemic contact. Bismarck, for example, is acquainted with himself. At the other extreme, one makes direct contact, not with a particular, but with a constellation of purely qualitative universals, the sort of thing expressed by a purely qualitative definite description. If such a constellation of universals is uniquely instantiated, by an external material object or another person, say, then one might be said to be making a kind of inferior, mediated epistemic contact with that thing.

There is an intermediate case. One might make direct contact with a constellation of universals *and* acquainted-with-particulars, the sort of constellation expressed by a hybrid description like 'the person who is my only daughter' (e.g. as used by me). Such a constellation affords me a mediated but still intermediate-level epistemic access to my daughter, for she is being presented as related to a particular with which I am directly acquainted, in this case, me.

It is crucial to note here that Russell links this intermediate epistemic access to *knowing who*.[22] Not only Bismarck's friends but even someone who knows Bismarck only through history can be said to know "who Bismarck was." Russell's idea here, I think, is that if I am competent with the name 'Bismarck', then either I have personally been introduced to Bismarck by name, or I have learned to use the name by interacting with others who use it. Either way, I stand in the intermediate epistemic position discussed above. That is, I am acquainted with a constellation of universals-cum-particulars that together specify Bismarck. If I have met Bismarck, the relevant particulars with which I am acquainted are "certain sense-data which [I] connect (rightly, we will suppose) with Bismarck's body."[23] For those of us who have not met Bismarck, the relevant objects of acquaintance consist in "testimony heard or read."[24] In either case, thinks Russell, as in the case of "my daughter," I have an epistemic fix strong enough for it to be reasonable to say that I *know who* is in question.[25]

Russell maintained that ordinary names were surrogates for hybrid descriptions, descriptions that provide intermediate-level epistemic contact with the denotations. One who is competent with an ordinary name, he further held, *knows who* it names. It begins to look as though Russell took there to be a strong epistemic requirement for the use, not only of genuine names, but even of ordinary names. *The use of ordinary names, no less than genuine ones, requires identifying knowledge on the part of the competent speaker.* One who uses a name, genuine or ordinary, must know about whom he is speaking. One who uses a genuine name must, of course, satisfy a much more stringent epistemic requirement than one using an ordinary name. Only the former requires direct acquaintance with the referent.

We now almost understand why Russell insisted that ordinary names could not abbreviate purely qualitative definite descriptions but necessarily abbreviate hybrid descriptions. I say "almost" because the epistemic constraint just mentioned does not yet fully explain why names cannot disguise purely qualitative descriptions. The epistemic constraint does entail that the name user be in possession of identifying knowledge, but this is compatible with the name's abbreviating a description that is purely qualitative, a description that does not convey such identifying knowledge. Let the name user, for example, know that some appropriate hybrid description, for example, 'the person causing this sense datum', applies to the denotation of the original purely qualitative description, for example, 'the longest living person'.

The mere presence of an identifying knowledge requirement for ordinary names, then, while it seems related to Russell's insistence on the hybrid-descriptions picture, does not by itself do the trick. The missing link—what is needed to see why names could not abbreviate purely qualitative descriptions—is provided by what I take to be Russell's intuition that not only do names require identifying knowledge for their use but the names themselves must indeed capture or convey that knowledge. They do this by abbreviating hybrid descriptions that formulate this knowledge. What names do for us—and this is Russell's "datum," the epistemological intuition that fuels the insistence on the hybrid-descriptions model—is to *identify* their bearers or denotations, to indicate *which things* are in question.

Russell, in motivating his idea that ordinary names conceal hybrid descriptions, misspoke. His point was not, if I understand him, that there is any sort of knowledge that one cannot have concerning the denotation of a purely qualitative description. His point was rather that the use, or understanding, of such a description—as opposed to the use, or understanding, of an ordinary name—does not capture or convey or express the sort of knowledge in question.

Russell's views about ordinary proper names seem to me underexplored. I have been focused upon the epistemic motivation for Russell's hybrid-description account, but there is still more. There is in "Knowledge by Acquaintance and Knowledge by Description" a distinct, semantic motivation for his view of ordinary names. Consider these two passages.

Suppose some statement is made about Bismarck. Assuming that there is such a thing as direct acquaintance with oneself, Bismarck might have used his name directly to designate the particular person with whom he was acquainted. In this case, if he made a judgment about himself, he himself might be a constituent of the judgment. *Here the proper name has the direct use which it always wishes to have, as simply standing for a certain object, and not for a description of the object.* But if a person who knew Bismarck made a judgment about him, the case is different. [In this case, since the speaker is not acquainted with Bismarck, the name must stand for a description.][26]

It would seem that, when we make a statement about something only known by description, we often *intend* to make our statement, not in the form involving the description, but about the actual thing described. That is to say, when we say anything about Bismarck, we should like, if we could, to make the judgment which Bismarck alone can make, namely, the judgment of which he himself is a constituent. In this we are necessarily defeated, since the actual Bismarck is unknown to us.[27]

Russell's remarks are confusing. In the first passage he tells us that all names, even ordinary ones, want, so to speak, to reach out and touch someone. What does this mean?

Russell suggests, in the second passage quoted, that when we use ordinary proper names, we wish to directly refer to their bearers but that our referential wishes are frustrated by our epistemological situation. Surely, however, Russell is not speaking seriously here about referential intentions and their frustration; surely what he says is not analogous, say, to the remark that the ancient Greeks intended to refer to Zeus but were frustrated in this intention due to Zeus's lack of existence. Imagine that I really intend to use an ordinary name as a genuine name, that is, I do not mean to put forth a descriptive characterization of the object of reference. If I am not, however, in an epistemic position to directly refer, then my intended reference should turn out to be a real reference failure, not a successful use of a device that abbreviates a definite description. What, then, is Russell's point?

Perhaps Russell has in mind, in this second passage—the first remains mysterious—not referential *intentions*, but rather referential *wishes*. Perhaps his point is that we would like to directly refer to Bismarck, which is not to say that we utter the name with the intention of directly referring to him. As much as we would like to so refer to him, we cannot, and so we do what is second best and express a descriptive characterization of him. How coherent is this? I am not sure. It seems to unrealistically assume great semantic sophistication on the part of ordinary speakers: they would like to refer directly, but since (they know that?) this is impossible, they go in for the descriptive mode of expression. Referential wishes do not seem to help here, any more than did referential intentions.

I want to suggest a different interpretive direction. Russell gives voice in both of these passages to a lingering sense that somehow names, ordinary ones, do not quite *feel* descriptional. Isn't it just this sense that Russell attempts to evoke with the remark that 'Bismarck', as Bismarck himself uses it, has the direct use *that it always wishes to have*, or with the comment that when *I* use 'Bismarck', *the name tries to directly get through to the man himself*? If not for what we know about the epistemic conditions for real naming, we can imagine Russell musing, it would be tempting to treat all names, ordinary ones included, as directly referential. Russell, if I am not mistaken, felt a conflict between the dictates of his semantic ear,[28] according to which names are directly referential, and his epistemological conscience.

I see in Russell's discussions of ordinary names, then, a tension between two conflicting pictures of the semantics of ordinary names. Russell's dominant tendency, the one that gets all the press, is to treat ordinary names as disguised definite descriptions. One may begin to get the scent of a conflicting tendency when Russell so often uses ordinary proper names as examples of genuine names, and characteristically remarks in such contexts that he is speaking *as if* mere ordinary names were real names. Perhaps, but Russell's direct reference impulse shines through most clearly, I think, in the quoted passages.

Russell's idea that ordinary names are descriptional, but not purely so, might well represent, at least in part, his attempt to do justice to the conflict between his semantic ear and his epistemological scruples. "Russell's compromise," as we might refer to his position on ordinary names, was to make ordinary names halfway houses between genuine names and purely qualitative definite descriptions. They fail to make the most direct sort of semantic contact with the things to which they apply—as dictated by epistemology. Yet they do not merely talk about things by indirection, as do purely qualitative definite descriptions. Ordinary names, since they abbreviate definite descriptions that contain genuine names of particulars, make a kind of semidirect contact with their bearers by specifying them in terms of directly referred-to particulars.

I have explored two philosophical motives for Russell's hybrid-descriptions theory of ordinary names, epistemic and semantic. Russell's ideas here are, as usual, ingenious and intriguing, as well as very frustrating. Russell is a source of great insight and suggestion, but also of ideas that are, at best, half worked out. I find his epistemological ideas especially frustrating. Perhaps this is because they presuppose a Cartesian-inspired epistemology that does not recommend itself to me. But it is also because of Russell's sloppiness, the easy use he makes, for example, of extremely obscure notions like *knowing who*.

One cannot deny, however, the richness of Russell's epistemic ideas, the idea, for example, that there are epistemic requirements for the use of even ordinary proper names, that the use of a name requires some kind of identifying knowledge. This idea is independent of, although, of course, not unrelated to, the thesis that names are description-surrogates. The epistemic requirement thesis, like so many of Russell's ideas, shows up, albeit in different dress, in contemporary discussions.[29]

It is striking how differently Frege and Russell respond to the challenges names present. Russell, unlike Frege, was impressed, almost obsessed, with proper names, even ordinary ones. Ordinary names, as we have seen, constituted a very special category to Russell. Indeed, if my reading of Russell is on track, ordinary names—both semantically and epistemologically—are much more like genuine names than the usual talk of the "Frege-Russell description theory" would suggest. Frege, by stark contrast, introduces a category of "proper name" with the remark "The designation of a single object can also consist of several words or other signs. For brevity, let every such designation be called a proper name."[30] Frege is thus not all that worried about what is distinctive about actual proper names. Semantically, they are of a piece with definite descriptions.

It is unfortunate that Russell never really develops, or even makes fully explicit, his semantic motivation for the hybrid-descriptions view of ordinary names, what I have referred to as the dictates of his semantic ear. Here, in a way that is entirely independent of his Cartesian epistemology, Russell's deepest differences with Frege are highlighted. And here Russell anticipates a most influential idea in the contemporary philosophy of language, the idea that an *ordinary* name is a "mere noise or shape conventionally used to designate a certain [thing]; it gives us no information about that [thing], and has nothing that can be called its meaning as opposed to denotation."

More on Russell's Representationalism: The Theory of Descriptions

Despite the deep differences uncovered between Russell and Frege, there remains, at least so far, this substantial agreement: ordinary singular terms, like names and indexical expressions, refer by expressing concepts. Perhaps "concepts" is not quite right for Russell. Ordinary singular terms, after all, express constellations of universals-cum-(acquainted-with-)particulars, and referring to these as concepts is perhaps distorting Russell's view, excessively assimilating it to Frege's.[31] Still, Russell apparently shares with Frege the idea that ordinary singular terms make mediated contact with their referents. The mediating agents may be Fregean senses, or Russellian universal-cum-particular constellations, but they mediate nevertheless. Or so it seems. The problem is that Russell's famous theory of descriptions suggests otherwise, for according to it, definite descriptions do not really express constellations of universals and particulars, nor do they even really refer to anything.[32] Let us see why.

One thing that is novel, and particularly relevant here, about Russell's approach to the semantics of definite descriptions is his idea that a sentence of the form "The F is G" is, to dramatize a bit, almost ill formed. Less dramatically, the grammatical structure of such a sentence, its subject-predicate form, gives a misleading picture of the content of the sentence, of what the sentence is actually putting forth as true. Such a sentence does not, contrary to grammatical appearances, attribute a property, G, to a thing, F, as do sentences of the form "a is G," where 'a' is a logically proper name. How, then, are we to understand such sentences? What exactly do they assert?

Russell's well-known answer[33] is that the content of such sentences is perspicuously formulated thus: one and only one thing has F, and that very thing also has G; or, more long-windedly, something has F, anything that has F is identical to the first thing (so that no more than one thing has F), and that very thing also has G. One who says, "The President of the United States who emancipated the slaves was a Republican," should not be thought of as, strictly speaking, attributing the property of being a Republican *to Lincoln*. Do not think of this utterance as mentioning Lincoln at all. Think of it as saying something very general about the universe: there is one and only one thing that has a certain property, *being a President of the United States who emancipated the slaves*, and, further, this very thing has an additional property, *being a Republican*.

While the general direction of Russell's approach is clear, the details are quite another matter. For one thing, the example just given, like many of the examples that spring to mind, including many of Russell's examples, would be extremely complicated to work out in detail. We might symbolically represent the reformulation just discussed as

$$(Ex) \{(Px) \ \& \ (y) \ [Py \rightarrow (y = x)] \ \& \ Rx\}$$

What property does 'P' designate? Remember, the predicate 'is a President of the United States who emancipated the slaves' embeds another description, 'the slaves', as well as the name 'United States'. The latter name in turn abbreviates a hybrid description, according to Russell. So we should think of the above reformulation as a mere first step toward a final version in which all descriptions are eliminated.

Even more troublesome is obtaining a precise account of the semantics of Russell's perspicuous formulations. This would involve, among other things, an account of the semantics of quantifiers, and Russell himself talks about this question in confusing, and on different occasions quite different, ways. Who knows how all of this is to ultimately get spelled out?

Let us be content, then, with Russell's basic idea, that the old, description-containing sentence ought to be scrapped in favor of one that employs quantifiers, variables, and so on, so as to perspicuously formulate the proposition.

I want to focus upon the great gap between the look of the original sentence and that of the reformulation. A radical metamorphosis seems to have transpired. The definite description does not simply get replaced by some other expression that better exhibits the description's function. We might think of Frege's view in a less radical way: a name, according to Frege, fails to make explicit its informational content, and so, to replace it by a definite description would have the virtue of making the content explicit. This kind of reformulation leaves the basic structure intact.

Russell's reformulation, by contrast, yields a radically new structure. What looked like (but never really was) a reference to Lincoln is gone, and instead we have references to various properties, acquainted-with-particulars, and so on (including whatever references are involved in the use of quantifiers, possibly propositional functions, second-order properties, and who knows what). The result is a new sentence that, as a whole, is supposed to be functionally equivalent[34] to the original, but not at all, so to speak, piece by piece. The basic structure of the propositions we express by ordinary sentences is, according to Russell, radically different from the structure suggested by the grammar of those sentences, and radically different from what, Russell admits, one would have naturally assumed.[35]

Consider now a Russellian reformulator, one who takes his Russell very seriously. (There is one in every crowd.) The Russellian reformulator looks at definite descriptions as mere artefacts of the misleading grammar of ordinary language. Definite descriptions do not really exist for him, at least not at the level of, as he likes to say, logical form. When a Russellian reformulator hears someone utter a sentence that contains one or more definite descriptions (or description abbreviations), he barely hears the vulgar form(s) of expression. What registers is "what the speaker is 'really' saying," the perspicuous Russellian reformulation. (Think of yourself "translating" a child's poorly constructed remarks.)

It makes no sense, argues the Russellian reformulator, to speak of "the constellation of universals-cum-particulars expressed by a definite description." If we took the unanalyzed sentence at face value, if we left the grammatically unified definite description intact, it would be natural to speak of "what *it* expresses," a concept, a constellation, or whatever. We are, however, not leaving this expression intact. When we straighten out what is being said, there is no unified expression that plays the role of the description. The Russellian reformulation *eliminates* the description and disburses those expressions that derive from it. There is thus no expression left that can be thought of as expressing such a constellation. Nor, to speak more ontologically, is there any such constellation of universals-cum-particulars that enters as a unit into the proposition.

Talk of names and descriptions expressing semantically mediating entities, while it fits hand in glove with Frege's approach, does not seem felicitous with respect to Russell's perspicuous reformulations. Strictly and philosophically speaking, then, Russell does not think of descriptions, nor of the ordinary names and indexicals that abbreviate descriptions, as expressing constellations of concepts and particulars. What has become of what we took to be Russell's Fregean tendency, his representationalism?

It will be instructive here, before we get carried away with strict and philosophical talk, to take brief note of Russell's introduction of the notion of "denotation." Russell maintains that although it is no part of the linguistic function of a definite description to pick something out (how could it be, since these expressions do not exist at the level of logical form?), we can still speak of the "denotation" of a description. The perspicuous reformulation of "The President of the United States who emancipated the slaves was a Republican" may not contain any expression that refers to Lincoln, but there is still a sense in which it is "about" Lincoln. That sense emerges when we note that there is a unique individual particularly relevant to the truth or falsity of the perspicuous formulation. Let us, suggests Russell, call this individual, if indeed such exists, "the denotation."

> Thus if 'C' is a denoting phrase [e.g. a definite description], it may happen that there is one entity x (there cannot be more than one) for which the proposition 'x is identical with C' is true, this proposition being interpreted as above. We may then say that the entity x is the denotation of the phrase 'C'.[36]

Definite descriptions may not really function to pick something out, but it is harmless enough to speak as if they did, since, in the felicitous case at least, there will be a unique individual particularly relevant to the truth or falsity of the perspicuous formulation.

Russell's "philosophy of 'as if'" approach to "denotation" seems applicable as well to talk of the concept or constellation expressed by a definite description. The Russellian reformulator, although he may balk at talk of definite descriptions expressing concepts, is not altogether ignorant of what *we* might reasonably call "the meaning" of individual descriptions (even considered "in isolation," perish the thought). For any definite description, there will be universals, acquainted-with-particulars, and so on that will get mentioned, albeit in a disbursed fashion, in the perspicuous reformulation. We can, if we like, mentally collect these disbursed remains of a description and speak as if there were a unified entity expressed. Such talk, properly understood, is harmless, and it facilitates recognition of what still can be called the "representationalist character" of Russell's approach. Just as the description can be said to be about someone, in the sense of having a denotation, it can be said to be about that individual in virtue of the individual's fitting the reconstituted constellation.

Russell's representationalism, it turns out, is a trickier business than Frege's, trickier than we had supposed. Indeed, it is, in one important respect, a more severe representationalism than is Frege's. Not only can one not speak of, for example, external things (more generally, anything that is not an object of acquaintance) in a conceptually unmediated way; one can never really mention such things at all. Such an epistemically removed item can never be the subject of a subject-predicate proposition, at least not one that we can understand. One can "talk about" such things only in the oblique fashion of Russell's perspicuous reformulations. We can, in this oblique sense, "talk about" Lincoln by asserting that one and only one thing was a presidential slave emancipator, and that thing was a Republican.

Concluding Remarks

Frege and Russell seem so far apart on so many of the questions at issue that it becomes difficult to discern a Frege-Russell approach to semantics. They are worlds apart on the nature of propositions, the intelligibility of direct reference, the viability of the sense-reference distinction, and the integrity of the syntax of natural language. Even where they seem to agree, moreover, one needs to take a closer look. They seem to agree, for example, that ordinary proper names have descriptive content. What this comes to, though, is very different for Frege than it is for Russell.

It may be useful, nevertheless, to revert to a level of abstraction at which they do agree. If, as many argue nowadays, ordinary proper names fail to bear any close relation to definite descriptions, then descriptivism, in both its Fregean and Russellian embodiments, is incorrect. Nor is descriptivism, contrary to what is usually supposed, their most significant area of agreement. Their deepest, most fundamental point of contact, as I see things, concerns what I will call the "intentionality intuition." This is the traditional idea that if one is to speak or think about a thing, one must possess a discriminating cognitive fix on the thing, that something about one's cognitive state must distinguish the relevant item from everything else in the universe. Otherwise, so the intuition goes, what would make *this* thing the referent?[37]

Even here, however, Russell and Frege approach the matter in very different ways. They disagree on what counts as the appropriate sort of cognitive fix, on just what sort of cognitive relation is required between thinker and object of thought. Frege's idea was that reference to an object required that the object be brought under an individuating concept, that only the possession of an individuating concept puts one in a position to refer to that which satisfies the concept.

Russell was, by comparison with Frege, a fanatic about intentionality. Russell was most dissatisfied with the idea that the mere possession of a concept might supply the required cognitive grip. One might possess a purely qualitative concept that in fact applies to a certain entity, maintained Russell, and yet have absolutely no idea who or what satisfies that concept. On the other hand, were one to be directly acquainted with an object, were one to have the object, as it were, smack up against one's mind, one would really know which thing was in question.

The Frege-Russell controversy about direct reference takes place against the background of a shared belief that reference to an object requires a discriminating cognitive fix. Frege's approach to the cognitive fix requirement makes direct, conceptually unmediated reference an impossibility. Russell, given his Cartesian epistemology with its conception of epistemic intimacy, thinks that direct reference is indeed possible, even if only reference to epistemically select items.

I stated above that the most fundamental point of contact between Frege and Russell is not, to my thinking, their agreement on the descriptive character of names. Russell, for one thing, does not espouse a description theory for what he took to be the real names, a fact that is too often noted but quickly set aside in our enthusiasm for (or against) their shared descriptivism. While Russell's descriptivism is thus mitigated, his view about the necessity of a strong cognitive fix, especially for genuine names, is not. Russell's tendency, moreover, was not to assimilate names to descriptions—as was Frege's—but to emphasize the differences. Even ordinary names, Russell held, involve a kind of epistemic intimacy with their referents not characteristic of purely qualitative descriptions, or so I have argued. If I am correct, moreover, about Russell's semantic ear, he would have loved to find a way to view ordinary names as entirely nondescriptive, if only their epistemology would have taken care of itself.

Nor is it even clear that descriptivism is at the heart of Frege's approach. Indeed, there is a controversy in the literature about whether Frege was a descriptivist at all, whether Frege took the senses of names to be given by purely qualitative definite descriptions. What is uncontroversial is that Frege took modes of presentation to be essential to reference. While it is difficult to imagine Frege as movable on the latter question, it is much easier to see the description theory as negotiable. For both Frege and Russell, then, it is not the description theory, but the cognitive fix requirement, that goes deepest.

Our quest has been for a perspective shared by Frege and Russell. After locating many areas of disagreement, we have located a fundamental point of agreement, indeed, one that Frege and Russell share with many philosophers, past and present, one that may indeed look unassailable. I have underscored it, rather than descriptivism, because I believe that it furnishes, or ought to furnish, a more important target for contemporary critics of Frege and Russell. Its radical rejection, I want to suggest, is the deep lesson Hilary Putnam sloganized as "Meaning ain't in the head."

NINE

Has Semantics Rested on a Mistake?

GOTTLOB FREGE motivates his famous distinction between sense and reference by formulating what amounts to a condition of adequacy for a semantic account of singular terms. Frege's idea is that any such account must provide an answer to a crucial question concerning the cognitive significance of language: the question of how identity sentences in which proper names flank the identity sign can both state truths and be informative. Subsequent Fregeans—and in this respect Bertrand Russell was himself a Fregean—fully concurred that a semantic account should yield answers to questions like Frege's. Indeed, Russell's somewhat Fregean treatment of ordinary proper names, his view that such names are not really names—not really tagging devices—but rather disguised definite descriptions, derives from a sensitivity to the sorts of epistemic problem one encounters if one treats proper names as John Stuart Mill's remarks suggest and as Russell himself treats "logically proper names," as purely designative, or nonconnotative, singular terms. Contemporary neo-Fregeans, moreover, make such epistemic concerns central to their arguments against the Mill-inspired view recently called "the new theory of reference." New theorists like Keith Donnellan, David Kaplan, Saul Kripke, John Perry, and Hilary Putnam—and my own work falls into this tradition—proffer an

---

Reprinted by permission from *The Journal of Philosophy* 83, no. 4 (April 1986): 185–209.

account that, according to their neo-Fregean critics, is insensitive to the sorts of epistemic puzzles that Frege and Russell took to be central. It is a scandal, or so it has seemed, that new theorists argue so vigorously against Frege's positive account yet have had so little to say about the kind of problem that both dominated Frege's attention and motivated his view.

New theorists have not been unimpressed either with the puzzles in question or with the argument that the new theory, as Alvin Plantinga says, "founders on these rocks."[1] Indeed they have been too impressed, too Fregean, or so I shall argue. They have not quite treated these concerns about cognitive significance as conditions of adequacy, as do the Fregeans. This would be to give up the game; for the anti-Fregean approach just does not yield an account of cognitive significance, at least not in any direct, straightforward way. Nevertheless, the anti-Fregeans have at least paid lip service to the need for a semantic account that does justice to the *Frege puzzles*, as I shall call them. Indeed, a few stabs were even made at showing how the Frege puzzles were, after all, no problem for the new approach.

The point of this paper is to challenge Frege's condition of adequacy. This condition cannot, however, be challenged in isolation. That an adequate semantics must be epistemologically sensitive is no separable, isolable feature of Frege's semantical enterprise, a feature that might be rejected while retaining the spirit of Frege's approach. Rejecting Frege's adequacy condition, on the contrary, involves rejecting Frege's conception of the semantical enterprise. I will urge that we replace Frege's conception of semantics with a radically different conception that was implicit, even if deeply buried, in the new theory from the outset.

The New Theory of Reference and Why It Has Seemed Wrong

Central to the new theory is the rejection of Frege's explication of the notion of "proposition" and its replacement by something like the Russell-Kaplan notion of "singular proposition."[2] Let us, following Kaplan, represent such propositions as ordered pairs (more generally, ordered *n*-tuples) of the object(s) referred to and the property (or relation) predicated. Why has this notion of "proposition" been thought to be epistemologically inadequate?

First, there is the problem of nondenoting singular terms.[3] Consider a sincere assertive utterance of "Vulcan is a large heavenly body," where, unbeknownst to the speaker, 'Vulcan' does not refer. Alternatively, to give an example involving indexicals, one might say, hallucinating a new Macintosh computer across the room, "I want that." The new theorist seems committed to the apparently absurd claim that in such cases, since there is no referent, no complete proposition has been expressed. The contrary—and apparently overwhelming—Fregean intuition is that the thought content of an utterance cannot depend upon whether or not the uttered expressions refer.[4] Along similar lines, such speakers presumably express determinate beliefs. The new theorist cannot account for this, or so it seems, since on his view there are no complete propositions to serve as objects of belief.

A second Frege puzzle concerns the informational content of directly referential singular terms. The new theorist holds that 'Cicero was an orator' and 'Tully was an orator' express the same proposition, that believing what the first sentence expresses just *is* believing what the second expresses. This seems plainly wrong, since the *cognitive* contents of the two sentences seem very different. One can understand both sentences and accept the first as expressing the truth while not accepting the second. Similarly, the new theorist is committed to the view that 'Cicero = Cicero' and 'Cicero = Tully' express the same proposition. This seems wrong, however, since it is surely plausible to suppose that virtually everyone believes the first proposition, but only a select few believe the second.[5]

The new theorist's difficulty here, just as with the first Frege puzzle, has nothing essential to do with proper names. Imagine that I see a man about to be mugged by a prominent philosopher of language. Unbeknownst to me, I am witnessing the scene by means of a series of mirrors, and, in fact, *I* am the intended victim. It is plausible that in such a context different propositions are determined by 'He is about to be attacked by a neo-Fregean' and 'I am about to be attacked by a neo-Fregean'. Presumably, in the case described, I believe the first of these propositions, indeed I know it to be true, but not the second.[6]

A third Frege puzzle concerns the explanation of action. If singular propositions are objects of belief, then they ought to figure in explanations of action. Singular propositions, however, as John Perry has emphasized, seem singularly unsuited for such explanations. Consider again utterances of '*He* is about to be attacked by a neo-Fregean' and '*I* am about to be attacked by a neo-Fregean', where he and I, unbeknownst to the speaker, are really one. The beliefs expressed by such utterances typically lead to dramatically different actions. But the propositions believed, at least according to the new theorist, are the same.

Let us characterize in a general way the Fregean argument that these three puzzles embody. The argument proceeds by specifying certain *data* (hereafter, *Frege's data*) concerning the cognitive significance of sentences: that one who utters the Vulcan sentence asserts a complete, determinate proposition or expresses a complete, determinate belief; that one who utters the Cicero sentence asserts a different proposition (or expresses a different belief) than one who utters the Tully sentence; that when one believes what 'I am about to be attacked . . .' expresses, one characteristically acts differently than one does when one believes what 'He is about to be attacked . . .' expresses. Second, the Fregean advances what I shall call *Frege's insight*, the idea that Frege's data, which seem to be nicely explained by the Fregean hypothesis that singular terms have not only references but also senses, cannot be accounted for by appeal simply to the level of reference.[7]

How Not to Develop the New Theory

I shall now consider two strategies that have been employed in defense of the new theory, strategies that maintain that the new theory has within it the resources to account for the cognitive significance of language. I believe both strategies are unsatisfactory. Indeed, the first is more or less hopeless, and I mention it only to highlight what needs to be done. The second is more promising. The discussion of why it fails will point toward a new way of looking at the relation between semantics and cognitive significance.

First, the new theorist might bite the bullet. New theorists have indeed been known cheerfully to deny that in the non-denoting-term cases a complete proposition was expressed.[8] Similarly, new theorists have insisted that utterances of the Cicero sentence and the corresponding Tully sentence are assertions of the same proposition, expressions of the same belief, or, turning to the puzzle of informative identities, that the proposition expressed by 'Cicero is Cicero' is none other than that expressed by 'Cicero is Tully'. Pending some further explanation, however, such insistence surely seems ad hoc and unintuitive. Tyler Burge, in a fit of subtle humor, states that "where 'a' and 'b' are proper names, a belief that $a = b$ is really the same belief as the belief that $a = a$ (so that one believes both or neither) seems to be completely implausible. I shall therefore ignore it."[9] Again, the intuitions to which the Fregean appeals certainly seem substantial.

A much more promising strategy derives from the work of John Perry and David Kaplan. Perry, in his seminal paper "Frege on Demonstratives,"[10] suggests that the apparatus Kaplan developed for the semantics of indexicals might be utilized for the solution of puzzles about cognitive significance. Although Perry's central focus in this paper is not the solution of any of the puzzles I have mentioned, his remarks are intriguing because they suggest a general approach to the problems of cognitive significance.[11]

Perry, unlike other new theorists, recognizes that singular propositions are not adequate to the phenomena of cognitive significance. He concedes, moreover, that these phenomena can be explained only by appeal to something very much like Frege's "modes of presentation." Frege's mistake, according to Perry, consisted in taking modes of presentation to be purely qualitative characterizations that, given the facts of the world, apply uniquely to some individual. On this mistaken view, when I say to you, "You look happy," there must be an operative mode of presentation that specifies you in a purely qualitative way, that selects you from everything else in the universe in terms of your qualitative properties—from God's point of view, so to speak. But surely when I refer to you pronominally, I need to have at hand no such purely qualitative way of distinguishing you from everything else. Frege, then, advanced an unrealistic view of modes of presentation, of the cognitive perspectives from which we view the referents of our terms.

Why not, asks Perry, appeal to linguistic meanings, as Kaplan has explicated this notion, for an account of modes of presentation? 'I', for example, in virtue of its Kaplanian "character," conveys a particular *way of presenting a referent*. 'I' and 'he' may be used to refer to the same thing, but will present it in radically different ways, 'I' as the speaker or writer, 'he' as (roughly) the indicated male. Thus we can explain the difference in behaviors noted in the third Frege puzzle in terms of the different linguistic meanings of 'I' and 'he'.

In order to emphasize the non-Fregean character of Perry's proposal, a proposal endorsed and developed by Kaplan, let us note the vast difference between Frege's modes of presentation and those of Perry and Kaplan. The cognitive perspective under which I am presented when I use the first-person pronoun is, according to Perry and Kaplan and contrary to Frege, exactly the same as that under which you are presented when you use 'I'. Since the linguistic meaning of 'I' stays constant from your utterance of it to mine, the way it presents the referent also stays constant. What makes my utterance count as a reference to me, and yours count as a reference to you, are the facts that in one case *I* uttered it, and in the other case *you* did. These are facts not about our mental states, or the senses we apprehend, but about the context of utterance.

A second difference from Frege is that Perry and Kaplan insist that their modes of presentation are not constituents of the propositions expressed. When I refer to myself as "I," in assertively uttering, say, "I am happy," I apprehend myself as the speaker or writer, but this does not mean that I assert that the speaker or writer is happy. What I assert is rather the singular proposition ⟨Wettstein, property of being happy⟩. Thus Perry and Kaplan are led to sharply distinguish the proposition asserted from the speaker's cognitive perspective on that proposition, or, as Perry often puts it, the proposition believed from the "belief state."

The Perry-Kaplan strategy seems easily generalizable to the other Frege puzzles. Consider the puzzle of nondenoting singular terms. A soldier in an enemy prison camp hallucinates that a fellow soldier is coming to rescue him. "You are wonderful," he says. I noted above that the new theorist's account of such an example—that no singular proposition is asserted—seems to violate Frege's quite reasonable demand that the thought content of such an utterance should not depend upon which things actually exist. Perry and Kaplan can apparently meet Frege's demand, however; despite the fact that the speaker's words fail to determine a singular proposition, they do determine, in virtue of their linguistic meaning, a definitive cognitive state or perspective. In fact, as Frege demanded, the speaker is in exactly the cognitive state in which he would have been had his singular term, 'you', referred.

The new theorist has not quite met the challenge of the first Frege puzzle, for that challenge, as I formulated it in the section above, is to give an account of the proposition asserted or believed in the hallucination case. The new theorist remains committed to denying that there is any proposition asserted or believed in such cases, and on this, the Perry-Kaplan-based strategy agrees with the bite-the-bullet strategy. The Perry-Kaplan strategy goes beyond the latter, however, by removing the sting from the Fregean argument. It does this by supplying an account of the indisputable fact that the utterance has cognitive significance. The new theorist can now argue that the Fregean has confused the real datum with the theoretical consequences of the Fregean view. The real datum is not that belief in a determinate proposition is expressed by the utterance in question. It is rather that such an utterance has determinate cognitive content.

Let us turn to the second Frege puzzle. The Fregean maintains that, in some relevant context, the belief expressed by, for example, "I am about to be attacked," is quite different from that expressed by "He is about to be attacked," even though 'I' and 'he' are co-referential. Armed with the Perry-Kaplan strategy, we can reply that although there is a single proposition asserted by both utterances, there is indeed a difference in the cognitive significance of the utterances. 'I', in virtue of its linguistic meaning, presents the referent in a very different way than does 'he'. Again, the real datum that underlies the Fregean challenge, the idea that these utterances differ in cognitive significance, has been explained.

Finally, the new theorist can now explain how utterances of identity sentences can express truths and, at the same time, be informative. Although the singular propositions corresponding to my utterances of 'I = I' and 'I = him' are the same, the relevant cognitive perspectives are very different. The second utterance can be informative, since unlike the first, the modes of presentation associated with 'I' and 'him' are different.

I believe, however, that the Perry-Kaplan strategy, tantalizing as it is with regard to certain well-chosen examples, fails to resolve the Frege puzzles in the general case.[12] I shall first discuss some problems with the application to utterances involving proper names and then return to indexical utterances.

The Perry-Kaplan approach individuates cognitive states by linguistic meanings. The application of this approach to utterances involving names depends, then, upon our grasp of the notion of the linguistic meaning of a name. New theorists, however, have not told us much about the linguistic meaning of names. Indeed, it might be tempting to think that the new theory, since it holds that names are "purely denotative," that they lack sense, or Millian connotation, holds that names lack linguistic meaning. If so, the Perry-Kaplan approach would be of no use here.

Such a conclusion, however, would be hasty. For one thing, the new theorist need not deny that names have linguistic meanings, only that they have descriptive meanings. For another, the Perry-Kaplan approach can be formulated without mention of linguistic meaning. Cognitive significance, Perry and Kaplan hold, is determined by semantic significance, by the semantic rules that govern the expression. Names, no less than other singular terms, have semantic significance in this sense.

The difficulty, though, is that the new theorists have not yet developed a clear conception of the rules or conventions that govern names. New theorists, following Donnellan and Kripke, typically subscribe to some form of historical explanation (or "causal")[13] theory of names, and it might thus seem that an account of the semantic rules would be forthcoming. The historical-chain approach, however, really is, as Kripke says, a picture rather than a theory. I mean this not only in the, by now, obvious sense that necessary and sufficient conditions for the reference of names have never been given but also in the more basic sense that the historical-chain approach fails to give us any clear indication of the nature of the rules for names. Indeed—

and this is a related point—advocates of this approach have never provided an account of what exactly the *semantic* function of the historical chain is.

One possibility is to treat the chain of communication as a semantic determinant, on a par with the contextual features that determine the reference of an indexical. The reference of a token of the first-person pronoun, for example, depends upon who produced the token, and this is what the semantic rule for 'I' specifies. Similarly, on the view in question, the reference of a token of 'Aristotle' depends (roughly) upon which individual is historically connected, in the "appropriate" way, to the production of the token (or to the speaker's acquisition of the name), and this is what the semantic rule for 'Aristotle' tells us.

Treating names as similar in this way to indexicals, however, has its drawbacks. New theorists generally, and Kripke specifically, take themselves to be developing Mill's "connotationless tag" conception of names. Talk of historical chains is notably absent from Mill, nor are they, in any obvious way, part of his idea. How, indeed, is Mill's conception of a pure tag supposed to be integrated with the thesis that the reference of a name is determined by a chain of communication? The thesis, in giving an important semantic role to the historical chain, apparently must deny that, as Millians sometimes put it, "all there is to the semantics of names is reference."

Kaplan's emphasis on the difference between indexicals and Millian tags highlights the difficulty just noted. Indexicals, he urges, but not Millian tags, have "descriptive meanings," formulable by semantic rules that include the appropriate descriptive information. This is, of course, not to say that the rule gives us the Fregean sense of an indexical. It rather specifies, in descriptive terms, how the reference of the indexical is determined. In Kripke's terms, the description merely fixes the reference of the indexical. If the semantic rules for names incorporate the description 'the individual that stands in the appropriate historical relation. . . ', as they do on the indexical model, then names are not just tags, any more than indexicals are just tags. Perhaps Kripke gives voice to this intuition when, at least in some passages, he expresses skepticism that any description might play even the meager semantical role of fixing the reference of a name.[14]

There are difficulties, then, with this construal of the semantic rules governing names. It is far from clear, moreover, that this construal of the semantic rules, even if correct, would be adaptable to the Perry-Kaplan treatment of cognitive significance. It is one thing to suggest that the semantic rule governing the first-person pronoun captures the cognitive perspective of one who utters it. Perhaps I do cognize myself as "the speaker" when I use 'I'. It is quite another thing to suppose that everyone who uses 'Aristotle' to refer to the ancient Greek philosopher must be thinking of him as "the individual that stands in the appropriate historical relation . . ." Most competent users of that name have never even heard of the Donnellan-Kripke account of names and do not think of the referents of names in such terms. Nor is there much reason to suppose that even one who believes that the semantic rule in question is correct typically thinks of, say, Aristotle in this way. Perhaps the rule accurately represents the *semantics* of 'Aristotle', although for reasons given in the last paragraph, I doubt it. If it does, however, then the idea that *semantic rules* capture *cognitive significance* seems to break down.

Let us sketch an alternative treatment of the semantics of names, one that takes more seriously the idea that the semantic significance of a name is exhausted by its reference. There is a suggestion in Kaplan's "Demonstratives," a suggestion recently developed by Joseph Almog, that the historical chains play a "pre-semantic" role and that the semantics of a name is completely specified by noting its referent.[15] Such a suggestion fits better with Mill's "tag" picture, and even with some of Kripke's more Millian remarks. Here we have the makings of a very different account of the semantic conventions for names. Those conventions do not specify the referents of names in terms of historical chains. They simply specify a referent for each name. A referent is *assigned* directly to each name.

We have seen that the first, "indexical" model for thinking about the semantic rules governing names was not adaptable to the Perry-Kaplan treatment of cognitive significance. How about the present, "assignment" model? Again, the Perry-Kaplan approach runs into grave difficulty. If the semantic significance of a name consists simply in the fact that it has a certain referent, then if two names have the same referent, they have the same semantic significance. If, however, the names have the same *semantic* significance, then, on the Perry-Kaplan approach they have the same *cognitive* significance. Accordingly, the Perry-Kaplan proposal cannot explain the Frege puzzles when they are formulated with proper names.

The application of the Perry-Kaplan strategy to the case of proper names, then, presents severe difficulties. Even if we restrict our attention to cases involving indexicals, however, the Perry-Kaplan approach is not in the end satisfactory. The crucial problem for this account, given its thesis that cognitive states are to be individuated by linguistic meanings, is revealed by examples in which synonymous utterances differ in cognitive significance.

Imagine two utterances of "He is about to be attacked," where a single individual is being referred to, but where it is not at all obvious that this is so. Indeed, let us suppose, it appears to both the speaker and his auditors that two very different individuals are being referred to. No doubt the cognitive significance of these utterances is dramatically different. One who understands these utterances might take only one of them to express a truth. This is, of course, the second Frege puzzle again. The third puzzle arises here as well, for one might well behave in one way if one takes the first utterance to be true and in quite a different way if one takes the second to be true. Perry and Kaplan *ought to say* that two different cognitive states are in question. If cognitive states, however, are to be individuated by linguistic meanings, then Perry and Kaplan cannot say that there are different cognitive states in question, since there is no difference in linguistic meaning. Thus they cannot explain "Frege's data" here.[16]

The same problem arises with regard to Frege's original problem about informative identities. The Perry-Kaplan approach can handle informative cases of "I = he," but what about "He = he"? Imagine that our speaker is watching a rock singer from the hallway outside an auditorium. The singer is so outfitted and made up that one cannot tell from his right profile and from his left profile that the same person is in question. Our speaker first observes him from a small window in a door on the side of the auditorium and then walks to another doorway and sees what he takes to be an entirely different performer, performing in what he takes to be a different auditorium. Dragging our original speaker down the hall from one doorway to the next, we point the singer out to him, saying, "He is the same person as he is," or "That one is none other than that one." The cognitive significance of the first 'he' is clearly different from that of the second, but, again, the Perry-Kaplan approach cannot explain this, since the term occurs twice with the same linguistic meaning.[17]

Semantics and Cognitive Significance: A New Perspective

The Perry-Kaplan approach, despite its shortcomings, points the way to a new perspective on the problems of cognitive significance. I begin by reformulating that approach in a way that will bring out its novelty better than do Perry's formulations or Kaplan's. Perry and Kaplan offer us a distinction between propositions believed and cognitive states, or, as they both often put it, thoughts apprehended, on one hand, and cognitive perspectives on those thoughts, on the other. The former way of putting the point stands in need of clarification, but the latter is, to my mind, positively misleading.[18]

Let us review some of the properties of the Perry-Kaplan "thoughts," or singular propositions. First, such thoughts are individuated by the referents of the singular terms used, along with the properties (or relations) predicated. Second, and closely related, among the *constituents* of these thoughts or propositions are the referents of the singular terms, things like you and me, as well as the properties predicated. Third, in virtue of the way these thoughts or propositions are individuated, it is quite possible for a competent and attentive speaker to assert the same thought on two occasions without being in any position to realize this. Ignorant of the Cicero-Tully identity, he may comment, "Cicero is often referred to by Quine," as well as "Tully is often referred to by Quine," while mistakenly, but quite reasonably, taking himself to be expressing two very different thoughts. Similarly, it is quite possible for one to accept and reject the same thought without being in any way illogical. Our speaker may affirm "Cicero is an orator," while denying "Tully is an orator."

What peculiar "thoughts" these are! Perhaps it was somewhat misleading even for Frege to use the term 'thought' as he does, since 'thought' may suggest presence in the mind. Frege, however, is on much safer ground than is the new theorist, for Frege's "thoughts" are at least relevant to explaining various cognitive phenomena. Indeed, if the new theorist adopts this vocabulary of "thoughts," then when he rightly admits that an utterance of, say, "Vulcan is my favorite planet" fails to express such a thought, he might seem to be admitting that the utterance has no "thought content," that it is without cognitive significance. I suggest, then, that the Perry-Kaplan insight is better expressed if we drop all talk of thoughts. Talk of singular *propositions* is less misleading, but perhaps not entirely so. The Perry-Kaplan thoughts or propositions are more like *states of affairs* than they are like anything we might reasonably call thoughts, nor are they much like those putative entities that have been called propositions, entities constituted by something like concepts. Talk of states of affairs is also pedagogically useful here. It helps us distinguish what is going on, on the side of the world from what is going on, on the side of the mind. States of affairs, of course, are not exactly "out in the world," for presumably they are abstract entities. They are, however, abstract entities that are composed of objects that are out in the world, objects like you and me, as well as of properties.

This is not to say that the notion of state of affairs is unproblematic. Indeed, on some views, states of affairs, being abstract entities, cannot contain individuals, any more than propositions can. Nevertheless, there is a view of states of affairs that is congenial to the Perry-Kaplan picture. As Ruth Barcan Marcus notes:

Knowing and believing have been characterized as "propositional attitudes." The vagaries of the many uses of 'proposition' have been a considerable source of epistemological confusion. There is a seemingly naive as well as much maligned view, to which I subscribe, Russell's for example, where knowing and believing are attitudes toward states of affairs (not necessarily actual), which may have individuals and attributes as constituents. The "propositional content" of a sentence on an occasion of use is (are) the (those) state(s) of affairs that would make that sentence true.[19]

My point here is not that Marcus's idea furnishes the best way to work out the anti-Fregean intuition that the referent itself, rather than a concept of it, figures in what was said. We would, I think, probably do better without states of affairs *or* singular propositions, indeed, without any unified upshot of an act of assertion—that is, the proposition or state of affairs asserted—and without any unified entity to serve as the object of belief. I have in mind here another Russellian theme: the idea that when I believe that Aristotle is smart, there is no entity that is the thing believed, the proposition *that Aristotle is smart*, for example, but rather (roughly) that I am related by the belief relation to Aristotle himself and to the property of being smart.[20] In any case, this is not the place to pursue this theme, which would take us far from our current concern with the Perry-Kaplan approach, according to which there are singular propositions, which are unified objects of belief and assertion. Still, states-of-affairs talk is at least often pedagogically superior to singular-propositions talk, and so I will frequently utilize it in what follows.

Adopting states-of-affairs talk, we can sharply distinguish the state of affairs determined by an utterance from the speaker's cognitive perspective on that state of affairs. The three features of the new theorist's "thoughts" mentioned above, features that seemed very strange indeed as features of thoughts and may even have seemed strange as features of propositions, now become quite natural features of states of affairs. First, they are to be individuated in terms of objects and properties. Second, those objects and properties are the very constituents of the states of affairs. Finally, a competent, attentive speaker may affirm the existence of the same state of affairs on two occasions without having the slightest clue that these are the same. How should such a speaker, after all, know that he affirms the same state of affairs when he says, "Cicero is often referred to by Quine," as when he says "Tully is often referred to by Quine"? Similarly, he may both affirm and deny what is, unbeknownst to him, the same state of affairs when he says, for example, "Cicero was an orator, but Tully was certainly not."

So much for my reformulation of the Perry-Kaplan approach. What can we learn from that approach? The most important lesson is the crucial distinction between states of affairs and the ways in which they are cognized. Perry and Kaplan express this distinction confusedly when they refer to the former as "thoughts." They err further when they take the latter to be retrievable from the sentences uttered. Nevertheless, the landscape has been altered. In place of the Fregean picture, according to which cognitive significance is to be absorbed into the proposition, we now have a distinction between singular propositions (or states of affairs) on the side of the world and cognitive perspectives on the side of the mind.

This new picture gives a sensitive hearing to Frege's original problem. One thrust of Frege's opening remarks in "On Sense and Reference" was completely correct. Notions like "singular proposition" and "state of affairs" are just not adequate to the *cognitive* significance of language. Having seen this, Frege went on to reject (a view of a piece with) the new theory, for he believed that an adequate semantic account must explain cognitive significance. Perry and Kaplan, anti-Fregean in other respects, approach the question of cognitive significance under the influence of Frege. Semantics, they agree, must provide an account of cognitive significance. They object to Frege's criticism of the new theory, however, for they believe that the new theory's semantic account is indeed adequate to the cognitive problems. Admittedly, cognitive significance cannot be explained by reference to singular propositions, but it can be explained by reference to another notion available from the new theorist's repertoire, the notion of linguistic meaning, explicated along the lines indicated by Kaplan.

I have, however, rejected the Perry-Kaplan attempt to explain cognitive significance. Linguistic meanings, I have urged, will not, in general, do the job. Am I not admitting, then, that the new theorist's *semantic* account fails to provide anything like a solution to the *cognitive* puzzles? Isn't this in violation of Frege's condition of adequacy? My suggestion is that at this point we make a more radical break with Frege's outlook. The new theorist should reject Frege's adequacy condition outright.

Why did Frege take it for granted that semantics ought to provide an explanation of cognitive significance? Frege, unlike the new theorist, was not concerned—or at least not primarily concerned—with what we might call the *anthropology* of those institutional arrangements that constitute natural language, the uncovering of the semantic rules that govern our linguistic practices.[21] His main interest was rather in thought contents, in the "eternal structure of thought," as Tyler Burge puts it.[22] Michael Dummett attributes the following three theses to Frege: "first, that the goal of philosophy is the analysis of the structure of *thought*; second, that the study of *thought* is to be sharply distinguished from the study of the psychological process of *thinking*; and, finally, that the only proper method for analysing thought consists in the analysis of language."[23] We do not have to imagine Frege's reaction to a proposed semantic account that, from his point of view, leaves opaque the relation between language and thought contents, one that fails, for example, to explain the fact that 'Hesperus = Hesperus' and 'Hesperus = Phosphorus' express different thought contents. To leave the cognitive significance of language untouched is, for Frege, to leave the philosophical study of language virtually untouched.

There is here a fundamental, but not generally appreciated, contrast between Frege's conception of semantics and that of the new theorist. It is easy to see, and new theorists have repeatedly pointed out, that the new theory contrasts with Frege's approach in its rejection of senses and in its substitution of a more direct picture of the language-reality relation. More fundamental, however, is the distinct project the new theorist advances for semantics. Where Frege's primary focus was on the connection between language and the mind, or, more accurately, between language and objective thought contents, the new theorist is largely unconcerned with matters cognitive. His interest is in the connection between language and the world, the realm of referents. He is doing the anthropology of our institutions of natural language, and he wants to understand the institutionalized conventions in accordance with which our terms refer. Indeed, many of the new theorist's arguments against Frege take the form of pointing out that the sense-reference model, no matter what its apparent advantages with regard to problems of cognitive significance, just cannot be correct, since it is incompatible with actual linguistic practice.

New theorists, often not keenly aware of this fundamental difference between what they were in fact doing and Frege's project, have been embarrassed by the failure of their positive account to be responsive to the problems of cognitive significance. These problems seemed to them, given their Fregean upbringing, crucial for the semantics of natural language. Given the perspective just delineated, however, there was little reason to think that the new approach to semantics would have any immediate implications for the problems of cognitive significance and, therefore, any reason to be embarrassed by this failure. There is no reason to suppose that, in general, if we successfully uncover the institutionalized conventions governing the references of our terms, we will have captured the ways in which speakers think about their referents.

Has Semantics Rested on a Mistake? 125

Examples concerning names and indexicals help to concretize the point. Let us suppose for a moment that Mill gave the correct account, unadorned with causal-historical chains, of the conventions regarding names. These conventions associate names, not with properties, but directly with individuals. Notice that this account gives us no help at all with the question of a particular speaker's cognitive perspective on the referent of a name he utters. Nor, as noted above, does the Donnellan-Kripke historical-chain variant illuminate the cognitive significance of names. That account, like the unadorned Millian view, attempts to specify the conditions under which an utterance of a name counts as a reference to an individual. It does not attempt to characterize, nor does it characterize, a speaker's way of thinking about the referent of a name. We do not typically think of Aristotle as "the individual that stands in the appropriate historical relation . . ."

Consider the following three competing accounts of the semantics of 'that'.

(1) The reference of 'that' is the unique individual that stands in the appropriate causal relation to the utterance of 'that'.
(2) The reference of 'that' is the unique individual that the speaker has in mind in uttering 'that'.
(3) The reference of 'that' is the unique individual that is indicated by the cues that are available to the competent and attentive addressee (where the relevant cues include pointing gestures, the fact that some individual is perceptually salient, etc.).[24]

The debate between the proponents of (1), (2), and (3) concerns the question of which rule governs our linguistic practice. It does not concern, nor does it have any obvious implications for, the question of how speakers cognize the referents of their demonstratives. None of these rules gives us a plausible candidate for that role.

I have argued that there is no prima facie reason to suppose that the rule of reference for an expression should provide the key to speakers' cognitive perspectives on the reference of that expression. A look at some plausible candidates for being the correct rules has, moreover, reinforced the point. Leading candidates for correct rules, at least for names and demonstratives like 'that', do not, on the face of it, provide characterizations of speakers' cognitive perspectives. Considerations concerning the epistemic status of semantic rules reinforce the point further.

Notice that the rules that govern our referential practices need to be *uncovered* by the anthropological semanticist. There is an important sense in which masters of a practice, in this case, competent speakers, often, even typically, do not "know" the rules that govern the practice, in this case, the semantic rules. Perfectly competent speakers are often in no position *either* to specify the rules that determine the references of expressions *or even* to select a correct rule from a list of plausible candidates. Consider the three competing accounts of the semantics of 'that'. Most people would have no idea which of these rules, if any, governs our practice, or, indeed, how one would go about finding out. How plausible is it, then, to take the rule, so far removed from consciousness, as specifying the way the speaker is thinking about his referent?[25]

Imagine that Jones is attending a lecture given by a great mathematician. After hearing the lecture, Jones says, "That is a brilliant man," gesturing to the mathematician. Is it at all plausible to suppose that how Jones is thinking about the mathematician is affected by which rule in fact correctly specifies the semantics of 'that' as he uses it? The differences between rules emerge only with respect to recherché cases about which Jones has probably never even thought. Why should Jones's membership in a community that uses the demonstrative in one of these ways rather than another affect how he thinks about the mathematician?[26]

It was natural for Frege, given his conception of the semantic enterprise, to require that an adequate semantic account yield the epistemological riches in question. Remarks like Dummett's "a theory of meaning is a theory of understanding," John Searle's "the philosophy of language is a branch of the philosophy of mind," and Stephen Schiffer's "the basis of a theory of reference must . . . be a theory of the thought in the mind of a person using a singular term" all issue from such a perspective.[27] The seeds of a radically different conception of semantics can be found in the work of the new theorists. An account of linguistic meaning is no longer to be seen as an account of anything like what the competent speaker understands by his terms but rather as an account of the practices he has mastered. Given this new, quasi-Wittgensteinian perspective, the most natural course for the new theorist is not to accept the burden of Frege's epistemological condition of adequacy and then try to show that somehow we can retrieve an account of cognitive significance from our new semantic account, which is what Perry and Kaplan do. The most natural course for the new theorist, given the nature of his project, is to reject outright Frege's condition of adequacy. The problems of cognitive significance are real and important, but their solution does not lie within the province of semantics, at least not as the new theorist conceives, or ought to conceive, his subject.[28]

Afterword: Belief Sentences and Cognitive Significance

I have argued that the new theorist qua semanticist need not worry about the problems of cognitive significance. There are, however, closely related puzzles that cannot be excised from semantics. My remarks have been restricted to simple, unembedded sentences. What about the well-known puzzles concerning belief sentences and other attitudinal embeddings, the genuinely semantic problem, for example, created by the alleged fact that substituting one name for another in the embedded sentence of a belief report often fails to preserve truth? If 'John believes that Cicero was an orator' expresses a truth, then so should the corresponding Tully sentence, according to the new theorist. But, urges the Fregean, if John assents to 'Cicero was an orator' but forcefully dissents from 'Tully was an orator', the respective belief reports will have different truth-values.

Attitudinal embeddings seem to be a place where cognitive and semantic questions converge. These sentences might therefore seem to place great strain on my idea that we can separate semantic questions from questions concerning cognitive significance. Nor does my apparatus—the distinction between states of affairs, linguistic meanings, and cognitive perspectives—promise any immediate solution to this semantic problem. What can be said here on behalf of the new theorist? Unfortunately, the questions involved take far more space than I have, and so I can only indicate the direction of my thinking.

New theorists should not respond, as some have,[29] by denying the putative Fregean datum that, in the sort of example considered above, the truth-values of the respective belief sentences differ. This response has all the charm of biting the bullet. Perhaps the data here are less than absolutely hard, but it is far from clear that the Fregean intuition is mistaken. New theorists' arguments against Frege often give great weight to ordinary intuitions about truth-values, and so they ought not to dismiss the apparently unfriendly intuitions to which Fregeans appeal here. The consequences of those intuitions, however, may not be what they have seemed.

It is interesting to note, to begin with, that the Fregean argument from belief sentences depends upon a highly selective view of the "data." Perhaps our practices of substituting one name for another are not nearly as liberal as the new theory seems to demand. They are not nearly as restrictive, however, as Fregeans would lead us to believe. In many, many ordinary contexts of reporting what other people say, think, believe, and so on, substitutions of embedded singular terms preserve truth, and so do substitutions of names for other names, even names for definite descriptions, definite descriptions for names, or definite descriptions for definite descriptions, as the following examples illustrate.

Nigel, an Englishman, says, "Tully was an orator" (imagine that the British use only this name for Cicero—Nigel has never heard the name 'Cicero'), and I report him to you (an American who has never heard the name 'Tully') as believing that "Cicero was an orator." Tom, a new faculty member, is told about all the new funding that the dean has arranged for faculty research. He says, not having any idea of who the dean is, "The dean is obviously very smart." I report to Barbara that Tom believes that Mike is very smart or that Jonathan's soccer coach is very smart (in case Barbara, say, characteristically refers to the relevant individual as "Mike" or is most familiar with him in his role as Jonathan's coach).[30]

Such substitutions, at least in the sorts of contexts indicated, are perfectly acceptable. Nor do we, in making such substitutions, have to worry about preserving or reporting the Fregean sense of the original remarks.[31] In such contexts at least, the truth or falsity of the report depends, not upon accurately capturing the Fregean thought believed, but simply upon correctly formulating who it is the believer has a belief about and what the believer believes about him. New theorists, also selective in their choice of data, have occasionally appealed to such examples as defeating the Fregean orientation and as establishing their own notion of a singular proposition as the object of belief.³² Belief reports have thus sometimes been seen as the main battleground between the Fregean and the anti-Fregean.³³

I believe that this aspect of the debate has been misguided. Belief reports are extremely resistant to neat theoretical treatment—and this is so on either the Fregean or the anti-Fregean orientation. Perhaps a neat treatment is not even possible if, as Kripke suggests in "A Puzzle About Belief," there are deep puzzles and paradoxes surrounding our reporting practices. Belief sentences, as Kripke emphasizes, present problems for all sides.³⁴

I want to recommend a more fruitful and natural battleground: the study of simple, unembedded sentences. Before concluding with such a recommendation, however, I will offer something of a diagnosis, a suspicion about the (or at least a) source of the problems created by belief reports. My diagnosis will further motivate the policy of not giving pride of place to belief reports.

My diagnosis begins with the thought that the problems posed by belief sentences derive from the thesis, jointly accepted by Fregeans and new theorists, that belief sentences report propositional content believed, that 'S believes that p' attributes to S belief in the proposition denoted by 'that p'. Such an account of belief sentences is natural enough, but it is not inevitable, even granting that belief consists in a relation to a proposition. Ordinary reports are, after all, *ordinary* reports, and it is not obvious ahead of time that our reporting practices must be aimed at the philosophically favored purpose of capturing propositional content believed. One might, then, defend a Fregean account of propositions or a Kaplan-Russell account, along with the idea that belief consists in a relation to a proposition, and still deny that ordinary belief sentences report the content believed.

Nor is this just a theoretical point. Both accounts of propositional content, when embedded in the traditional picture of belief sentences as reporting propositions believed, face recalcitrant data. This complicated array of data³⁵ thus suggests that what is reported is not (at least not exclusively) propositional content believed. Indeed, the truth of belief reports does not seem to depend upon *any* single sort of factor. What the relevant factors are, moreover, seems highly context-dependent, dependent, that is, upon the communicative purpose for which the report was issued. Sometimes what predominates is the end of indicating the referent of the belief, that is, what the belief is about, along with the property predicated. These, of course, are the contexts in which truth is preserved by the substitutions in question. On other occasions, those to which Fregeans have drawn attention, a report can be false even if it gets the reference and predication correct, false because it, in effect, puts the wrong words in the believer's mouth or the wrong ways of thinking about the referent into his head. These, of course, are just a sample of the sorts of relevant factors.

Fregeans and new theorists, not particularly attuned to the social character of our reporting practices, have generally taken for granted the traditional view of belief sentences. Giving up the traditional view may open the door to a more adequate account of the semantics of attitudinal embeddings.[36] Whether either or both approaches are adequate to the explanation of all the data remains, of course, to be seen. We ought not to be too quick in ruling out either orientation because of as yet inadequate treatment of belief reports. This suggests what seems plausible anyway, that such embeddings are not the obvious starting points for the semantics of natural language.

It is, moreover, far from obvious that belief reports even constitute the natural place to begin a study of the problems of cognitive significance.[37] I say this in part because of how difficult and messy the study of attitudinal embeddings turns out to be. A more important reason, however, is my suspicion that the substitutivity puzzles, and related problems, do not exclusively, or even centrally, reflect difficulties about the cognitive significance of the embedded singular terms. That 'Cicero' and 'Tully' play different cognitive roles for many people is a fact about the cognitive significance of these names. That 'Cicero = Tully' is often informative is a fact about the cognitive significance of that sentence. What about the fact that with respect to 'John believes that Cicero was an orator' there are some contexts in which we can substitute 'Tully' for 'Cicero', *salva veritate*, as in the Nigel case above, and other contexts in which such substitution fails to preserve truth? Is this a fact about the cognitive significance of the names? Or is it rather a fact about the social and communicative purposes served by belief reports? Indeed, if we had a good explanation of the cognitive significance of the names, if we had, for example, a general idea about how the explanation of the informativeness of identity ought to proceed, would that automatically explain the substitutivity phenomena, the explanation of which would seem to involve a central social component? Conversely, if we had an account of the substitutivity phenomena, an account that centrally involved the social character of belief reports, is it obvious that this would explain the cognitive significance of the names for the believer?

It is interesting to note that the Perry-Kaplan strategy, explicitly an approach to cognitive significance, was aimed at providing an account of the cognitive significance of simple sentences exclusively.[38] It is perhaps even more interesting to note that Frege, as opposed to some recent neo-Fregeans, seems to locate the central problem of cognitive significance at the level of simple, unembedded sentences. His objection, at the beginning of "On Sense and Reference," to a view that is of a piece with the new theory, is *not* that it cannot handle *belief contexts*. It is rather that the view cannot handle the cognitive significance of simple, unembedded sentences, specifically the informativeness of factually true identity sentences in which the names flank the identity sign. I believe that this is where the Fregean should focus his attack. Blunting the force of such a Fregean attack has been the point of this paper.

TEN

Cognitive Significance Without Cognitive Content

> *Imagine how it must appear to the Martian making his first visit to earth. Let us suppose that he too is an intelligent being, whose intelligence has, however, evolved without the mediation of language, but rather, say, through the development of ESP. So he is something like the angels who, according to St. Thomas, can see things directly in their essences and communicate thought without language. What is the first thing he notices about earthlings? That they are forever making mouthy little sounds—clicks, hisses, howls, hoots, explosions, squeaks—some of which sounds name things in the world and are uttered in short sequences which say something about these things and events in the world. . . .*
>
> *Instead of starting out with such large, vexing subjects as soul, mind, ideas, consciousness, why not set forth with language, which no one denies, and see how far it takes us toward the rest.*
>
> —Walker Percy, "The Delta Factor"

Introduction: Two Conceptions of Semantics

In the beginning, there was Gottlob Frege, who approached the philosophical study of language with his gaze firmly fixed upon one of those "large, vexing subjects," the "eternal structure of thought."[1] Michael Dummett attributes the following three theses to Frege:

first, that the goal of philosophy is the analysis of the structure of *thought* [that is, the objective and eternally existing contents of thought]; second, that the study of *thought* is to be sharply distinguished from the study of the psychological process of *thinking*; and, finally, that the only proper method for analysing thought consists in the analysis of *language*.[2]

Reprinted by permission from *Mind* 97 (January 1988): 1–28.

Cognitive Significance Without Cognitive Content

A central aim of semantics, for Frege, is thus the elucidation of how language expresses thought contents. 'Hesperus is Phosphorus', maintained Frege, expresses a significant piece of information, a nontrivial thought content. Our semantic account of names must explain how this is so. Frege concluded that the contribution of the two names to the thought content must be different.

Frege's sense-reference approach not only explains the contributions of names to thought contents but does so in a way that respects what I will call the "intentionality intuition." This is the powerful traditional idea that in order to be thinking about something, one must have a *cognitive fix* on it, that something in one's thought must correctly distinguish the referent from everything else in the universe.[3] 'Hesperus' and 'Phosphorus', then, not only contribute differently to the thought content, but, holds Frege, what each name contributes is its distinctive mode of presentation, its own cognitive fix on the referent. That a semantic account of a name must make plain the cognitive perspective on the referent that is associated with the name is another crucial feature of the Fregean perspective, one intimately related to Frege's emphasis on thought.

Frege's outlook on the business of semantics thus eliminates semantical accounts like Mill's "pure denotation" view of proper names, recently championed by many of us. Millian accounts make the semantics of the two names the same, and so will not be able to explain what Frege took to be the very datum, that sentences like 'Hesperus is Phosphorus' express nontrivial thought contents. The Millian approach to names, moreover, fails to explain the speaker's cognitive fix on the referent. Even worse, that approach, at least as it has been recently developed, implies that the speaker need not have much of a cognitive fix, perhaps none at all. Saul Kripke, to mention one prominent example, takes it to be plain that one can refer by proper name even if one has very little information about the referent—not nearly enough to individuate it.[4] So much the worse, from Frege's point of view, for cognitively insensitive Millian accounts.

One might, though, approach the philosophical study of language in a radically different spirit, that suggested by Walker Percy's remarks. Let us focus for a moment, not upon language vis-à-vis thought, but upon language vis-à-vis the realm of things language is used to talk about, or, even better, vis-à-vis our practices of talking about things.

The social practices that constitute natural language are, after all, pretty fascinating in and of themselves. Articulated speech is indeed distinctively human, the first thing that Percy's Martian notices about us. And thought is one of Percy's "large, vexing subjects," one that might better be approached a bit later—which is not to say that the two subjects are not, in the end, intimately related. My semanticist thus fixes his gaze upon language as a social, institutional arrangement, and upon speakers as participants in a social practice.

Speaking, it occurs to him, like other kinds of practical mastery, does not presuppose theoretical understanding of the practice. We are indeed fortunate—God, so to speak, has been good to us—that articulable insight is not necessary, for it is extremely difficult to attain. Indeed, speakers, and other practitioners, may well find their own practices theoretically impenetrable. Adequate theoretical characterizations of one's practices will typically not be available to introspection. Nor will competent practitioners typically be able even to select some correct characterization from a list of fairly plausible candidates.[5]

The semanticist thus sees himself as engaging in an anthropological study of the institutional arrangements that constitute natural language.[6] His charge, more specifically, is to provide an account of the semantics of our linguistic practices. Which features of the total communication situation do our practices count as determining the references of proper names? What, as our practices go, links up a particular name (or utterance) with a particular referent? This is the sort of question in which he is interested.[7]

Frege's sense-reference account might be seen as providing an answer to the latter question. Contemporary anti-Fregeans have argued that Frege's is not a good answer. It fails to reflect accurately the character of our practices. Perfectly competent speakers often fail to have available the sort of information required of them by Frege's account. They often lack anything like purely qualitative individuating beliefs about the referents of the names that they use. The beliefs that they do have, moreover, often correctly apply to individuals other than the referents of the relevant names, and so on.

Frege, moreover—and this is a point of importance for distinguishing the two conceptions of semantics—does not put forth his sense-reference account as an answer to our anthropological semanticist's question: what, according to actual linguistic practice, determines the reference of proper names? Frege's picture provides, inter alia, an answer to this question, but this is not his focus at the beginning of "On Sense and Reference."[8] His primary concern is with explaining the contribution of names to thought contents. If we use 'semantics' in the second, and non-Fregean, way, we can say that Frege's interest was not primarily semantical.

Someone with a Fregean conception of semantics, on the other hand, might well wonder about the very relevance to semantics, in his sense, of Millian-style accounts of names. The thesis that the reference of a name depends upon, as Keith Donnellan and Saul Kripke urge, a historical chain of communication—even if this thesis formulates some yet-to-be-classified kind of truth about our practices with proper names—fails to answer the specifically "semantic" questions about the contribution of names to thought contents and about the cognitive fix involved in the use of names. If, as we are sometimes told, a theory of meaning is a theory of understanding, then it is far from clear that John Stuart Mill, or the Donnellan-Kripke approach, tells us anything about meaning.

Mill's contemporary sympathizers have indeed often been attacked for the alleged cognitive insensitivity of their view. Millians have not been conscious of deep differences between their conception of semantics and Frege's, and so they have often been embarrassed by the apparent failure of their semantics to yield illumination of the sort demanded by Frege. Alternatively, they have twisted and turned to show that *their* semantic apparatus can be pressed into cognitive service.[9]

The anthropological conception of semantics yields a natural response on behalf of the Millian. The aim of the anthropological semanticist is not, after all, to solve Frege's problems. Nor does the anthropological semanticist presume that his work will yield such solutions. It is not at all obvious that elucidating the social-reference-determining conditions will explain the cognitive dimension, for example, the informativeness of 'Hesperus is Phosphorus'. The explanation of that might, for instance, turn upon, in Hilary Putnam's terms, what is in the head of the speaker. Reference, on the other hand—at least if the Millian is correct—has little to do with the head of the speaker. The anthropological semanticist, however, need not assume that his work will be of no help in illuminating the cognitive dimension. He can adopt, as they say, a wait-and-see attitude.

Philosophical debates in which adversaries argue at cross-purposes, as in the present case, are typically fuelled by deep, unarticulated differences. My suggestion has been that, contrary to the appearances, we should not think of the two approaches as engaged in a single explanatory project. Indeed, their explanatory projects, while displaying considerable overlap, differ substantially. This difference in explanatory projects, the difference in conception of the semantic enterprise, does not, however, exhaust the deep, unarticulated differences of which I spoke. That their semantic projects sharply diverge is itself a symptom of a much deeper divide between Fregeans and anti-Fregeans. My central aims here are to call attention to differences at the level of broad philosophic outlook and to draw some implications for the area of intersection of philosophy of language and philosophy of mind in which Frege and his followers have been so interested.

The anti-Fregean view, it turns out, is far from cognitively insensitive. That view, seen in the context of the broad outlook to be proposed here, does provide a most natural way of thinking about the cognitive dimension. Mill's remarks on names, and those of Donnellan and Kripke as well, do indeed fail to provide for the sort of account of the cognitive dimension that Frege sought. Their not providing for such an account is indeed a virtue, for a Frege-style account, I will argue, presupposes a Cartesian perspective that we have reason to reject.

Frege's Cartesianism

Frege, like his recent critics, never does formulate, or even gesture toward, a comprehensive philosophical outlook. His semantical work, at the same time, is grounded in strong intuitions about intentionality, the contents of thought, and related matters in metaphysics, epistemology, and the philosophy of mind. There is, I submit, a big picture just out of sight. I see in Frege's work the deep influence of the Cartesian tradition. I have in mind here not so much specific Cartesian doctrines as a tendency of mind, a way of approaching the philosophy of language and the philosophy of mind. Frege's sense-reference perspective, his emphasis on the connections between language and objective thought contents accessible to the mind, rather than on, say, the connections between language—thought of as a public, social institution—and the world, bespeaks this Cartesian influence.[10]

Frege might well seem, however, a most unlikely neo-Cartesian. Frege himself, as Michael Dummett emphasizes, has played a crucial role in the twentieth-century anti-Cartesian revolution. Frege's own revolutionary contribution, as Dummett notes, consisted in making the philosophical study of meaning, rather than skepticism and the theory of knowledge, the starting point in philosophy. Frege, moreover, emphasized what we might call "the publicity of thought content," the idea that the thoughts we express with language are not in principle private to the minds of individual thinkers but are in the public, albeit nonphysical, domain.

Consider, however, the Fregean semantic perspective vis-à-vis the Cartesian "mirror of nature" tradition in the philosophy of mind. That tradition, it is often noted, sees the mind as set against nature, as the repository of images and conceptual representations of things. Pieces of language become meaningful by being associated with the conceptual representations. Leaving aside the question of images, and the probably related Fregean "ideas," is not this picture at least a very close relative of Frege's?

One difference, already noted, is Frege's anti-psychologistic platonism, his insistence that senses do not reside in the mind, but rather in a third, objective realm. Still, there is for Frege a realm of representations, distinct from the things represented and accessible to the mind, and linguistic expressions become meaningful only by being associated with these representations.[11]

Frege's making the representations abstract and therefore public entities may obscure, moreover, an important individualistic strain in his view. The reference of a proper name depends, for Frege, not upon anything like the role of the name in the public language, but rather upon the individual's associating a particular sense with the name.[12]

Frege's view shares other characteristic features of a Cartesian orientation. It is, Frege tells us, the representations—senses and not words—that refer in the primary instance.[13] The reference of words is thus derivative from the reference of senses.[14] Proponents of a Cartesian orientation also characteristically emphasize the clarity and distinctness of the representations and make mathematical concepts the paradigm, and again, Frege is no exception.

So much for Frege's Cartesian perspective on individual terms and the conceptual representations with which they are associated. The same themes reappear, perhaps more strikingly, when we consider Frege's treatment of language at the level of whole sentences. Just as the vitality—to use Wittgenstein's metaphor—of individual expressions derives from their association with senses, so the vitality of whole sentences derives from their association with sentential senses. Just as the senses of singular terms, rather than the terms themselves, are the things that refer in the most basic sense, so sentential senses, the thought contents, are the primary bearers of truth and falsity. Fregean thoughts, like their constituent senses, are well defined and eternally existing. They constitute, Frege tells us, the "common treasure of mankind."

Frege, although his focus is directed toward Plato's heaven and not toward social practice, would acknowledge the platitude that natural language is a social, institutional arrangement. That certain sentences get correlated with certain thought contents is, he would surely agree, an artefact of human institutional arrangements. Frege would insist, however, that one's thinking a certain thought content is no matter of human convention, institutional arrangement, or anything of the like. It is a matter of one's mind grasping an objectively existing content. More important, then, at least in a sense more important, than the fact that sentences express such "thoughts" is the fact that by uttering sentences we assert them, we give voice to the thought contents that we are thinking. The traditional Fregean account of the "propositional attitudes," for example, the idea that belief consists in a relation between a person and a thought content, emerges directly.

A Social, Naturalistic Alternative

Frege, we might say, puts forth a thought-driven picture of language.[15] Language, if we overlook its imperfections, is thought externalized. Frege's conception contrasts dramatically with the one I want to develop, the one I see rationalizing the work of Frege's recent critics. My picture shares much with, and owes a great deal to, that of Wittgenstein.[16] Wittgenstein, although some Fregeans are fond of claiming him for their own, gives voice to a radically different perspective, one less representationalist, and arguably more naturalistic. I do not want here to engage in Wittgenstein exegesis, an even trickier business than the question of how best to read Frege. So let me just sketch my alternative.

The approach I have in mind, in stark contrast to the Cartesian tradition, denies that pieces of language become meaningful by being associated with representations, mental *or* objective. It is here that the connections between Wittgenstein and contemporary anti-Fregeans emerge most clearly. Consider Putnam's slogan, slightly adapted: "meaning ain't in, nor is it available to, the head." Indeed, a central lesson of the *Philosophical Investigations*, at least as I read it, is that there is less available to the head than one might have supposed, and further that whatever is intellectually available is less relevant to philosophers' questions about language (and even thought) than one might have supposed.[17]

If the vitality of linguistic expressions is not a function of associated representations, of what is it a function? The broadly Wittgensteinian answer is that the significance of a piece of language is a function of its embeddedness in social, linguistic practice. The problem for those of us—virtually everybody—brought up Cartesian is to make this more concrete, to somehow allow us to get a feel for how meaningfulness could be a function of anything other than representations.

The Donnellan-Kripke historical-chain picture, whether or not it provides the last word on its subject matter,[18] can be pressed into service here as suggesting a model of how significance might depend upon social practice and not upon representations. An introductory philosophy student, quite ignorant about Aristotle and his accomplishments, asks, "Who was Aristotle? Was he the one who believed that everything was water?" The name 'Aristotle' as it occurs in the student's questions, surmises, and assertions makes reference to Aristotle, our Aristotle, in virtue of—as the Donnellan-Kripke sketch goes—a historical chain of communication that stretches back to something like an original baptism. Notice that the Donnellan-Kripke account gives the name a role in the *public language*; it functions as part of a public, name-using practice. The name, as uttered on these occasions, has a *conventional* referent.[19] The name connects to the referent, then, in virtue of a communal practice of using *this* name as a name for *him* and not in virtue of conceptual associations.[20]

Wittgenstein, in the service of a social practice picture, sometimes appears to urge that we drop talk of "meaning" in favor of talk of "use." I do not know that we need to follow this advice strictly, but there is surely something to be said for the idea. Talk of "meaning" tends, for one thing, to suggest the very representationalist picture we are at pains to supplant. It tends to conjure up images of "grasping meanings," when there are—think about names from a Millian perspective—no meanings to grasp. And thinking about linguistic competence in terms of grasping meanings encourages us to emphasize the theoretical knowledge involved in competence, to think in terms of *knowing that* as opposed to the more appropriate *knowing how*.

It is natural enough, moreover, to speak of "meaning" both in connection with communal linguistic practice *and* in connection with individual speakers' conceptual associations. So meaning-talk, instead of helping us keep these topics distinct, encourages conflating them. Keeping them distinct is, of course, absolutely crucial from the point of view taken here.[21]

The moral I want to draw is, not that we need to banish talk of meaning, but that we handle it with care. Wittgenstein himself at times appears to urge, not that we drop talk of meaning in favor of talk of use, but that we identify meaning with use. We want to be careful, though, not to suggest that there is nothing more to meaning, in any of its manifestations, than communal linguistic practice. We might settle for the more modest methodological exhortation that insofar as we do talk of meaning, we give pride of place to the social, specifically to communal practice, rather than to individual, or even community-wide, representations. Even when we turn to the Fregean's favorite questions about individual cognition—and we ought not do this too quickly, so the methodological sermon continues—our prior study of meaning *as* use will be focal. It is to court disaster to look first toward what is available to the individual consciousness for the clarification of virtually anything that comes under the rubric "meaning."

Crucial to the outlook that I am recommending, then, is its rejection of Frege's thought-driven conception of language.[22] One implication of the conception, an implication noted above, is that it is the conceptual representations rather than their linguistic embodiments that, in the first instance, refer. The real action, as it were, takes place at a good distance from our social practices. Such a conception makes it natural to suppose that the first step toward understanding how words refer is to understand how thoughts do so.[23] Nothing could be further from the truth according to our new picture. What we semanticists study is, not thought, but our social practices of talking about things. Indeed, it becomes tempting, although it is no doubt too simple, to construe silent thought on the model of internal utterance.

So far we have the bare bones of the more socially sensitive, naturalistic picture that I want to recommend. I will soon turn to implications for the area of intersection of the philosophy of language and the philosophy of mind to which Fregeans have riveted our attention. First, however, I want to sketch my picture more fully. The additional features of my view that I will mention are important to the overall perspective, but they do not figure directly in the account of the cognitive dimension that I will offer. I thus want to mention and motivate them here, but a full discussion will not be possible.

Clarity and distinctness. Frege attributes to the third-realm entities that he takes to stand behind language, entities like senses and thought contents, an extreme, perhaps even absolute, refinement; they are necessarily clear and distinct. Think here of Frege's comment, for which he took some chiding from Wittgenstein,[24] that a concept without boundaries is no concept at all.

Frege, of course, is not alone here. There is a deep tendency in the representationalist tradition to attribute such purity to the representations, a tendency that has consequences for one's conception of language. The ways in which the conception of language may be affected are various. Philosophers have sometimes seen language, or at least its more "respectable" parts, as itself possessing a kind of clarity and distinctness—as being associated, for example, with clear criteria that specify necessary and sufficient conditions of application. Alternatively, language may be seen as a mere dim reflection of the pristine realm, and the messiness of language attributed to our all-too-human ways of getting at the clear and distinct concepts.[25] Either way, the background conception of perfectly refined representations plays a dominating role.

Rejecting the representationalist picture may open the door to a different way of thinking about linguistic practice. It is here that we anti-Fregeans have most to learn from Wittgenstein. A truly social, anti-representationalist picture will not merely reject the ontology of objective or mental concepts. It is not even enough to embrace the idea that meaningfulness is to be cashed out ultimately in terms of linguistic practice. One might go this far but remain in the grip of a picture of practice and its governing rules (or RULES) that derives from the rejected Cartesian perspective. One might well presuppose, and see semantics as the attempt to uncover—as indeed we anti-Fregeans have—a kind of rigidity on the part of the phenomena, a fixedness that the phenomena may in fact fail to exhibit.

A detailed look at actual practice is out of the question here, but it will stand us in good stead to remind ourselves that our practices with words do not evolve from the attempt to capture in words, or communicate to others, pre-existent concepts that, almost by definition, possess the required refinement.

In the beginning—if the reader will indulge me one more time—there were the primitive brutes, bumping into each other and grunting by way of indicating to their fellows salient features of the environment. Linguistic practice, on this impressionistic picture, gets more articulated, more refined, as suits the practical, social, and eventually intellectual needs of the brutes and their successors. The crucial point is that whatever precision, articulation, refinement, does evolve is a result of pressures of the sorts mentioned, and not a result of the desire to capture in words some absolutely precise Cartesian concepts. The precision achieved is thus never "absolute," whatever that might mean, nor is there any absolute standard, like the Cartesian concepts, by which we might assess the precision of usage.

To the extent one thinks that such a sketch roughly represents the way things really go, to that extent one will be skeptical of philosophers' tendency to impute clarity and distinctness to usage, or to usage-when-it-is-up-to-snuff. And to that extent, one will be sympathetic even to Wittgenstein's more radical "lack of regimentation" claims.

Consider, for example, the putative "family resemblance" phenomenon. Reflection upon actual linguistic practice with many general terms, 'game' for example, fails to reveal—urges Wittgenstein—what the traditional picture led us to expect: a set of features common to all games, features that are individually necessary and jointly sufficient for something to be a game. Given our new picture, Wittgenstein's claims do not seem outlandish. Why indeed can't there be terms whose utility does not depend upon there being something substantive shared by the things to which the term applies? Mightn't there well be utility to having a term that collects a range of things that are roughly similar to one another, things that fail to share any single feature but that share a kind of family resemblance?[26]

Consider a related "lack of refinement" phenomenon, vagueness, the fact that, for example, there are no sharp boundaries separating games from nongames. The Cartesian can try to account for vagueness in any number of ways,[27] but, to be sure, this phenomenon does not fit hand in glove with the Cartesian picture, and something will have to be said.

Far from being a source of pressure to our more naturalistic, social account, vagueness is entirely to be expected. Remember, we do not start with pre-existent, sharply demarcated concepts, the common treasure of personkind.[28] Our practices with words are only as refined as they are, and there is no external standard (such as how well they capture our conceptual representations) by which to measure them. If there are cases that in practice rarely occur, for example, borderline cases of the applicability of a term, then it is likely that even a master of the term will not be able to say that the term either clearly does or clearly does not apply. This inability reflects, not a lack of mastery, but rather the fact that, as Wittgenstein says, the borders have not yet been drawn.[29]

An important component of the anti-representationalist picture is thus its expectation that usage will turn out to be considerably less regimented than we have supposed. This is not to say that we can expect Wittgenstein's family resemblance picture to provide a generally applicable model. The primitive brutes and their successors, after all, can become attuned to relatively stable aspects of their natural environments, for example, the water that they drink and bathe in, and come to have terms that apply in an at least somewhat, and perhaps dramatically, less openended way. Even pieces of language that seem more deeply institutional than do natural-kind terms like 'water' may presumably vary widely in the degree of regimentation they exhibit. Perhaps we should expect a continuum here. The point, though, is that we cannot simply proceed as we have, taking Kaplan's "The reference of the first-person pronoun is the agent of the context" as the model of what the semanticist should aim to uncover.[30]

Propositional content. Propositions, it is often noted, have been wanted as the bearers of truth, and as the "objects of propositional attitudes." Frege's representationalist picture makes it natural to let the sentence-level representations, the Fregean thoughts, play these roles. What, though, if we reject representationalism in favor of the kind of perspective I am advocating? What becomes of propositions?

The topic is, however, gigantic. I can only sketch what I take to be the natural response, that a truly social and naturalistic conception will want to do without propositions. I will briefly mention two sorts of considerations that seem to me to militate against propositions.

1. *Naturalism.* Kaplan has recently objected to the Platonistic conception of the individuation of words. We suppose, he argues, that the distinction between word tokens and abstract types is the basis of the individuation of words. Not so! What makes your utterance of 'Aristotle' and mine two occurrences of the same word is not the supposed fact that both occurrences stand in a relation to some abstract stereotype that they instantiate, or are members of an abstract type that inhabits Frege's third realm. The worldly occurrences need to be linked in some more naturalistic way; their being occurrences of the same word must be a function of our social, linguistic interactions.[31]

I want to reject, in this same spirit, the notion that thought, belief, and assertion, for example, consist in relations to abstract entities. The anti-Fregeans' "singular propositions" may appear to be more innocuous than Fregean thoughts, for singular propositions are abstract entities that have been, so to speak, brought down to earth. Among their constituents, after all, are things like you and me. Even such propositions, however, seem to me objectionable from a naturalistic point of view. Had we anti-Fregeans not started with Fregean thoughts and then made the appropriate amendments—replacing Frege's propositional constituents, senses, with referents—would it have seemed natural to construe thought, belief, and assertion as involving relations between minds (or even persons) and abstract entities? The very idea that thought et al. involves such relations may well be a legacy of the Fregean-Cartesian picture.

2. *The messiness of linguistic practice.* How does the propositions picture—explicated in terms of either Fregean thoughts *or* singular propositions—comport with that other implication of our social orientation, the fact that usage often fails to be sharply bounded, that usage is only as clear as it needs be? Assume, for a moment, that Wittgenstein was correct and that 'game' is a family resemblance term. What proposition is expressed by 'That is a game'? What, specifically, are we to make of the predicate constituent? The idea that the predicate constituent is the property of being a game surely does not comport well with our "family resemblance" account.

My question is whether the apparatus of propositions is compatible *in spirit* with the social orientation. There is no question that it can be made compatible. One might insist that the proposition does contain the property of being a game (or the sense of 'game'), that it is just a fuzzy property (or sense), or something of the like. Surely we can hang on to the notion of a proposition if we want to. The question is whether the most natural way to work out a socially sensitive conception of language involves the notion of a proposition.

These remarks raise many questions, of course, questions about how, without propositions, we are to do the work traditionally assigned to them. Are we to try to do without truth-bearers? If not, what will play that role? How are we to construe belief if not as involving a relation to a proposition? I cannot, of course, begin to deal with these questions here, but I will do so elsewhere.[32]

Intentionality: The Missing Cognitive Fix

I turn now to the problems that have seemed to make life so difficult for anti-Fregeans. Let us begin with what may appear to provide the anti-Fregean's most severe headache, the Cartesian intuition concerning intentionality, the problem of the missing cognitive fix. The Cartesian idea that reference requires mental discrimination of a referent initially looks unassailable. Indeed, I have heard it said that this alone disqualifies the anti-Fregean's semantical views. The Cartesian intentionality intuition takes on a very different look, however, when reconsidered from the vantage point of our more social, naturalistic picture.

If we *look* at our actual practices as Wittgenstein urged, rather than think about what they must be like, the "cognitive fix" requirement immediately begins to look suspicious, perhaps just plain wrong. People often simply do not have much of a fix on the things to which they refer. For one thing, as has been pointed out time and again, the beliefs that a speaker has about the referent of a name that he is using may be very far off the mark, and yet his reference is not affected.[33] A philosophy student may mistakenly associate with 'Aristotle' the properties of having taught Plato and having died of hemlock poisoning, and yet his utterances of the name, in an exam, say, count as references to Aristotle, our Aristotle.

There are many cases, moreover, in which a competent speaker does not begin to possess the sort of information about his referent that would single out that referent, that would distinguish it from many other things. Felipe Alou, I know, was a major-league baseball player. I do not know much else about him, surely not enough to individuate him in any serious way from many others, and yet I can use his name to say things about him. Similarly, as Kripke points out, all that many people know about Cicero is that he was *a Roman orator*.[34] Consider also Kripke's Gell-Mann and Feynman example, in which a speaker competent with two names associates precisely the same (meager) information with each. Such a speaker refers to Gell-Mann when he uses the latter's name and to Feynman when he utters 'Feynman', despite the fact that the only salient thing he knows about either of them is that each is *a leading theoretical physicist*. Putnam makes the same point with respect to the natural-kind terms 'elm' and 'beech'.

Reference in the absence of an accurate cognitive fix looks miraculous, I submit, only to the Cartesian, or to the residual Cartesian strain in us. If pieces of language refer only in virtue of their being associated with representations, then it is miraculous that someone should refer to something in the absence of an appropriate representation. This sense of miraculousness fades fast, however, when we bring the conception of a public language into sharp focus, a conception suggested by the sorts of examples mentioned above. What connects the student's utterance to Aristotle is not the student's cognitive fix on Aristotle. What connects utterance to referent is rather the fact that the student is using a linguistic device that, as our social practices go, refers to Aristotle. Linguistic expressions, as parts of a public practice, attain a kind of life of their own. One who uses a proper name participates in an institutionalized practice and refers to the name's *conventional* referent.[35] Indeed, so far from their being an epistemological requirement of the sort supposed by the traditional picture, it rather seems that one of the crucial functions of proper names is to allow us to bridge great cognitive gulfs. The public language thus makes it possible for us to speak about things even when our beliefs about them are very scanty, confused, even badly mistaken. The examples that seem to show that reference does not require anything like a discriminating conception should not, then, seem astounding, or indeed at all surprising, at least not on our social picture.[36]

Someone with Cartesian intuitions might admit that underscoring the social and institutional character of natural language is the best way for the anti-Fregean to proceed. His argument might run as follows:

> Emphasizing that proper names are part of a public, institutional practice might well seem to make sense of the idea that a speaker need not have much of a cognitive fix on the things about which he speaks. The effect of the anti-Fregean proposal, though, is to make speech and thought radically discontinuous—for such a cognitive fix is surely indispensable to *thought*—and such a radical discontinuity is just not

acceptable. If, in the Aristotle-Socrates case above, for example, it is clear that the descriptions the speaker would offer really do take us to Socrates, then he surely was *thinking* about Socrates. If, moreover, a speaker uses a name in the absence of a cognitive fix, then he really cannot be *thinking* about anyone.

So much in philosophy depends upon which phenomena one takes to be fundamental, where one starts. The anti-Fregean focus has admittedly not been on thought but on language, public language. The Cartesian, believing as he does that this is the wrong place to begin, might well conclude that notwithstanding the apparent counterexamples drawn from actual communicative practice, linguistic reference, unless it is to be divorced from thought, *must* require discriminating knowledge.

Alternatively, if someone with Cartesian intuitions is impressed enough with the social and institutional character of natural language *and* with the anti-Fregeans' counterexamples, he might be willing to endorse the alleged discontinuity between thought and speech.[37] "I'll give you speech," we might imagine him saying, "but thought is quite another thing." The idea is that the correct interpretation of speech is perhaps, in the final analysis, in the public domain. It is a matter of the conventions of the linguistic community and really not a matter of what is in the head of the speaker. What one *thinks*, on the other hand, is very much a matter of what is in (or available to) the head of the thinker. An utterance of "Aristotle wrote the *Ethics*," in a philosophy class, say, counts as a reference to Aristotle, but if the speaker takes Aristotle to be the teacher of Plato and so forth, his *thought* is directed upon Socrates. What about one whose beliefs about Aristotle are so indefinite that they fail to discriminate anyone? Perhaps such a speaker fails to be thinking about anyone.[38]

Emerging here again is the deep difference between a broadly Cartesian orientation and the more social, naturalistic view. It is no accident, no mere oversight, that anti-Fregeans have tended to begin with the study of public practices of communication, practices that we tend to see as, so to speak, relatively out in the open. Thought seems to us, or at least to me, a much more difficult and elusive topic, one with which we might do better had we some grip on our public communicative practices.

It thus makes good sense that the Cartesian would worry that we anti-Fregeans have distanced speech from thought in an extreme way. My worry, on the other hand, is that the Cartesian, on the basis of his philosophical picture of thought, either denies what seems plain about speech (for example, that reference does not require a cognitive fix) or else grants the latter but insists on distancing thought from speech. I do not believe that there is any such radical discontinuity between thought and speech or that the approach taken here suggests such a discontinuity. What seems dubious to me is what the Cartesian takes to be so obvious, the idea that if we restrict our attention to the question of about whom the speakers are *thinking*, it is clear that the background descriptions provide the decisive answer.

Let us begin with examples in which speakers fail to have any sort of real cognitive fix, examples in which the background descriptions fail to individuate. Someone says, "Cicero was a Roman orator," and cannot identify Cicero much further. It seems very farfetched, indeed altogether ad hoc, to suppose that such a perfectly competent and sincere speaker who fails to believe very much about Cicero ipso facto fails to be thinking about him. Surely, in the example above, I was thinking about Felipe Alou. The phenomenon of reference in the absence of individuating information is so pervasive that the supposition in question would deny thought content to an extremely wide range of sincere utterances produced by reflective people. This surely seems like the proverbial philosophers' view, as opposed to what seems plain to just about everyone.[39] Thinking about something, it would seem, no more requires a cognitive fix than does speaking about something.

Now suppose we turn to the case of the speaker who has "mistaken beliefs," whose background descriptions fit, not the referent of the uttered name, but rather someone else. Consider the Aristotle-Socrates case above. There are, no doubt, examples of this sort with respect to which it would be perfectly natural to say that the speaker was thinking about the denotation of the background descriptions. The question is whether this is necessarily so, whether the simple fact that the background descriptions take us to Socrates itself establishes that the speaker was thinking about Socrates. It seems pretty clear, at least if we take our cue from our ordinary judgments, that the background descriptions do not play any such decisive role. We would ordinarily say, after all, in many such cases, that the speaker expressed a mistaken *belief*, even a mistaken *thought*, about Aristotle.[40]

Let us turn from our ordinary judgments and get philosophical. The Fregean, in making the background descriptions decisive, gives a kind of cognitive priority to descriptions over names. This is natural enough, given the Fregean outlook, including the cognitive fix requirement, modes of presentation that are supposed to capture the cognitive perspective, and so on. The question is, however, whether *we* ought to accept this inegalitarian treatment of names vis-à-vis descriptions.

The situation, after all, is that the speaker actually uttered a name that, as our practices go, names *Aristotle*. If asked of whom he was speaking, it is true, our speaker would have provided a description that fits Socrates. How does this make it the case that he was thinking of Socrates? Why not say instead that he was thinking about the person named by the name that he used, that is, Aristotle, and the background descriptions merely reveal his (in this case false) beliefs about that person? In any case, the uttered name takes us to one person, the to-be-uttered-if-asked descriptions to another. What, other than the disputed Cartesian picture, makes it so obvious that we should favor the latter?

My point here, as already indicated, is not that we ought always to give priority to the uttered name over the background descriptions, or that, more generally, whatever singular term is uttered should furnish the key to the referent-in-thought. Sometimes, we ought indeed to privilege unuttered, background terms. One might, for example, utter the name 'Jones' as a mere slip of the tongue while thinking about, and intending to say something about, Smith. Alternatively, one might mistakenly take 'Brown' to be the name of Harris, and thinking about and intending to say something about Harris, one might use the name 'Brown'. So a name other than the uttered name may deserve priority, and so may a background description. Someone might, for example, be thinking about 'the ugliest and nastiest professional wrestler, whoever that is'. Thinking that the person in question is none other than Brutus Beefcake, the speaker may make a remark mentioning the latter by name. If B.B. does not really fit the description, however, there may well be circumstances in which it would be appropriate to say that the speaker was really thinking of 'the ugliest and nastiest professional wrestler, whoever that is', or even that he was thinking about the Iron Sheik, if the latter is indeed uglier and nastier than any other.

We should not, then, expect a single formula in answer to the question of how, in general, we are to determine which item it was about whom someone was thinking.[41] My point here was not to provide such an answer, one that favors, say, uttered names over background descriptions. It was merely to dispel the illusion that at least cognitively—if not semantically—names must be backed up by individuating concepts and that the question of about whom someone is thinking when he utters a name is to be resolved by reference to such a background concept. Whatever we do, in the end, with the thorny problem of reference in thought, it is far from clear that the Cartesian-spirited Fregean idea, the contention that the descriptions-to-be-uttered-if-asked must be decisive, has much merit.[42]

I will conclude this section with some remarks on the implications of my view for another topic that deserves book-length treatment, that of silent thought. It is sometimes supposed that the Cartesian intentionality intuition has a kind of obvious plausibility when it comes to silent thought episodes, that somehow silent thought, as opposed to overt speech, is a most natural candidate for the Cartesian picture. Consider again someone who, although ignorant of Cicero's accomplishments (say, other than being a Roman orator), uses the name pretty much as we all do. We are ordinarily willing to ascribe thoughts about Cicero to such a person when he says things like "I know who Cicero was. He was a Roman orator." Isn't it equally clear that he is in a position to have silent thoughts about Cicero? Surely it is not the verbalization that makes thought about Cicero possible.

Being a participant in a name-using practice, specifically, being competent with 'Cicero', our speaker is in a position to use the name not only in overt speech episodes but also in silent thought. Do names, then, actually occur in silent thought episodes? Are there at least some such episodes that amount to internal utterance? My point does not depend on positive answers to these questions. Whether or not his silent thought that Cicero was an orator amounts to his silently rehearsing this sentence—indeed, however we understand silent thought episodes—his competence with the name, his participation in the practice, puts him in a position to have the thought that he would express, were he to put it into words, as "Cicero was an orator." Not only does the reference of an utterance not depend upon one's cognitive fix but the reference of one's silent thought similarly does not depend upon "what is in the head." This will, of course, seem preposterous from a Cartesian point of view.

How Puzzling Is Frege's Puzzle?

Frege's discussion of cognitive significance, at the beginning of "On Sense and Reference," is focused upon his famous puzzle about informative identity sentences. How, Frege wants to know, are we to explain the difference in "cognitive value" between the trivial 'Hesperus is Hesperus' and the informative 'Hesperus is Phosphorus'—the fact that these sentences formulate different thoughts?

Frege's focus on identity sentences is not altogether salutary, for contrary to its suggestion, the fundamental problem about the cognitive dimension of language with which Frege was centrally concerned has nothing special to do with identity. Frege's fundamental problem was that of accounting for the fact that a mere change of one co-referring name for another can effect a change, indeed a very significant change, in the thought content of a sentence. Frege might well have avoided identity, with all its attendant perplexities, and have asked for the explanation of the difference in cognitive value between 'Hesperus is a planet' and the corresponding Phosphorus sentence.[43]

Frege's discussion—let us focus on the two sentences just mentioned—draws attention to what I shall call "Frege's data," to cognitive phenomena of undeniable importance: one might understand both sentences, for example, but be willing to assert only one of them, even emphatically deny the other. Alternatively, one might find, say, the Hesperus sentence old hat but the Phosphorus sentence highly informative. Finally, one might behave quite differently depending upon which of these sentences one accepts.

Frege's data are both uncontroversial and uncontroversially important, but the lessons Frege would have us learn from them are far from uncontroversial. The most notorious lesson, quite obviously controversial, is Frege's sense-reference approach to semantics. There is, however, a more subtle, prior message that Frege takes the cognitive phenomena to convey, a putative implication that can be made to seem almost like a datum itself. Notice that in formulating Frege's puzzle in the first two paragraphs of this section, I gloss "difference in cognitive value" as "difference in thoughts expressed." Frege's contention that the two sentences express different thoughts, distinct propositional contents—a natural enough contention given Frege's thought-oriented approach—is far from uncontroversial.

One might, for example, insist, in the spirit of the Russell-Kaplan singular-propositions picture, that 'Hesperus is a planet' and 'Phosphorus is a planet' express the same proposition. Alternatively, one might, in the spirit of the naturalistic approach I have been advocating, try to make do without propositions, without unified things that are, as Strawson once put it, the upshots of assertive utterances. Frege's quasi datum is surely contestable. What we cannot contest, however, and what I want to explain, are what I have dubbed "Frege's data," the cognitive phenomena that, for Frege, made it plain that different thought contents were indeed expressed by the respective sentences.

Let us keep in mind that our project is not to make good on the alleged cognitive failures of the anti-Fregean semantic approach. Having made the distinction between semantics, on the anthropological conception, and the study of cognitive significance, the anti-Fregean ought not to be embarrassed that, say, Mill's remarks on names (or those of Donnellan and Kripke) do not immediately address Frege's data. At the same time, the output of anthropological semantics ought to cohere with a more general account of language and thought, one that must address Frege's data. How, then, might one approach the cognitive phenomena if one takes a broadly Millian approach to the semantics of proper names?

It is striking that even those who have led the revolt against the Fregean orientation have approached the explanation of the cognitive phenomena in a way more suited to the Fregean, representationalist picture. To the representationalist, the obvious and only way to explain differences in the cognitive roles of expressions is in terms of differences in associated representations. Kaplan, to mention a prominent example, tries to account for the difference in cognitive roles of indexical expressions by resurrecting modes of presentation, not Fregean senses, mind you, but more kosher "ways in which agents represent the references of their terms."[44]

The appeal of the representationalist picture, here as before, is a function of the fact that we are its captives. It is difficult to so much as conceive an alternative, even in bare outline. If 'Hesperus is a planet' differs cognitively for an agent from the corresponding Phosphorus sentence, doesn't this have to be because he is thinking of the referent in two different ways, because he is employing two different cognitive perspectives? If someone finds 'Hesperus is Phosphorus' informative, doesn't this have to be because he associates a different way of thinking (or mode of presentation or cognitive perspective) with the left-hand side of the equation than he does with the right-hand side? How else might we begin to explain the obvious cognitive differences?

I have argued elsewhere against the Kaplan-Perry approach to the cognitive significance of indexicals.[45] While I stressed there the Fregean flavor of that approach,[46] I was not sufficiently focused upon what I now see as the most salient similarity with Frege, Kaplan's representationalism. Kaplan, no less than Frege, explains cognitive differences between expressions as differences in their associated modes of presentation.[47] Here I want to urge that we abandon representationalism even in the study of the cognitive significance phenomena. Modes of presentation, no matter how liberalized and attenuated, remain spiritual descendants of the Fregean approach. Reflection on some of the anti-Fregean discussions of proper names, moreover, should convince at least these discussants that no such representationalist approach, no matter how benign its representationalism, has any future.

I have in mind here Kripke's Gell-Mann–Feynman case and Putnam's Elm-Beech story. The original point of these examples was to show that reference does not depend upon what is in the head, upon the information that the speaker associates with the expressions.[48] Don't these examples indicate, no less forcefully, that cognitive significance does not depend upon the associated information? 'Gell-Mann' and 'Feynman', after all, can play cognitively inequivalent roles for a speaker despite the fact that the speaker's associated "conceptual files" are identical.

We can make the same point—that cognitive significance is not a matter of associated information—with names that, unlike 'Gell-Mann' and 'Feynman', co-refer. Someone might acquire the names 'Cicero' and 'Tully', associating with them precisely the same information, say, 'a famous Roman'. Still, the names may differ in "cognitive value." It may never strike the speaker that only one person may be in question, and so he may react very differently to sentences that contain one name than to those that contain the other. The anti-Fregean explanation of the cognitive difference between 'Cicero' and 'Tully', then, given our own examples, had better not rely upon necessary differences in associated information, that is, upon different modes of presentation.[49]

My proposal, then, is that we forget modes of presentation and take a fresh look at the data to which Frege drew our attention. I urged in the last section that the Cartesian intentionality intuition—remember how unassailable it seemed at first—takes on a very different look when considered from the vantage point of our more social, naturalistic picture. The same can be said for the highly-plausible-if-you-have-been-brought-up-on-Frege idea that to explain a difference in the cognitive roles of expressions, one must appeal to a difference in cognitive perspectives.

Let us begin with the reflection that the more epistemology one builds into linguistic competence with names, that is, the more of a cognitive fix one requires, the more it will seem that Frege's data present not merely interesting and important phenomena to be explained but a prima facie problem, a *puzzle*. Why is this? The thesis that linguistic competence with names requires mental apprehension of their referents induces a tension between two names' co-referring and their being cognitively inequivalent. If in using each of the two names one must be in cognitive touch with their single referent, how can this identity of reference have escaped notice?

Indeed, if one raises the epistemic stakes enough, it will be impossible to have co-referring names that differ cognitively. Imagine, to take a fanciful example, that we required that a name user be omniscient about the referent. It would then be impossible to be competent with two co-referring names without realizing that only one referent was in question. Co-referring names could, then, not differ in cognitive significance.

Let us go to the other extreme. Although for present purposes we can consider this another fanciful example, anti-Fregeans have sometimes suggested a "no epistemology" picture of linguistic competence. One might, on this view, possess *radically* mistaken beliefs about the referent of a name, or virtually no beliefs at all, and still be in a position to use the name as a name for its socially determined referent. Smith, on the periphery of a conversation between mathematicians in which the name 'Joan' is used as a name for a theorem, mistakenly takes Joan to be a woman. Alternatively, Smith comes away completely unsure of who or what Joan is. In either of these cases, on the no-epistemology view, one may still be in a position to say things about the referent, that is, the theorem, by using the name. One might, for example, speculate about Joan's properties, or ask who or what Joan is.

If one thus does not need to know virtually anything about the referent, it is very easy to see how one could pick up two co-referring names and not know that they had a single referent. The no-epistemology theorist, since he does not think that competence requires mental apprehension of the referent, will thus not see Frege's data as presenting a serious and difficult problem, a real puzzle. Indeed, the explanation of the fact that 'Cicero' and 'Tully' might play different cognitive roles—and not much of an explanation is really needed—would involve simply pointing out that competence with two names does not put one in a position to know whether or not the names co-refer. How could it, given that competence requires no knowledge of the referent?

Frege advanced a view, intermediate between "omniscience" and "no-epistemology," that a name user need attach to the name a purely qualitative concept that he takes to single out a referent. This is, of course, far from requiring omniscience—much further, say, than Russell's direct-acquaintance requirement[50]—and it allows for a cognitive difference between co-referring names. Like the omniscience view, however, it demands a substantive cognitive fix—something intellectually available to the speaker must mentally focus him on the referent. A consequence is that, compared to the no-epistemology view, a more substantive explanation of two co-referring names differing cognitively is required. If one is really mentally focused on the same thing twice, why doesn't one know it? Frege's view yields a natural answer, of course. Someone might not know that a single thing is in question because his focus is not direct, so to speak, as it was for Russell, but is mediated by a concept. If he is focused upon the same thing twice, but by means of different concepts, he may well not realize that the same thing is in question.

We are now in a position to see how the perspective I have been outlining in this paper yields a distinctly non-Fregean approach to the cognitive phenomena. While I have not plumbed the depths of how little need be in the head in order to use a name—I have not subscribed to the *no*-epistemology view—the use of a name, on my account, emphatically does not involve a substantial cognitive fix, the mental apprehension of a referent. Indeed, one of the functions of names is to allow a speaker (or thinker) to bridge great cognitive gaps, to allow a person to speak about things in the absence of anything like individuating conceptions. A consequence is that, just as on the no-epistemology view, the cognitive phenomena no longer have the air of paradox. The use of a name does not require mental apprehension of its referent, and so there is no *puzzle*, no special problem, about how a speaker might be competent with co-referring names and yet not know that they co-refer. Given how little one needs to know (or even believe) about the referent to be competent with a name, there is no presumption that a speaker will know of two co-referring names in his vocabulary, that they in fact co-refer.

I have been emphasizing the fact that the more social outlook dispels any sense of paradox concerning Frege's data. What seems even more important is that we now have a new form of explanation of Frege's data, one radically different from that suggested by the traditional representationalist account. The powerful grip of the representationalist account led us to suppose that the only way to explain a cognitive difference was in terms of a difference in mode of presentation. And anti-Fregeans, laboring under this supposition, have been raking the leaves, as it were, to somehow retrieve such representational differences. Notice that cognitive perspectives, modes of presentation, have no role in our new form of explanation. We do not look into the speaker's head and find two different conceptual files in terms of which we can now see why 'Cicero' and 'Tully' play different cognitive roles for him. We rather reflect upon the fact that given how little need be in his head, his mere competence with the names puts him in no position to decide the question of whether or not these names co-refer. Indeed, as noted above, were we to look inside his head, we might find identical conceptual files for each of two *cognitively distinct* names. We might, of course, find different conceptual files, say 'being a famous Roman orator' associated with 'Cicero', and 'being a famous Roman politician' with 'Tully'. Such a difference, however, does not affect our explanation of what makes it possible for him to wonder whether Cicero was Tully. Such wonder is not rendered more intelligible by the difference in conceptual files. A competent speaker, given how little he need know or even believe about the references of names, might well raise the question even if both files had included merely 'is a famous Roman'.[51]

I began this essay with the distinction between two conceptions of semantics, Fregean and anthropological. The attention of the anthropological semanticist, I argued, is not focused upon the cognitive dimension that, under Frege's influence, has seized center stage. If it turns out that the anthropological semanticist's work fails to provide much help in the explication of the cognitive dimension, so be it. Much to our surprise, however, the anti-Fregean semantical outlook, at least when embedded in the sort of perspective I have been recommending, yields a most natural approach to the cognitive dimension. Central to this approach is the outright rejection of the Cartesian intentionality intuition, argued for in the fourth section above (Intentionality: The Missing Cognitive Fix). To put the point in a more positive way, linguistic contact with things—reference, that is—does not presuppose epistemic contact with them. Underscoring this deep lesson of the anti-Fregean revolution leads, as we have just seen, to a radically non-Fregean account of the Fregean's favorite topic, the cognitive significance of language.[52]

ELEVEN

Turning the Tables on Frege, or How Is It That "Hesperus Is Hesperus" Is Trivial?

Introduction: The Charge of Cognitive Insensitivity

The following challenge, offered me by a friend some years ago, still represents the sense of at least a large sector of the philosophical community. This, as I will argue, is not as it should be.

For some twenty years now philosophers have been carping about the inadequacies of the semantical approaches of Frege and Russell. It must be admitted that many counterexamples to the views of Frege and Russell have been offered, some of considerable intuitive merit. It is nothing less than scandalous, though, that the anti-Fregeans have never given due weight to the sorts of considerations that were absolutely central for Frege and Russell, considerations about "the cognitive significance of language." Indeed, these questions, like the puzzle about informative identities with which Frege begins "On Sense and Reference," are barely mentioned by many leading anti-Fregeans.

Philosophers may have quite a number of things in mind when they speak of the cognitive significance of language. I will focus, in this paper, upon two central facets of cognitive significance, two central ways in which the approach I favor, that of the anti-Fregeans,[1] has been thought to be cognitively insensitive.

1. The anti-Fregean orientation seems to violate an intuition that runs very deep in traditional thinking, the "intentionality

---

Reprinted from *Philosophical Perspectives*, vol. 3 of *Philosophy of Mind and Action Theory*, ed. J. Tomberlin (Atascadero, Calif., 1989), pp. 317–39, by permission of the publisher.

intuition," as I will call it. The idea is that in order to be thinking or speaking about something, one must have a substantial *cognitive fix* on the thing in question, that something in one's thought must correctly distinguish the relevant item from everything else in the universe.

One might motivate a cognitive fix requirement in several different ways. Russell's motivation was explicitly epistemic. One cannot think or speak about a thing, Russell maintained, *without knowing which thing is in question*. Frege's motivation was less explicit, but it seems plausible that an important strand in Frege's thinking was a very different intuition, one which Russell emphatically did not share, that conceptually unmediated reference is impossible, maybe even incoherent. Reference to a thing, on this view, essentially involves entertaining a concept. It may be useful here to compare Frege's semantical view with the view of the perceptual dualist: one cannot, according to the latter, immediately perceive physical objects. Perception of a thing, for the dualist, *just is* the apprehension of a sense datum that, in some sense, represents the thing. So too, for Frege, reference to an object cannot be unmediated, but rather consists in the apprehension of a sense that is satisfied by the object.[2]

Frege and Russell differ not only about the motivation for the intentionality intuition; they differ also about what exactly is required of the speaker or thinker. Russell demands, and this seems closely connected with the fact that his motivation was epistemic (and his epistemology Cartesian), that the speaker or thinker stand in an extremely strong epistemic relation to the referent, namely, that of direct acquaintance. Reference requires that the referent needs to be, as it were, smack up against one's mind. Otherwise, held Russell, the thinker or speaker would not really know which thing was in question, even if he possessed a concept that uniquely applied to it. Frege, motivated not so much (perhaps not at all) by epistemic considerations, but likely by what we might call his "referential dualism," maintains more modestly that one need merely (merely?) possess a uniquely denoting concept.

However one motivates the requirement, and whatever the details of the requirement, some such requirement might well appear obviously in order. We anti-Fregeans, on the other hand, often proceed as if we do not have to spend a moment worrying about this problem. Indeed, many of our examples seem simply to presuppose the incorrectness of any such requirement. Think, for example, about our claim that one who possesses a name, say, 'Cicero', may refer to its bearer even if one's beliefs about the relevant individual are very far off the mark, indeed, even if one has very little "in the head" on this topic.

Fregean sympathizers have often focused their attention on other alleged cognitive failings of the anti-Fregean approach, but the intentionality intuition, I submit, is a deep source of the sense so many have had that no matter how good the criticisms we anti-Fregeans have made of the traditional approach, our view remains deeply incoherent.

2. An arguably more famous, and certainly more specific "cognitive insensitivity" problem is posed by Frege's well-known discussion of nontrivial identity sentences like 'Hesperus is Phosphorus'. It is a commonplace that neither the Millian idea that, as Ruth Barcan Marcus puts it, a name is a tag, or the Donnellan-Kripke way of reviving Mill, yields any simple, straightforward way of understanding the informativeness of 'Hesperus is Phosphorus', or the obvious difference in informativeness of 'Hesperus is Hesperus' and 'Hesperus is Phosphorus'. Frege's view, on the other hand, yields a straightforward explanation.[3] On Frege's view, each name contributes its own distinctive sense to the thought content expressed, and so 'Hesperus is Phosphorus' can express a nontrivial content. The Millian approach, eschewing as it does anything like modes of presentation, or connoted properties, seems to give us no intellectual apparatus out of which we might fashion an explanation.

My aim in this paper is to reveal as baseless the contention that, as Alvin Plantinga once put it, the anti-Fregean approach founders on the rocks of cognitive significance.[4] Others in the anti-Fregean camp have presented putative solutions to puzzles about cognitive significance. What I have in mind, though, is not another solution but rather a dissolution. (If the reader, to paraphrase Santayana, is tempted to smile, I can assure him that I smile with him.) That the phenomena to which Frege draws our attention seem so puzzling is a tribute to the grip of the traditional way of thinking about language represented by the work of Frege and Russell, or so I will argue. Attention to what is perhaps the deepest lesson of the anti-Fregean revolution will suggest a very different way of sorting what is puzzling from what seems perfectly natural.

Conservative Versus Reform Anti-Fregeanism

I want to distinguish two ways of developing the anti-Fregean approach, one relatively conservative and one more radical. The conservative theorist, whose views I describe in more detail below, wishes to avoid what he sees as the obvious pitfalls of Fregean orthodoxy. His hope, though, is to capture, in a less objectionable form than did Frege and Russell, the motivating spirit of the tradition, embodied in the idea that the connection between words and things is intellectually mediated, a matter of the way the referent is presented to the mind.

The more radical approach that I will advocate wants nothing of the spirit of Fregean orthodoxy. The conservative, as he himself emphasizes, has admittedly moved a substantial distance from orthodox Fregeanism. Some of the conservative's moves, moreover, and especially some of his examples, contain the seeds of genuine intellectual revolution. What the conservative fails to discern, excited as he is about his distance from Frege and Russell, is the extent to which he remains tied to traditional patterns of thought. The conservative's Fregean side, his emphasis on the way the referent is presented to the mind, obscures the natural approach to questions concerning the connection between words and things, as well as to questions about the cognitive significance of language.

The Problem of the Missing Cognitive Fix: The Conservative Response

There are many ways to develop a conservative strategy, and one finds what I have called the fundamental Fregean idea cropping up again and again throughout the anti-Fregean literature. I will focus here on its presence in the work of David Kaplan, where it is quite explicit, and in the work of Saul Kripke, where it is more surprising in light of Kripke's sometimes explicit rejection of intellectually mediated reference.

Let us begin with what might well seem a natural place for an anti-Fregean with conservative leanings to begin, with indexical expressions, the first-person pronoun, for example. Why might indexicals, as opposed to proper names, make for a natural conservative starting point? The answer is provided, in effect, by Kaplan in "Demonstratives," which might serve as a conservative handbook.[5] Kaplan argues that while proper names are, as John Stuart Mill taught, "purely denotative"—they lack descriptive meanings—indexicals, like 'I', typically have descriptive meanings. Indeed, continues Kaplan, they have "easily stateable descriptive meanings." Descriptive meanings are, of course, grist for a Fregean's mill. Such meanings, maintains Kaplan, are known to the competent speaker and provide the speaker with a kind of mode of presentation, a cognitive fix on the referent.[6]

Frege's orthodox notion of "sense" and his attendant conception of cognitive fix (not to speak of Russell's "direct acquaintance" approach to the appropriate sort of cognitive fix) were, according to Kaplan, too crude, too naive. We often do not carry around with us anything like purely qualitative individuating characterizations of the things about which we wish to speak. Indeed, we may lack such conceptions even of ourselves. Nor must our concepts, or even our self-concepts, be accurate. I have a friend whose self-concept fits God better than it fits himself. Still, he speaks of himself when he uses 'I'. His ability to so refer to himself, despite his transcendent ego, reflects the fact, according to Kaplan, that associated with 'I', *by linguistic convention*, is a mode of presentation, although not a Fregean one. The crucial difference between Fregean and Kaplanian modes of presentation is this. Senses determine references "absolutely," while Kaplan's "characters" do so in a *context-relative* way; a character determines an object as reference only relative to a context of utterance. The character associated with 'I' is, for Kaplan, (roughly) "the speaker of the context."

Kaplan's approach to indexical reference is thus compatible, at least in spirit, with the dictates of the intentionality intuition. The reference of an indexical is certainly not independent of the speaker's cognitive fix on the referent. Kaplan's conception, however, is of a context-relative cognitive fix, one that, by contrast with Frege's conception, has been brought down to earth.

I have formulated Kaplan's approach so as to emphasize its

continuities with Frege. There are, of course, substantial and impressive discontinuities that have been emphasized by Kaplan and others.[7] One important qualification that deserves explicit mention is that Kaplan never suggests, as some have, that indexicality is ubiquitous, that his treatment of indexicals can serve as a paradigm for the treatment of, say, proper names and natural-kind terms. Kaplan emphasizes, on the contrary, that names, entirely devoid of descriptive meaning, seem to require a very different sort of treatment.[8]

Nevertheless, the Fregean flavor of Kaplan's approach is striking. Kaplan's theoretical repertoire includes "ways of apprehending," conventionally associated with expressions, that provide a cognitive fix (relative to a context) and thereby determine the reference. Thus Kaplan, with Frege—and this is the point of great importance—gives great weight, with respect to the determination of reference, to the way the referent is represented to the mind.[9]

Not only Kaplan but many others as well have either embraced or at least been tempted by the conservative strategy. The feeling that reference must be intellectually grounded goes very deep. And the possibilities for attenuating the Fregean picture are extensive. One can, as we saw, try bringing the senses down to earth by making them context-relative. Another popular variation, tempting for one not quite ready to see proper names as entirely without descriptive content, is to assign to that content a semantically more humble role than did Frege, that of merely "fixing the reference" of a name, rather than that of providing a synonym for it.

Let us distinguish two ways in which the notion of "reference fixing by description" has been used, by Kripke as well as by others. First, one hears it said that names are sometimes, typically, or even always *introduced* by reference-fixing definite descriptions. This, it should be noted, is a thesis about how names get going, so to speak, and not an account of how they later function. One who advances such a thesis need not maintain that later users of the name, or even later uses by the person who introduced the name, utilize a description to fix the reference. A second, and stronger, reference-fixing-by-description thesis consists in the claim that users of a name, even if they do not use the name synonymously with a description, must be fixing the reference of the name by some description.

This distinction is important for our purposes. It is the second and stronger reference-fixing thesis in which I am here primarily interested and which I see as most clearly exemplifying the conservative strategy.[10] Taking the reference of each use of a name to be determined by descriptions available to the speaker retains the intellectual character of the name-referent tie and thus avoids the specter of semantic action at an epistemic distance.[11]

Kripke has, from time to time, explicitly disavowed this conservative position. He roundly asserts, in "Identity and Necessity," "I . . . think, contrary to most recent theorists, that the reference of names is rarely or almost never fixed by description. And by this I do not just mean what Searle says: 'It's not a single description, but rather a cluster. . . .' I mean that properties in this sense are not used *at all*."[12] Some, though, have taken Kripke to be, in my vocabulary, a conservative theorist, to be advancing the very view that Kripke denies in the passage just quoted. Indeed, Kripke himself sometimes seems much less definite on the matter. Lecture 3 of *Naming and Necessity* seems to place great emphasis on reference fixing by description. Consider the following passage: "Usually, when a proper name is passed from link to link, the way the reference of the name is fixed is of little importance to us. It matters not at all that different speakers may fix the reference of a name in different ways, provided that they give it the same referent."[13] The Fregean tone of this passage should not escape us. Frege, you remember, emphasizes that in natural language at least, different speakers will typically attach different senses to a name, but this will not matter much as long as reference is preserved.

Kripke, moreover, in his later "A Puzzle About Belief," in which he again rejects the reference-fixing-by-description approach to the semantics of names, suggests that it would not have been out of the question to read *Naming and Necessity* as suggesting the disputed view.

[In *Naming and Necessity*] I presupposed a sharp contrast between epistemic and metaphysical possibility: Before appropriate empirical discoveries were made, men might well have failed to know that Hesperus was Phosphorus, or even to believe it, even though they of course knew and believed that Hesperus was Hesperus. *Does not this support a Fregean position that 'Hesperus' and 'Phosphorus' have different "modes of presentation" that determine their references?* . . . So it appears that even though, according to my view, proper names would be *modally* rigid— would have the same reference when we use them to speak of counterfactual situations as they do when used to describe the actual world— they would have a kind of Fregean "sense" according to how that rigid reference is fixed.[14]

A Radical Rejoinder

The radical sees philosophical backsliding in anti-Fregean attempts to satisfy the spirit of the intentionality intuition.[15] Doesn't the conservative strategy miss what the striking anti-Fregean counterexamples so strongly suggest? Recall the Donnellan-Kripke examples concerning proper names, examples in which a speaker, competent with a name, nevertheless has beliefs about the name's referent that are badly mistaken or extremely meager, for example, that Cicero was "some famous guy I think I heard about at school." What drives reference, such examples teach us, is not the mind's grip on the referent. The point, to particularize it to Frege, was not that we need to find more proper senses—to bring senses down to earth. The point was that we can do without anything like senses, that the intentionality intuition is simply mistaken. The radical thus takes seriously the rhetoric about an anti-Fregean *revolution* and proposes the following motto (every revolution needs one): Semantic Contact with Things Does Not Depend upon Substantive Epistemic or Conceptual Contact with Them.[16]

The following remarks of Kripke, in *Naming and Necessity*, may help provide a feel for the contrast between the conservative, Frege-inspired outlook and the more radical one.

The picture which leads to the cluster-of-descriptions theory is something like this: One is isolated in a room [Descartes's study, we might add]; the entire community of other speakers, everything else, could disappear; and one determines the reference for himself by saying— "By 'Gödel' I shall mean the man, whoever he is, who proved the incompleteness of arithmetic." Now you can do this if you want to. There's nothing really preventing it. . . .

But that's not what most of us do. Someone, let's say a baby, is born; his parents call him by a certain name. They talk about him to their friends. Other people meet him. Through various sorts of talk the name is spread from link to link as if by a chain. A speaker who is on the far end of this chain, who has heard about, say, Richard Feynman in the marketplace or elsewhere [Question: where does Kripke shop?] may be referring to Richard Feynman even though he can't remember from whom he first heard of Feynman or from whom he ever heard of Feynman. . . . He doesn't know what a Feynman diagram is. . . . Not only that: he'd have trouble distinguishing between Gell-Mann and Feynman. So he doesn't have to know these things, but, instead, a chain of communication going back to Feynman himself has been established by virtue of his membership in a community which passed the name on from link to link, not by a ceremony that he makes in private in his study: "By 'Feynman' I shall mean the man who did such and such."[17]

My point here is not to endorse the particulars of Kripke's sketch, the idea that reference is determined by means of "chains of communication." I am increasingly skeptical about the adequacy of the Donnellan-Kripke sketch.[18] My point is rather that however the details go, it is the community's practice of using this name as a name for *that* man that allows particular speakers to use the name to refer to him. What drives reference is thus the institutionalized practice of the linguistic community and not the way the individual is represented to the mind of the speaker (even where this is relativized to a context). The word-referent tie, as I put it above, is not an intellectual tie. I thus want to take very seriously the platitude that names are social instruments for making their bearers subjects of discourse.[19]

What of indexicals? Indexicals, I said above, might seem to supply a natural habitat for Kaplan's brand of conservatism. Although a full discussion is not possible here, I do want to argue that Kaplan's approach to indexicals is far from trivial; indeed, I believe it to be implausible.

Kaplan's idea is that competence with an indexical involves knowing the rule that specifies the features of the context that determine the referent of the indexical, and that this rule, in turn, captures the speaker's cognitive perspective on the referent. Competence with indexicals, though, seems more a matter of getting the hang of them, of *knowing how* to use them, than it does of intellectually grasping some rule that determines reference. Semantic theorists, not to speak of ordinary mortals, seem to have quite a time discerning the sorts of contextual features relevant to the determination of references of demonstratives like 'that'. Imagine confronting an ordinary, competent speaker with an array of candidate rules, for example, that the reference of a demonstrative is determined by a certain sort of causal chain, or rather by the referential intentions of the speaker, or rather by the cues available to the competent and attentive auditor. Such a speaker, I submit, would not know where to begin. It is implausible, then, to suppose, as Kaplan does, that the semantic rules that govern our practices with indexicals are intellectually available to the competent speaker, and capture the speaker's cognitive perspective on the referent.[20]

One might find oneself sympathetic to the radical's reading of the original Donnellan-Kripke counterexamples, and to the considerations briefly mentioned that militate against Kaplan's approach to indexicals, but feel that more needs to be said. The feeling may well linger that some deep incoherence attaches to the idea of epistemically unmediated reference. How indeed, to paraphrase Russell, can one speak of something without knowing what it is of which one speaks? Perhaps, then, the radical, in emphasizing the apparent lesson of the Donnellan-Kripke examples, has merely underscored what seems so perplexing about his view.

Second, even putting to one side the problem of the missing cognitive fix, is there any hope for dealing with the more specific problems of cognitive significance, Frege's famous puzzle, for example, without recourse to something like modes of presentation? I turn now to Frege's puzzle, the discussion of which will afford us another chance to say the more that needs to be said.

Frege's Puzzle

Frege's discussion of cognitive significance, at the beginning of "On Sense and Reference,"[21] calls attention to cognitive data of undeniable importance, to what I'll call "Frege's data." I will discuss Frege's data in the context of ordinary subject-predicate sentences, rather than, as Frege himself does, in the context of identity sentences, so as to avoid any special problems having to do with identity.[22] Consider, then, 'Hesperus appears in the morning' and 'Phosphorus appears in the morning'. Or, for an example that involves indexicals, 'I am on fire' and 'He is on fire' (where unbeknownst to me, he and I are one). Here are Frege's data:

(1) One can understand both sentences but assent to only one.
(2) One might find one of these old hat but the other highly informative.
(3) One's nonverbal behavior may change depending upon which of these one accepts.

Frege moves quickly from these uncontrovertible pieces of data to something much more controversial, to a theoretically infused way of describing the data, albeit one that looks harmless enough. Indeed, it sometimes has not been noticed that there is any movement here at all. Frege maintains that these sentences *express different propositions*, that they *have different thought contents*.

That Frege's description of his own data is far from inevitable is perhaps obvious enough once stated. Propositions, indeed the very category of propositional content, as acceptable as it is nowadays, was much less so just a few years ago. We can, though, reinforce this point—that Frege, in formulating his famous puzzle, imposes theory on the data—by reference to a view that takes propositions seriously but that takes issue with Frege's contention that the respective pairs of sentences express different propositions.

Consider, then, Kaplan's view according to which both 'I am on fire' and 'He is on fire' express the same Russell-Kaplan "singular proposition," a proposition that contains me (in the flesh) as the subject constituent and the property of being on fire as the predicate constituent. Kaplan, having posited a single proposition as the "content" of the two sentences, needs, of course, to address the obvious cognitive difference between the sentences. He needs to address, that is, Frege's data, (1), (2), and (3) above, and indeed he proceeds to do so. We may like his subsequent explanation of Frege's data, or we may not.[23] What is clear, however, is that the cognitive data do not force us to conclude that the propositional contents are, as Frege supposed, distinct.

The distinction I am drawing between the uncontroversial cognitive data to be explained and the data-as-described-in-terms-of-Fregean-categories seems to me important. If this distinction is not observed, it will not indeed appear that the "cognitive data" refute the anti-Fregean approach. To observe the distinction is not yet to exonerate the anti-Fregean from the charge of cognitive insensitivity. What the anti-Fregean needs, though, is an explanation of Frege's data, and not an explanation of how the respective propositional contents can differ. The challenge, then, is this. 'Hesperus' and 'Phosphorus', for example, are equivalent along the dimension of reference but may be strikingly inequivalent for a speaker along the cognitive dimension. How, given a Millian view of names, are we to account for this difference in cognitive role?[24]

The Conservative Approach to Differences in Cognitive Role

The conservative, we have seen, is not prepared to reject outright the traditional idea that reference depends upon what is in the head. The power of this Fregean intuition, however, pales before that of a related, perhaps even deeper Fregean impulse, the idea that the *cognitive significance* of an expression is a matter of how the referent is presented to the mind.

Imagine that we could induce the conservative to reconsider his attempt to recover something intellectually available to the speaker that determines the reference (or does so in a context, etc.). We might attempt to move him by appealing, as I did above, to the Donnellan-Kripke counterexamples and to the idea, suggested by these examples, that the correct interpretation of speech is, in the final analysis, in the public domain, a matter of the conventions of the linguistic community, and not, so to speak, in the jurisdiction of the individual speaker, not a matter of what is in his head.

Such an appeal, even if successful, would leave intact the more powerful Fregean impulse mentioned above—that cognitive significance is surely a matter of how the referent is presented to the mind. Even if reference is not a matter of what is in the head, how could the *cognitive significance* of an expression not be a matter of the individual's conceptual associations? Surely Frege was right about this much at least, or so thinks the conservative: 'Hesperus is Phosphorus' can be informative to a speaker only if he is thinking of the referent in different ways, one of which is associated for him with 'Hesperus' and one with 'Phosphorus'. Perhaps we can depart from the traditional account in more radical ways than we have envisaged, the conservative might (or might not) allow. Surely, though, we should not depart from what goes deepest in the tradition.

The challenge for the conservative, and it is not a trivial one, is to provide a non-Fregean account of these "ways of thinking," these modes of presentation. The conservative, despite his rejection of Fregean senses, still enjoys considerable latitude here, for his idea that cognitive differences are to be cashed out in terms of mode-of-presentational, or representational, differences does not commit him to any particular story about the relevant representational differences. One might look, for example, to the linguistic meanings of the relevant terms for the representational differences, as did Kaplan for the case of indexicals. This, however, seems implausible for the general case, since, as Kaplan noted, proper names lack descriptive meaning. Indeed, Kaplan's approach seems implausible even for indexicals when one considers examples like informative utterances of 'That is the same thing as that', where one cannot appeal to differences in the linguistic meanings of the indexicals.[25]

One might try a different conservative tack and, focusing upon proper names, look to descriptions that merely fix the reference for an account of the relevant cognitive perspectives. Or, disabused of the notion that descriptions have even this much semantic relevance, one might simply give up the idea that anything of semantic import will be of help in explicating the relevant cognitive perspectives. The idea now would be to still insist that if two names differ cognitively, the speaker must be thinking of the thing(s) in different ways. These different "ways of thinking" will no longer be tied to how the names achieve reference. One might think, that is, that the key to cognitive significance is indeed associated properties—without thinking that these properties have anything to do with the determination of reference.

The Conservative's Problem

A central theme of the anti-Fregean literature is underscored in the following passage from Kripke's "A Puzzle About Belief," a passage in which Kripke presents what he refers to as "the clearest objection [to the Frege-Russell description theory]."

Individuals who "define 'Cicero'" by such phrases as "the Cataline denouncer," "the author of *De Fato*," etc., are relatively rare. . . . Common men who clearly use 'Cicero' as a name for Cicero may be able to give no better answer to "Who was Cicero?" than "a famous Roman orator," and they probably would say the same (if anything) for 'Tully'. . . . Similarly, many people who have heard of both Feynman and Gell-Mann would identify each as "a leading contemporary theoretical physicist." Such people do not assign "senses" of the usual type [that uniquely identify the referent] to the names . . . (even though they use the names with a determinate reference). But to the extent that the *indefinite* descriptions attached or associated can be called "senses," the "senses" assigned to 'Cicero' and 'Tully', or to 'Feynman' and 'Gell-Mann', are *identical*.[26]

Kripke's remarks here resonate with Hilary Putnam's early admission that although he was certainly competent with 'elm' and 'beech'—he, like the rest of us, was in a position to use these terms to refer to the respective kinds of trees—he was entirely ignorant about what distinguishes elms from beeches.

This common anti-Fregean theme, that two terms can share their (often meager) associated information without being coreferential, is by now not only common but a virtual commonplace. What is less appreciated is that this commonplace presents a dramatic obstacle to the conservative strategy. Examples like Putnam's elm-beech example and Kripke's Gell-Mann–Feynman example indicate not only that *reference* is not a matter of what is in the head. They indicate just as clearly that (to take only a bit of dramatic license) *cognitive significance is not a matter of what is in the head*. The names 'Gell-Mann' and 'Feynman', after all, are far from cognitively on a par, despite the lack of any difference in associated properties. Indeed, Kripke's just quoted remarks continue thus:

Yet clearly speakers of this type [who associate the same indefinite information with both names] can ask, "Were Cicero and Tully one Roman orator, or two different ones?" or "Are Feynman and Gell-Mann two different physicists, or one?" without knowing the answer by inspecting senses alone. Some such speaker might even conjecture, or be under the vague false impression, that, as he would say, "Cicero was bald but Tully was not."

The conservative, wishing as he does to explain cognitive differences in terms of differences in associated properties, thus again seems to miss the point of the striking anti-Fregean examples. Nevertheless, it is not difficult to see what is driving the conservative, for the Fregean intuition that cognitive differences somehow *must* reflect representational differences runs very deep. If someone associates exactly the same properties with 'Cicero' as with 'Tully', then, wonders the conservative, how is it that he does not automatically take them to be a single person? Similarly, if one associates the same properties with 'elm' as with 'beech', then how can it be that one does not take them to be a single kind?

Dissolution of the Puzzle

To say that reference requires a substantive cognitive fix—a thesis common to traditionalists and conservatives—is to say, in effect, that reference requires a kind of mental apprehension of the referent. Think impressionistically for a moment of reference as involving a kind of intellectual gazing at the things of which we speak or think. This perspective immediately generates a puzzle from what I have been calling "Frege's data": how, a cognitive fix advocate will have to ask himself, can one be using two co-referring names—that is, be gazing at the same thing twice—without knowing that the same thing is in question?

One can, given such a mental apprehension conception, proceed in several directions. Russell's view was that if one is indeed gazing at the same thing (and it is genuine, unmediated gazing, i.e. direct acquaintance), then one cannot wonder about whether there are two things. One would know that there is only one thing in question. If two terms, for example 'this' and 'that', are really functioning as logically proper names of the same thing, then 'This = that' cannot be informative. Conversely, if one can wonder whether, as it were, this *is* that, then one cannot really be engaged in unmediated gazing, and the terms must be functioning, not as logically proper names, but as disguised descriptions.

Alternatively, Frege maintained that the relevant intellectual gazing is always mediated by the apprehension of a sense that uniquely individuates the referent. If the senses associated with the co-referring 'a' and 'b' are different, then one may be gazing at the same thing (under different aspects, we might say) and still not know that the referent is one and the same.

Notice the driving role of the mental apprehension picture in generating the sense of perplexity. Frege's data themselves—the idea that two names can, unbeknownst to the competent speaker, co-refer—do not seem all that dramatic. Is it, after all, so obvious that we should know of any two co-referring names that they co-refer? But put Frege's data together with the mental apprehension picture and sparks fly. What may prevent appreciation of this point is the feeling that some sort of mental apprehension conception is inevitable, that its radical denial is incoherent. I will try, then, to further loosen the hold of the mental apprehension picture. Whether or not I succeed, what I am really after is the sense that the mental apprehension conception is what impels the puzzle. Were we to radically deny the former and adopt an epistemically innocent way of thinking about reference, as I have suggested that we should, Frege's data would present no special problem.

The alleged difficulty with the radical's epistemically innocent conception of reference is that it makes reference entirely mysterious. What, or so the Fregean wants to ask, other than the mind's grip on a referent, could possibly secure reference? Where the Fregean sees a mystery, however, I see a fundamental and unproblematic feature of our name-using practices, indeed a feature that has enormous social utility.[27]

Imagine our plight if we could only make those things subjects of discourse about which we had individuating knowledge (or even individuating belief). If that were the case, if our practices were so restrictive, then people like me could not refer to people like Herod by name. Given how little I believe about Herod, I would not be able to ask, for example, who Herod was. Nor could I speculate that he lived in the first century. (To paraphrase Kripke, the idea that names like 'Cicero' must mean, for the competent speaker, something like "the Cataline denouncer," is a tribute to the excessive classical learning of some philosophers.) I can do these things now—refer to Herod by name, for example—just because our practices with names do not require anything like what the traditional picture presumes.

Names are thus not to be thought of as externalizations of inner gazings, mediated or not, but as social instruments, as tags that allow us to make into subjects of discourse those things with which the tags are conventionally associated. And it is crucial to the utility of these linguistic devices that they function even in the face of a referent's epistemic remoteness. Far from there being an epistemic requirement of any sort traditionally supposed, names allow speakers to bridge great cognitive gulfs. The mere possession of a name for an item, that is, *provides* a crucial kind of contact with it. One can now, as noted, ask questions, make assertions, and so on that are *about* that very item. Names, from an epistemic point of view, ask very little of us, but generously provide for our needs.

So much for my attempt to loosen the hold of the traditional picture, to encourage a kind of gestalt switch in our thinking. I argued above that Frege's puzzle, so called, is generated, not by Frege's data alone, but only in conjunction with the mental apprehension conception of reference. Is it so obvious, I asked, that there is something deeply puzzling about the very idea that a speaker can be competent with two co-referring names and not know that they co-refer? The radical change in perspective I have been encouraging makes the dissolution of the puzzle even more dramatic. If one can refer to something without anything like a substantive cognitive fix on the referent, if the use of a name can be virtually blind epistemically, then why should it be the slightest bit surprising that a speaker might be competent with two co-referring names but have no inkling that they co-refer?

A student who associates with 'Cicero' only that he was "a Roman orator," or "a famous Roman," subsequently hears about "Tully," another "famous Roman." He now stands in possession of two social instruments for making things subjects of discourse. *We* know that there is only one thing in question, but how in the world should he know this? Suppose he assumes that there are two people in question. Or suppose that he begins to wonder whether "Cicero is Tully." Why should anyone suppose that his wonder presents some special puzzle? Does the intelligibility of his wonder really require his associating *different* properties with the names? Why should it? Why can't he be thinking of both Cicero and Tully as "a Roman orator"?

To one in the grip of the mental apprehension picture, it will seem that the obvious and only way to explain what I have been calling "Frege's data," that co-referring names can be cognitively inequivalent, is in terms of a difference in cognitive perspectives, a difference in associated properties. Rejecting that picture, we can now see that there is no presumption whatever that co-reference should somehow be apparent to the competent name user, or that the possibility of its not being apparent is crucially dependent upon there being two different ways the referent is presented to the mind. That cognitive differences presuppose representational differences is a dogma, a product of the very conception that anti-Fregeans, at their best moments, have been at pains to reject.

Indeed, if there is any presumption to speak of here, it is in quite the opposite direction, that co-reference, except under unusual circumstances, will not be apparent. In general, then, "$a = b$" identities that are truths will nevertheless not be trivial, and this is no surprise. What is more surprising perhaps—and here we turn the tables on Frege—is that "$a = a$" identities are not, in general, trivial. One can, of course, simply repeat a name, intending to refer to the same person, thus—barring seriously mind-bending circumstances—guaranteeing that the same reference is in question. I can, for example, provide my class with an example of a triviality: "Susan [I point to a student] is, of course, Susan." But the mere presence of the same name, indeed the same name of the same party, surely does not make the identity trivial. One can pick up Susan's name on two occasions and not know that the same Susan is in question.

Nor does the same name, along with the same identifying information, guarantee that the same individual is in question. Imagine yourself hearing about "a famous Roman orator" named "Cicero" in circumstances that lead you to believe that "another Cicero" is in question, that is, a Cicero other than the one about whom we have all heard. You later forget just where you learned about this "other Cicero" and just what it was that induced the belief that another Cicero was in question. It may well be that you have no discriminating information about the "two Ciceros," yet you do not therefore assume that a single person was in question.

My conclusion, then, is that anti-Fregeans need not feel embarrassed by allusions to Frege's puzzle or the problem of the missing cognitive fix. We need neither to supply some missing epistemological link to bridge the cognitive gulf between speakers and the references of names that they use nor to supply intellectual apparatus out of which to fashion a solution to Frege's puzzle.

To say this is not to argue that the anti-Fregean has the upper hand in the larger debate. This depends upon much larger questions—methodological as well as substantive, questions in the philosophy of mind as well as in the philosophy of language—only some of which have I touched upon here and then all too briefly. It is not insignificant, though, that what was supposed to be *the* point of severe pressure for the anti-Fregean, his inability to face squarely the questions that Frege and Russell took to be central, turns out to be amenable to natural treatment.[28]

Notes

Notes

Introduction

1. My reading of Frege makes him an arch-representationalist and emphasizes the distance between his picture of language and thought and that of someone like the later Wittgenstein. This is, of course, controversial and perhaps depends upon which of the Fregean texts one emphasizes. In any case many philosophers have expressed agreement with the philosophical views of "my" Frege, and we can thus speak of the "Fregean tradition," even if, contrary to my view, Frege never did maintain this sort of outlook. David Kaplan remarks that when he presented a similar reading of Frege at Oxford, the response was that first, Frege never held any such thing, and second, if he had, he would have been correct.

2. It is a tribute to Saul Kripke's powerful intuitive case for the relevant modal distinctions that many feel ready to conclude on modal grounds that Frege must be wrong. Not that Kripke makes his criticisms of Frege and Russell only on modal grounds. In lecture 2 of *Naming and Necessity* (Cambridge, Mass., 1980), he offers a variety of other grounds.

3. I make mention of the Donnellan-Kripke historical-chain view of proper names not to endorse it—I am increasingly skeptical of its adequacy even as a picture of what is going on—but rather to emphasize the affinity between some central anti-Fregean ideas and a social practice conception of significance. (I discuss my ideas about how best to work out Mill's pure denotation conception of proper names in "Supplanting Linguistic Cartesianism," ch. 4, of my [as yet untitled] forthcoming book.)

4. Examples readily come to mind of philosophical proposals that seem not at all like natural responses to good questions, but rather like relatively unmotivated (except by a desire to save the theory), forced

responses to the most recent counterexamples. Some of the post-Gettier epistemological literature, and some of the recent literature on the semantics of belief reports, come especially to mind. The very appearance of such unnaturalness should give us pause, and cause us to take another look at fundamentals. Such is Wittgenstein's advice, if I have him right.

5. I wish to thank Joseph Almog, John Fischer, and Alex Rosenberg for helpful comments on this introduction.

Essay 1

1. This is taken for granted by, for example, P. F. Strawson in his *Introduction to Logical Theory* (London, 1952); see ch. 1, esp. pp. 3-4. Another who proceeds along these lines is Richard Cartwright; see his "Propositions," in *Analytical Philosophy* (1st series), ed. R. Butler (Oxford, 1962), pp. 82-103, esp. p. 103. Also see James J. Thomson, "Truth-Bearers and the Trouble About Propositions," *The Journal of Philosophy* 66: 737-47.

2. Those who find propositions objectionable simply because they are *abstract* entities will find sentences, that is, sentence types, objectionable as well. A natural move on behalf of such philosophers would be to claim that what a person asserts is a sentence token.

3. My argument will concern itself with sentence types, but it is applicable to tokens as well.

4. At least non-eternal sentences may be used to assert different things. For the distinction between eternal and non-eternal sentences see W. V. O. Quine, *Word and Object* (Cambridge, Mass., 1960), sec. 40.

5. In "Propositions," Cartwright attempts to supplement these arguments in order to show that what is asserted is in no case a sentence. As I will argue, there are difficulties with Cartwright's approach.

6. The argument about to be presented is an application of a line of reasoning used by Paul Benacerraf in "What Numbers Could Not Be," *The Philosophical Review* 74 (1965): 47-73.

7. The verb is to be understood "tenselessly."

8. I assume that the feature of completeness of formulation would be included in any proposed set of discriminating features. Hence the sentences from which we try to select one sentence (per thing asserted) would always be eternal sentences.

9. "Complete sentence" is Cartwright's term for eternal sentence. When in the passage quoted, Cartwright speaks of "these complete sentences," he means those eternal sentences which can be used to make the statement in question.

10. Cartwright, "Propositions," p. 99.

11. By such expressions as "eternal sentence counterpart," "corresponding eternal sentence," and "eternal sentence expression," I mean the result of replacing any indexical elements in the original sentence by using tenseless verbs, indicating time explicitly, and so forth so as to render the resulting sentence an eternal one. Of course, the same non-

eternal sentence will often have different "eternal sentence counterparts" for different contexts of utterance.

12. The view that I have claimed to be plausible has its difficulties, and these are not confined to the implication that sentences are what we assert. One fatal difficulty is the following. It is clear that a number of speakers may assert the same thing while uttering different non-eternal sentences, each of which when "eternalized" necessarily yields a different eternal sentence (e.g. one speaker may be speaking English and one French). But it *could not be that both assert the eternal sentence expansions* of what they utter, for what they assert is, *ex hypothesi*, identical, while their respective eternal sentence expansions are different.

Despite the fact that the view presented here cannot, in the end, be successfully defended, I have presented it because whatever difficulties there are with it, they have nothing whatever to do with Cartwright's absurdity claim. If Cartwright were correct in his absurdity claim, then such a view should have seemed obviously wrong and wrong for Cartwright's reasons.

13. Cartwright, "Propositions," p. 99.
14. Ibid., p. 100.
15. Benacerraf, "What Numbers Could Not Be," p. 56.
16. Benacerraf's position here seems to me to be intuitively obvious. However, I do not have an argument to show that it is correct. It is not clear to me that Benacerraf has an *argument* either. See ibid., pp. 57–58.
17. Cartwright, "Propositions," p. 100.
18. Benacerraf, "What Numbers Could Not Be," p. 68.
19. Cartwright, "Propositions," p. 100.
20. This claim is absurd, for it would imply that, say, the number 3 is identical to many nonidentical sets.
21. Indeed, in the interest of clarity we might do better to restrict our talk of *identifying x* with *y* to contexts in which *x* and *y* are *identical*. Accordingly, in formulating the second of these claims we would not speak of *identification* at all. However, in light of the fact that such terminology has become fairly standard (see, for example, Benacerraf, "What Numbers Could Not Be," pp. 67–68, and Quine, *Word and Object*, secs. 53 and 54), no harm is done if we adhere to such usage.
22. When I say that various explications might be expected, I do not mean to imply that in the case of an open concept, *philosophical analysis* necessarily consists in 'explication' (in the sense in which I have been using that term). For example, Benacerraf, who takes the concept of natural numbers to be open, goes on, not to offer an explication, i.e. to identify the numbers with some particular set, but rather to advance a sophisticated kind of formalism.
23. An earlier version of this paper was presented at the meetings of the American Philosophical Association, Eastern Division, in December 1975. I am indebted to a number of people for comments on earlier drafts. Special thanks are owed to Peter A. French, Dean Kolitch, Charles Landesman, Jr., Richard Mendelsohn, and the editors of *The Philosophical Review*.

Essay 2

1. Cf. Keith S. Donnellan, "Proper Names and Identifying Descriptions," in *Semantics of Natural Language*, 2d ed., ed. D. Davidson and G. Harman (Dordrecht, 1972), pp. 356–79, esp. p. 358. In the foregoing paragraph, I have relied on Donnellan's formulation of these matters.

2. Ruth Barcan Marcus, "Dispensing with Possibilia," in *Proceedings and Addresses of the American Philosophical Association, 1975–76*, vol. 49 (Newark, Del., 1976), p. 45.

3. Gottlob Frege, "The Thought: A Logical Inquiry," in *Essays on Frege*, ed. E. D. Klemke (Urbana, 1968), p. 516.

4. Only assertive utterances will be considered here.

5. Frege, "The Thought," p. 533; italics added. Along similar lines, Morris R. Cohen and Ernest Nagel state: "*The present governor of Connecticut is Dr. Cross* seems to be a proposition true for certain years, but surely not always. This, however, is an inadequate analysis. For the phrase 'the present governor' clearly presupposes a date; and as we complete our expression including explicitly the date, we obtain expressions for different propositions, some of which are true and some false" (*An Introduction to Logic and Scientific Method* [New York, 1934], p. 30).

6. W. V. O. Quine, *Word and Object* (Cambridge, Mass., 1960), pp. 193–94.

7. For an argument to this effect, see my doctoral dissertation, "What Propositions Could Not Be" (The City University of New York, 1976), ch. 6.

8. Jerrold J. Katz, *Semantic Theory* (New York, 1972), p. 126.

9. Ibid., p. 127.

10. This argument is an application of a line of reasoning used by Paul Benacerraf in "What Numbers Could Not Be," *The Philosophical Review* 74 (1965): 47–73. I make use of the argument in "Can What Is Asserted Be a Sentence?" (in this volume) in an attempt to show that propositions cannot be identified with sentences.

11. Here I am indebted to Herbert Heidelberger and J. L. Mackie, both of whom pointed out the inadequacy of an earlier formulation.

12. W. V. O. Quine, *The Ways of Paradox and Other Essays* (New York, 1966), p. 222.

13. Bertrand Russell, *An Inquiry into Meaning and Truth* (Baltimore, 1962), pp. 108–9.

14. Thus a view of this kind assimilates such uses of indexicals to "pronouns of laziness" in such sentences as "If the next Governor of New York were a Democrat, then he would be influential in the labor dispute." In sentences like the latter, the context, in this case the linguistic context, does take up the slack, that is, 'he' in the consequent does stand in for the phrase 'the Governor of New York'.

15. Frege, "The Thought," p. 516.

16. John Stuart Mill, "A System of Logic," abridged in John Stuart Mill, *Philosophy of Scientific Method*, ed. E. Nagel (New York, 1950), p. 26.

17. Ibid., p. 27; italics added.
18. Ibid., p. 71.
19. Ibid., italics added.
20. 'She' would not be an *appropriate* device for referring to a male. Whether full-blooded (semantic) reference is *possible* by the use of a conventionally inapplicable expression—for example, if the speaker mistakenly believes that the referent is a woman—is another and indeed controversial question. Donnellan has argued that such reference is possible. He maintains this in the case of definite descriptions in Keith S. Donnellan, "Reference and Definite Descriptions," *The Philosophical Review* 75 (1966): 281–304, and in the case of proper names in "Proper Names and Identifying Descriptions." For objections to Donnellan's position see David Wiggins, "Identity, Designation, Essentialism, and Physicalism," *Philosophia* 5 (1975): 28 n. 9; Michael Lockwood, "On Predicating Proper Names," *The Philosophical Review* 84 (1975): 485–86 n. 1; and especially Saul Kripke, "Speaker's Reference and Semantic Reference," *Midwest Studies in Philosophy* 2 (1977): 255–76.

Essay 3

1. Hector-Neri Casteñeda, "On the Philosophical Foundations of the Theory of Communication: Reference," in *Contemporary Perspectives in the Philosophy of Language*, ed. P. French, T. Uehling, and H. Wettstein (Minneapolis, 1979), pp. 125–46.
2. Ibid., pp. 171–72.
3. This is so, on Castañeda's view, only for some descriptions, those which are, in his language, "fully propositionally transparent." The point is that, for Castañeda, some descriptions fail to fully reveal the "identifying traits" of the referent which are "before the consciousness of the speaker." Such a description would not be fully propositionally transparent. An example, as we will see, would be a description which contains a proper name (which is being used as a genuine name).
4. "The denotation, I believe, is not a constituent of the proposition, except in the case of [logically] proper names, i.e., of words which do not assign a property to an object, but merely and solely name it" (Bertrand Russell, "Knowledge by Acquaintance and Knowledge by Description," in Bertrand Russell, *Mysticism and Logic* (Garden City, N.Y., n.d.), p. 216.
5. Castañeda, "On the Philosophical Foundations," p. 172.
6. Ibid.
7. Ibid.
8. Strictly speaking, this is only a necessary condition for successful communication, for it only specifies what successful communication is with regard to the subject constituent of the proposition. For simplicity, I assume that the sentence in question fully reveals the predicate constituent.

9. It should be noted that Castañeda sees the significance of Kripke's "causal theory" quite differently than I do. See footnote 5 of his paper.

10. More precisely, a definite description which contains no "propositionally opaque contexts," for example, no proper names used as genuine names. Otherwise, the description would again fail to fully reveal the propositional constituent.

11. We assume here that each of these characterizations is propositionally transparent, that is, that each fully reveals a set of uniquely identifying traits of the referent. Although I am not certain that the examples I gave above would, for Castañeda, qualify, those examples suffice to give an idea of the range of different characterizations of the referent that the speaker may possess.

Essay 4

1. Cf. Ruth Barcan Marcus's comment in "Dispensing with Possibilia," that proper names are "the long finger of ostension" (*Proceedings and Addresses of the American Philosophical Association, 1975–76*, vol. 49 [Newark, Del., 1976], p. 45).

2. See Keith S. Donnellan, "Reference and Definite Descriptions," in *Readings in the Philosophy of Language*, ed. Jay F. Rosenberg and Charles Travis (Englewood Cliffs, N.J., 1971), pp. 195–211.

3. Ibid., p. 198; italics added.

4. It is not essential that the speaker not know or have a belief about who the murderer is. For even if he believes that Jones is the murderer, his use of the description will still be attributive just in case that belief is irrelevant to the speech act, that is, just in case what he communicates is that the murderer, whoever that is, is insane.

5. Donnellan, "Reference and Definite Descriptions," p. 198.

6. P. F. Strawson, in "On Referring" (*Mind* 59, n.s., [1950]: 320–44), did not recognize an attributive use of descriptions (which occur in the subject position). A plausible application of Strawson's view to attributive cases, however, would be that in such cases the speaker presupposes that *something or other* is Smith's murderer (as opposed to presupposing of some particular thing that *it* is Smith's murderer) and that the statement has no truth-value if this presupposition is unfulfilled. It should be noted that Donnellan takes no position on whether to prefer a Russell-type approach or a Strawson-type approach in cases of attributive use.

7. Donnellan, "Reference and Definite Descriptions," p. 199.

8. Ibid., p. 207; italics added.

9. David Wiggins, "Identity, Designation, Essentialism, and Physicalism," *Philosophia* 5 (1975): 1–30.

10. Very roughly, the semantic referent is the item to which the term conventionally applies. See Saul Kripke, "Speaker's Reference and Semantic Reference," in *Contemporary Perspectives in the Philosophy of Language*, ed. P. French, T. Uehling, and H. Wettstein (Minneapolis, 1979),

pp. 6–27, for a detailed account of this and related notions and for Kripke's approach to the question of reference via a conventionally inapplicable expression.

11. Michael Lockwood, "On Predicating Proper Names," *The Philosophical Review* 84 (1975): 485 n. 21.

12. This point was brought to my attention by Lockwood in his "On Predicating Proper Names."

13. Donnellan makes the analogous claim for proper names in Keith S. Donnellan, "Proper Names and Identifying Descriptions," in *Semantics of Natural Language*, 2d ed., ed. D. Davidson and G. Harman (Dordrecht, 1972), pp. 356–79.

14. Castañeda, "On the Philosophical Foundations," p. 146 n. 7.

15. While the view that there are two such uses is intuitively plausible, it appears to crucially involve the notoriously difficult notion of *having a particular item in mind*. It may be, then, that a complete account of the distinction awaits an analysis of this notion, an analysis which has not yet been successfully provided. On the other hand, if the assimilation of "referential use" to "demonstration" which I attempt in the present paper is correct, the notion of referential use may be no worse off in this regard than is the notion of demonstration. (The assimilation of referential use to demonstration was suggested in David Kaplan, "Dthat," *Syntax and Semantics*, vol. 9, ed. Peter Cole [New York, 1977]. Although the present paper was virtually completed before "Dthat," then unpublished, came into my hands, I am indebted to Kaplan for some of the present formulations.)

16. In this sense the distinction has semantic significance, but as Donnellan notes, this is not to say that descriptions are semantically ambiguous as between referential and attributive *senses*. Rather, a univocal description can be utilized in accordance with two radically different kinds of intentions. The distinction has semantic significance, since a referential utterance of the (univocal) description will make a different contribution to the truth conditions (of the utterance of the sentence as a whole) than will an attributive utterance of the description. (Cf. Donnellan's remark that we might say that sentences containing descriptions are pragmatically ambiguous ["Reference and Definite Descriptions," p. 207].)

17. Saul Kripke, "Naming and Necessity," in *Semantics of Natural Language*, 2d ed., ed. D. Davidson and G. Harman (Dordrecht, 1972), p. 343 n. 3.

18. In "Speaker's Reference and Semantic Reference," Kripke expands on these earlier remarks. He maintains that the arguments Donnellan advances in "Reference and Definite Descriptions" fail to support his claims concerning the referential-attributive distinction. Kripke's attack is, however, directed upon that aspect of Donnellan's view which I do not share, that is, Donnellan's view concerning reference via a conventionally inapplicable expression. Kripke, moreover, states that there are phenomena which may be suggestive of a (seman-

tically significant) referential-attributive distinction. The phenomena he mentions are those which I investigate below, phenomena concerning "indefinite definite descriptions." (This is not, of course, to suggest that Kripke would agree with my findings.)

19. H. P. Grice, "Vacuous Names," in *Words and Objections*, ed. D. Davidson and G. Harman (Dordrecht, 1969), pp. 141–42.

20. See Keith S. Donnellan, "Putting Humpty Dumpty Together Again," *The Philosophical Review* 77 (1968): 204 n. 5.

21. Donnellan utilizes this sort of argument in Keith S. Donnellan, "Speaker Reference, Descriptions, and Anaphora," in *Syntax and Semantics*, vol. 9, ed. Peter Cole (New York, 1977), but the use he makes of it is, in my view, problematic. An account of Donnellan's argument there and my criticism of it are beyond the scope of this paper.

22. See Strawson, "On Referring," esp. pp. 14–15.

23. Gottlob Frege, "The Thought: A Logical Inquiry," in *Essays on Frege*, ed. E. D. Klemke (Urbana, 1968), p. 516.

24. My argument here, as well as in "Can What Is Asserted Be a Sentence?" and "Indexical References and Propositional Content" (both in this volume), has similarities to a line of reasoning used, for entirely different purposes, by Paul Benacerraf in "What Numbers Could Not Be," *The Philosophical Review* 74 (1965): 47–73.

25. See my "Indexical Reference and Propositional Content" for a more detailed discussion of indexical reference.

26. David Kaplan, "How to Russell a Frege-Church," *The Journal of Philosophy* 72 (1975): 716–29, and his "Dthat."

27. I speak here of the referential use of both indefinite definite descriptions and uniquely denoting descriptions. My view is that the demonstrative use of descriptions is not a phenomenon localized to indefinite definite descriptions. I defend this view in the next section of this paper, How General Is the Distinction?

28. See the concluding paragraph of Donnellan, "Reference and Definite Descriptions." As noted above, Donnellan does not commit himself to Russell's theory as an account of attributively used descriptions. He does, however, think it not implausible.

29. Frege's approach, as we saw, met with difficulty in cases of referential use of indefinite definite descriptions. That approach might appear better suited to cases of attributive use, as might Russell's theory of descriptions. The difficulty about to be introduced militates against Frege's approach as well as against Russell's.

30. In "Putting Humpty Dumpty Together Again," p. 204 n. 5, Donnellan states that when a description is used *attributively*, it is plausible to maintain that we can look to the circumstances of utterance to "supply further qualifications on the description to make it unique. . . . Someone says, 'The next President will be a dove on Viet Nam,' and the context easily supplies the implicit 'of the United States'." Contrary to Donnellan, such a defense of Russell is seldom, if ever, plausible. Even with regard to the case mentioned by Donnellan, it is not clear

that "the context easily supplies the implicit 'of the United States'," as opposed to, say, 'of our country'.

31. It might seem that since the description in question does not uniquely denote, there is no semantic referent. Surely the phrase 'the murderer', considered in isolation, has no semantic referent. Nevertheless, we can speak here of a semantic referent: it is (roughly) the item that fits this description *as used on this occasion*. To anticipate, since in the context in question the force of 'the murderer' is (something like) "The murderer of that one," the semantic referent is that individual (if there is one) who in fact murdered that person. (Cf. Kripke's mention of the "semantic reference *on a given occasion*" of ambiguous expressions, indexicals, etc., in "Speaker's Reference and Semantic Reference," p. 14.)

32. Moreover, Donnellan would not agree to my assimilation of referential use to demonstration, as is shown by some of his examples in "Speaker Reference, Descriptions, and Anaphora" (see esp. pp. 60–61). These examples indicate that the notion of "having a particular item in mind" bears much greater weight in Donnellan's treatment than it does here. (See also note 31 above.)

33. I am indebted to a number of people for comments on earlier versions. Special thanks are owed to Panayot Butchvarov, Peter A. French, R. A. Fumerton, Herbert Heidelberger, Dean Kolitch, Charles Landesman, Jr., Ernest LePore, and Richard Mendelsohn. My debt to the writings of Keith S. Donnellan should be evident. The support of both the American Council of Learned Societies and the Graduate School of the University of Minnesota is gratefully acknowledged.

Essay 5

1. Keith S. Donnellan, "Reference and Definite Descriptions," *The Philosophical Review* 75 (1966): 281–304.

2. Indeed, although in that essay I am agnostic about Donnellan's view that, in Kripke's terms, the semantic referent of a description can be an item to which the description does not even apply, it now seems to me likely that Donnellan's claim is mistaken. Were Donnellan correct, the same should hold of other singular terms, for example, proper names, demonstratives, and personal pronouns. Indeed, Donnellan extends his view that reference can go through, even when the term fails to conventionally apply, to proper names (in Keith S. Donnellan, "Proper Names and Identifying Descriptions," in *Semantics of Natural Language*, 2d ed., ed. D. Davidson and G. Harman [Dordrecht, 1972], pp. 356–79), as well as to the other categories mentioned (in conversation). I argue in "How to Bridge the Gap Between Meaning and Reference" (in this volume), however, that his view is incorrect with regard to demonstratives and pronouns. See Saul Kripke, "Speaker's Reference and Semantic Reference," in *Contemporary Perspectives in the Philosophy of Language*, ed. P. French, T. Uehling, and H. Wettstein (Minneapolis,

1979), pp. 6–27, for other criticisms. The point that one can have a referential-attributive distinction without Donnellan's controversial claim was, to my knowledge, first made by Michael Lockwood in "On Predicating Proper Names," *The Philosophical Review* 84 (1975): 471–98.

3. Nathan U. Salmon, "Assertion and Incomplete Definite Descriptions," *Philosophical Studies* 42 (1982): 37–45.

4. Thus the accounts of Russell and Frege, although intended to apply to all uses of descriptions, are at least roughly on the right track for the attributive use. See my "Demonstrative Reference and Definite Descriptions" (in this volume), pp. 45–48, for criticisms of the views of Frege and Russell even as accounts of the attributive use.

5. By a referential (attributive) utterance of this sentence, I mean an utterance in which 'the murderer of Smith' is used referentially (attributively).

6. David Kaplan, "Dthat," in *Contemporary Perspectives in the Philosophy of Language*, ed. P. French, T. Uehling, and H. Wettstein (Minneapolis, 1979), pp. 383–400, and his "Demonstratives," in *Themes from Kaplan*, ed. Joseph Almog, John Perry, and Howard Wettstein (New York and Oxford, 1989), pp. 481–563.

7. Gottlob Frege, "The Thought: A Logical Inquiry," in *Essays on Frege*, ed. E. D. Klemke (Urbana, 1968).

8. Frege employs this strategy with respect to indexicals, but if successful for the case of indexicals, there is no reason not to apply it to incomplete definite descriptions as well.

9. For a more complete statement of the argument see my "Demonstrative Reference and Definite Descriptions."

10. 'That' is not a surrogate for a uniquely specifying description for the same reason just given in the text that 'the murderer' was not elliptical for a more complete description, as I argue in "Indexical Reference and Propositional Content" (in this volume).

11. I consider here and throughout only "deictic" occurrences of pronouns.

12. I expand on this "contextual theory of reference" in "How to Bridge the Gap Between Meaning and Reference" and distinguish it from the causal theory of reference as well as from Donnellan's view that reference depends upon the referential intentions of the speaker.

13. Salmon, "Assertion," pp. 42–43.

14. Cf. Salmon's remarks quoted above that since 'the murderer' applies to no one in the possible world in question, then the sentence "The murderer is insane," as used on the actual-world occasion in question, cannot be true.

15. See John Perry, "Frege on Demonstratives," *The Philosophical Review* 86, no. 4 (October 1977): 474–97, and his "The Problem of the Essential Indexical," *Noûs* 13 (1979): 3–21.

16. Indeed, Salmon himself, in, for example, "Frege's Puzzle," supports the "theory of direct reference concerning proper names, demonstratives, and other single word singular terms." See the introduction to Nathan U. Salmon, *Frege's Puzzle* (Cambridge, Mass., 1986).

17. Briefly, Salmon's discussion raises two sorts of questions. First, it is not clear how seriously we are to take the notion of "assertion" in 'speaker assertion'. Several of Salmon's examples appear themselves to ride roughshod over another Gricean distinction, that between what a speaker says or asserts and what he "implicates" (implies, suggests, and so on). See Grice's discussion in H. P. Grice, "Logic and Conversation," in *The Logic of Grammar*, ed. D. Davidson and G. Harman (Encina, Calif., 1975), pp. 64–75. The message one communicates when one uses a sentence ironically or asks a rhetorical question is not, contra Salmon ("Assertion," p. 39), asserted by the speaker, it is not part of "what the speaker said" (as Grice would put it), but is rather implicated, in Grice's sense. Second, Salmon provides, in addition to the irony and rhetorical-question examples, several other examples of his distinction that raise serious questions. One example: Salmon maintains that whenever anyone assertively utters a sentence that formulates a general proposition, for example, "There is one and only one person that murdered Smith and that person is insane," he asserts not only the general proposition formulated by his words but also the corresponding singular proposition, in this case (assuming Jones is the murderer), the proposition that Jones is insane. This seems implausible. If I have never heard of Jones and have no reason to believe that *he* murdered Smith and say, "Whoever murdered Smith was insane," why should we construe my remark as the assertion of the singular proposition that Jones is insane? Even if, as Kaplan suggests in "Demonstratives," one *can* assert this singular proposition without knowing who the murderer is, it does not follow (nor is it even suggested by Kaplan) that one does assert this singular proposition every time one asserts some corresponding general proposition.

18. Salmon, "Assertion," p. 39.

19. Ibid., p. 40.

20. See the beginning of the second section of "Demonstrative Reference and Definite Descriptions," pp. 39–40.

21. Immediately following the passage I have been discussing, Salmon writes, "Wettstein's argument . . . can be reformulated to focus explicitly on semantic content. But when the issue is sharpened in this way, much, if not all, of the intuitive force behind his argument seems to vanish" ("Assertion," p. 40). My point is that my argument was focused on semantic content to begin with. Salmon's reason for his remark that "the intuitive force behind [my] argument seems to vanish" concerns his theses, disputed above, that the objects of evaluation with respect to alternative possible worlds are *sentences as used on particular occasions*.

This paper was written while I was an NEH Fellow (1981–82), and I am grateful to the National Endowment for the Humanities, the Graduate School of the University of Minnesota, and the Office of the Academic Dean of the University of Minnesota, Morris, for support. I am grateful to the Department of Philosophy of Stanford University, and especially to its former chair, John Perry, and to Patrick Suppes, Director of the Institute for the Mathematical Study of the Social Sciences at Stanford, for the hospitality shown me during 1981–82. I am especially indebted to Perry for many hours of extremely fruitful discussions of the sorts of questions I discuss in this paper, and I wish to thank him, Michael Bratman, Ernest LePore, and Julius Moravcsik for helpful comments on earlier drafts.

Essay 6

1. See Terence Parsons, *Nonexistent Objects* (New Haven, Conn., 1980), and his "Are There Nonexistent Objects?" *American Philosophical Quarterly* 19 (1982): 365–71.
2. My example of the historian's utterance is supposed to illustrate Parsons's approach rather than to make the strongest possible case for it. For Parsons's defense of his view see Parsons, *Nonexistent Objects,* pp. 32–38, and Parsons, "Are There Nonexistent Objects?"
3. The dialogues occur in Parsons, *Nonexistent Objects,* p. 113.
4. Ibid.
5. Ibid.
6. Jones's hallucinatory woman, the nonexistent entity to which Himmelfarb refers, should not be identified with Jones's sense data or any other mental contents. Sense data, if such are indeed needed to account for hallucination phenomena, are certainly not nonexistent objects. Dream objects, hallucinatory objects, and the like are, on Parsons's view, nonexistent objects. See note 7 below.
7. I have in mind, first, the general form of argument that many of our ordinary beliefs certainly *seem* to commit us to such things, for example, Himmelfarb's belief that "the woman Jones hallucinated was probably (alas) more beautiful than any woman I have ever seen." See Parsons's argument in *Nonexistent Objects,* p. 32. A second form of argument Parsons employs to establish that there are nonexistent objects is that such an assumption simplifies reports of experience. Parsons applies this argument to dream objects in Parsons, "Are There Nonexistent Objects?" p. 370, and the argument applies, mutatis mutandis, to hallucinatory objects.
8. Parsons, *Nonexistent Objects,* p. 207.
9. See David Kaplan's interesting (but brief) remarks on pretended reference in Kaplan, "Bob and Carol and Ted and Alice," in *Approaches to Natural Languages,* ed. J. Hintikka, J. M. Moravcsik, and P. Suppes (Dordrecht, 1970), appendix 11. Also cf. Kendall Walton's notation of "make-believe truths" in Walton, "Fearing Fictions," *Journal of Philosophy* 75 (1978): 5–27, and Walton's development of the idea in the papers he mentions there. Also see John Searle's discussion in Searle, "The Logical Status of Fictional Discourse," in *Contemporary Perspectives in the Philosophy of Language,* ed. P. French, T. Uehling, and H. Wettstein (Minneapolis, 1979).
10. Pretense here does not entail deception. Notice that the anthropologist (or the contemporary atheist speaking with a believer in some

form of Western religion) might make perfectly clear that he does not accept the beliefs in question and nevertheless refer to the God as "he."

11. I am counting acts of writing sentences as utterances.

12. Parsons argues that the occurrence of 'the Greek gods' in the sentence in question is a referential occurrence, for (1) "*a* worships *b*" is an extensional context, according to Parsons, and (2) even if "*a* worships *b*" were not extensional, the phrase 'the Greek gods' has a *de re* occurrence in the sentence in question. See Parsons, *Nonexistent Objects*, p. 32ff.

13. Ibid., p. 217.

14. Again, since the belief report is *de re* with respect to 'the Greek gods', this phrase has a referential occurrence.

15. Parsons, *Nonexistent Objects*, p. 28. See chapter 1 in his book for the discussion between nuclear and extranuclear properties.

16. An earlier version of this paper was presented at a symposium (the main paper of which was Parsons, "Are There Nonexistent Objects?") at the 1982 meetings of the American Philosophical Association, Pacific Division. The paper benefited from discussions with Alan Code, Julius Moravcsik, Terence Parsons, and John Perry. I am grateful to the National Endowment for the Humanities, the Graduate School of the University of Minnesota, and the Office of the Academic Dean of the University of Minnesota, Morris, for support. I also wish to thank Patrick Suppes, Director of the Institute for the Mathematical Study of the Social Sciences at Stanford University, for the use of the institute's facilities.

Essay 7

1. A Fregean answer, rejected by the new theorists, is that the gap is to be bridged by, so to speak, more meaning. One version of this answer is that the speaker relies on the context of utterance to supplement the meager lexical meaning of the indexical so as to yield a descriptive characterization which uniquely fits the referent. For criticisms see my papers "Indexical Reference and Propositional Content" and "Demonstrative Reference and Definite Descriptions" (in this volume).

2. This answer was implicit in my earlier work on the reference of indexicals, but not fully explicit—even to me. See the two papers mentioned in note 1.

3. It is by no means obvious that the causal theory of reference is the prevailing view among the new theorists. Saul Kripke is sometimes characterized in such terms, but this seems to me at least premature and probably incorrect. New theorists typically do proffer a causal or historical-explanation theory of proper names, but this is quite another matter. Kripke, in *Naming and Necessity* (Cambridge, Mass., 1980), for example, maintains that the use of a name by one who was not present at the dubbing involves the user's obtaining the name via a "causal chain of communication." Kripke maintains that such chains are crucial to the semantic account of, say, my use of 'Aristotle' (or to the semantic

account of 'Aristotle' in my idiolect). This is not to say, however, that such chains are always operative. One who speaks of one's own children does not refer, at least in many everyday cases, by means of such a chain of communication. One might tell some other kind of causal story for such uses of names, but Kripke, for example, does not do so. Adoption of a "causal theory of names" does not commit one to the causal theory of reference. An explicit defender of the causal theory of reference is Michael Devitt in his book *Designation* (New York, 1981).

4. While an intentional theory may be motivated by a dissatisfaction with a causal approach, it can be otherwise motivated. Indeed, the two theories may be held together, as they are by Devitt. A causal theorist can be an intentional theorist just in case he holds a causal theory of intention, that is, the view that to have a certain object in mind is for there to be "a certain sort of causal connection between his state of mind and the object" (Devitt, *Designation*, p. 33). Keith Donnellan, a leading advocate of the intentional theory, at least for reference by proper names, definite descriptions, and (in conversation) demonstratives, is hesitant about the causal theory. For Donnellan's general orientation see Keith S. Donnellan, "Reference and Definite Descriptions," *The Philosophical Review* 75 (1966): 281–304, and his "Proper Names and Identifying Descriptions," in *Semantics of Natural Language*, 2d ed., ed. D. Davidson and G. Harman (Dordrecht, 1972), pp. 356–79. For his hesitation about the causal theory see his "Speaking of Nothing," *The Philosophical Review* 83 (1974): 3–32.

5. Putnam's remarks on the division of linguistic labor for natural-kind terms and Kripke's remarks on proper names both stress the role of social interaction in determining the references of our words. See also Tyler Burge, "Individualism and the Mental," *Midwest Studies in Philosophy* 4 (1979): 73–122. I am grateful to Burge for focusing my attention on the fact that my view further socializes "reference."

6. It is a commonplace that the notion of "having in mind" stands in need of clarification. Such a task is not part of the current project, and I remain neutral on how the analysis of this notion should proceed.

7. See David Kaplan's long-awaited, finally published monograph "Demonstratives," in *Themes from Kaplan*, ed. Joseph Almog, John Perry, and Howard Wettstein (New York and Oxford, 1989).

8. In treating 'now', 'here', and 'today' as pure indexicals, I oversimplify for ease of exposition. I am inclined to think that 'I' is the only really *pure* indexical. The other expressions that Kaplan classifies as pure indexicals exhibit features that make them something like hybrids of 'I' and the demonstratives. 'Now', for example, does not simply pick out the instant of utterance (which would make it a pure indexical like 'I'); it picks out greater or lesser intervals of which this instant is always a constituent. The "breadth" of the intervals varies with the context.

9. Or so I assume. Consistent with my project in this paper, I do not here argue against other perspectives on the roles of the singular terms I discuss, say, the perspective according to which 'now' means "concur-

rent with the present utterance." Instead I assume a nondescriptivist perspective and try to work out the most coherent way to fill out the picture.

10. See Devitt, *Designation*, pp. 42–43.

11. Here I follow Kaplan in "Demonstratives."

12. This rule should not be seen as supplying a *synonym* for 'I', such as 'the agent of the context', but rather as utilizing this description only, so to speak, in the metalanguage, to systematically fix or specify the references of utterances of 'I'.

13. Donnellan has agreed in conversation that a Kaplan-like nonintentional account is correct for the pure indexicals, whereas, on his view, the havings-in-mind of the speaker are crucial for reference by names, demonstratives, and definite descriptions. I am not sure why, on his view, intentions should not also be decisive for the pure indexicals. In any case, the argument I develop here against the intentional view applies to demonstratives as well, as I argue in the next section.

14. David Kaplan, in his seminal paper "Dthat" (in *Contemporary Perspectives in the Philosophy of Language*, ed. P. French, T. Uehling, and H. Wettstein [Minneapolis, 1979], pp. 383–400) states: "A person might utter: 'I am a general' intending—that is, 'having in mind'—de Gaulle, and being under the delusion that he himself was de Gaulle. But the linguistic constraints on the possible demonstrata of 'I' will not allow anyone other than de Gaulle to so demonstrate de Gaulle, no matter how hard they try" (pp. 396–97). Kaplan's example, however, does not make it clear that the speaker not only believes that he is de Gaulle but really has de Gaulle in mind. After all, just as in the "I am hungry" case, the speaker could say, "I am a general," believing he is de Gaulle, and perhaps still have himself in mind. When I first read Kaplan's example, I had this picture: the speaker utters 'I' and thinks "*de Gaulle, de Gaulle, de Gaulle.*" He *tries hard*, as Kaplan says, to refer to de Gaulle. Having someone in mind, though, is surely not a matter of thinking about him actively, concentrating on him, when uttering the singular term.

15. Donnellan, in "Proper Names and Identifying Descriptions," considers a case that is similar to my Ahern case in that a speaker uses a singular term (in Donnellan's example, a proper name rather than an indexical) to refer to an individual whom he misidentifies and takes to be someone else. In Donnellan's example, a student meets a man at a party whom he mistakenly takes to be "J. L. Aston-Martin, the famous British philosopher." The student later describes the party to a friend and, in doing so, repeatedly uses the name 'J. L. Aston-Martin'. Is the referent of the student's utterance of the name the British philosopher so named, or rather the man at the party? Donnellan suggests that the answer depends upon the intent of the speaker. When the student says to his friend, "You'll never guess who I met last night—J. L. Aston-Martin," the point of his utterance concerns the person so named, the famous British philosopher, and so the philosopher is the referent.

When he says (something like), "... and Aston-Martin, who was by then quite drunk, tripped over Robinson's feet," his use of the name is, Donnellan says, "as it were, incidental," that is, incidental to the point of the utterance. The point of the utterance has to do with the man the student mistakenly takes to be Aston-Martin, and the referent is the man at the party.

16. There is a sense in which Ahern did refer to de Gaulle. If he succeeded in communicating about de Gaulle, which I agree may have occurred, then he must have, in some sense, referred to him. Still, there is another sense, a preferred sense, in which he referred only to himself. If what he said, strictly speaking, was false, then his assertion was about himself. *He* is the individual whose properties are relevant to the truth or falsity of what was said. In such a case, I shall say that the speaker, while he may have intended to refer to de Gaulle, referred to himself. Alternatively, we might adopt Saul Kripke's terminology in "Speaker's Reference and Semantic Reference" (in *Contemporary Perspectives in the Philosophy of Language*, ed. P. French, T. Uehling, and H. Wettstein [Minneapolis, 1979], pp. 6–27) and say that although the speaker has referred to de Gaulle, his words, on this occasion, do not so refer.

17. My argument here against the intentional theory depends crucially upon the intuition that what Ahern said was false. Intuitions about the truth-value of what was said may be less clear in the analogous Aston-Martin case of note 15 above, the case in which the speaker has the man at the party in mind and the point of the utterance is to say something about *him*. Intuitions are certainly less clear with regard to some cases involving utterances of definite descriptions. See note 27 below.

18. See, for example, Rod Bertolet's comments in "Demonstratives and Intentions," *Philosophical Studies* 38 (1980): 75–78.

19. This example slightly modifies Kripke's in "Speaker's Reference and Semantic Reference," see esp. pp. 14–15.

20. As do the parallel claims I made for the similar cases discussed in the previous paragraph.

21. As Kripke notes in "Speaker's Reference and Semantic Reference," p. 25 n. 28.

22. That the historian's intention to refer to himself as *subsidiary* is, no doubt, related to the fact that it is a *derivative* intention. The historian wishes to communicate about de Gaulle and must choose some linguistic means to his end. One such means, given his mistaken beliefs, is an utterance of 'I'. He knows, of course, that by uttering 'I' he will refer to himself and fully intends this as a means to his communicative end, speaking about de Gaulle. Thus his intention to communicate about himself is *derivative* from his primary intention to communicate about de Gaulle. Such a primary-derivative distinction was suggested to me by Michael McKinsey's "Names and Intentionality," *The Philosophical Review* 87 (1978): 171–200; see esp. pp. 176–77. McKinsey points out that Hector-Neri Castañeda is the father of the distinction.

See Castañeda's "Intentions and the Structure of Intending," *The Journal of Philosophy* 68 (1971), esp. p. 454.

23. But not inevitably. As Kripke notes in "Speaker's Reference and Semantic Reference," p. 25 n. 26, if one says, "Smith's murderer is insane," having in mind the (innocent) man on the witness stand who is acting bizarre, the speaker has only *that person* in mind and takes him to have a property he does not have, that is, the property of having murdered Smith. He is not confusing two individuals, both of whom he has in mind.

24. Thus the Ahern example shows that having someone in mind in the primary sense is not a sufficient condition for reference to him. The Ahern example further shows that having someone in mind in the primary sense is not even a necessary condition for reference to him, for Ahern referred to himself, even though he failed to have himself in mind in the primary sense.

25. 'Now', 'here', 'today', and so on, since (as suggested in note 8 above) they have a "demonstrative" component, require a more complicated positive account than does 'I', one in accordance with my remarks on demonstratives in the next section, Demonstratives: Positive Remarks.

26. Colin McGinn, "The Mechanism of Reference," *Synthese* 49 (1981): 157–86. The example occurs on page 161.

27. Another example might be provided by having our deranged history lecturer try to make a point about de Gaulle, not by saying 'I' but by saying 'that one', pointing to a student or colleague whom the lecturer takes to be de Gaulle. Kaplan, in "Dthat," provided much earlier a brilliant example of a somewhat different variety, his "Carnap-Agnew case" (p. 396). Notice that while intuitions about such cases, as well as about the Ahern case in the section above (Pure Indexicals), cases involving pure indexicals and demonstratives, are pretty clear, cases involving utterances of definite descriptions and proper names are much less so. Consider Keith Donnellan's example in which someone says, "The man drinking the martini looks happy tonight," intending to refer to "that guy over there," who indeed looks very happy but who, unbeknownst to the speaker, is not drinking a martini at all, but is merely drinking sparkling water in a martini glass. Another man, let us suppose, standing just off to the side, is the only man really drinking a martini in the room, and he looks quite miserable. Do we have any clear intuitions about the truth-value of what was said, strictly speaking, and therefore about the reference of the definite description? Donnellan, at least as I read "Reference and Definite Descriptions," thinks that what was said, the statement made, was true, and that the referent, indeed the semantic referent, is the man the speaker had in mind. (Donnellan has agreed in conversation that this was his intent, and he is explicit about this in his later paper "Speaker Reference, Descriptions, and Anaphora," in *Contemporary Perspectives in the Philosophy of Language*, ed. P. French, T. Uehling, and H. Wettstein [Minneapolis, 1977], pp. 28–44. Kripke, writing only about "Reference and Definite Descrip-

tions," reads Donnellan as being more cautious. See Kripke's remarks in "Speaker's Reference and Semantic Reference," p. 12.) Kripke expresses the contrary intuition. The same dispute, supported by the same conflicting intuitive judgments, occurs with respect to proper names. See Kripke's discussion in "Speaker's Reference" and Donnellan's in "Proper Names and Identifying Descriptions," sec. 9. Given a lack of undisputed intuitions about such cases, how might we proceed? Perhaps the arguments I have advanced are relevant, for my argument yields the result that there are at least some cases in which it is clear that (semantic) reference is not determined by what the speaker has in mind. Donnellan, it should be remembered, was developing a quite general point, not one related to the peculiarities, say, of definite descriptions. His view that what the speaker has in mind determines the semantic reference is applied by him to names, definite descriptions, and in conversation at least, to demonstratives (see note 13 above). My arguments, at least prima facie, make Donnellan's general picture implausible. If semantic reference and speaker reference can diverge in the case of, say, demonstratives, why can't they diverge in the case of names and descriptions? If the reference of a demonstrative does not depend upon what the speaker has in mind, why should the reference of names and descriptions so depend? (One should not conclude from this that there is nothing left to Donnellan's referential-attributive distinction. See my paper "Demonstrative Reference and Definite Descriptions" for Donnellan's distinction cleansed of Donnellan's views about the semantic role of havings-in-mind.)

28. For reasons of space, I cannot consider Kaplan's positive account of the determination of reference for demonstratives (presented briefly in "Dthat" and more fully in "Demonstratives"), his "Fregean theory of demonstra*tions*" (as opposed to the "Fregean theory of demonstra*tives*," which he rejects). I believe, to be brief, that Kaplan's view is inadequate, in part because it fails to assign a central-enough place to the contextual cues and allows no place for the extra-contextual ones.

29. More accurately, as we shall see, they, together with other cues, determine the reference.

30. The contextual cues go far beyond the fairly pedestrian ones mentioned in the text. When I say to my son, "That is the most disgusting thing I have ever seen," he knows that I am speaking of the dead and decaying frog he is holding. He knows this in part because of the cue provided by *the predicate* I have used. Considerations of stress and intonation are relevant as well. Cf. Stephen Isard, "Changing the Context," in *Formal Semantics of Natural Language*, ed. E. L. Keenen (Cambridge, 1974).

31. One way to put my thesis is that the referent of 'that' is the individual that is *salient* with respect to that demonstrative utterance. The idea is that something or other must make some item salient, that is, conspicuous or striking, with regard to each utterance of a demonstrative. I hesitate to formulate my thesis in terms of the notion of "sali-

ence," however, for doing so seems to divert attention away from the substantive thesis I am proposing and toward questions like whether the term 'salience' really captures my idea. I believe the term to be both helpful and appropriate, but defending it is probably more trouble than it is worth. For a similar use of the notion of "salience" see David Lewis, "Scorekeeping in a Language Game," *Journal of Philosophical Logic* 8 (1979): 339–59.

32. When I say that the speaker relies on certain cues, this is not to suggest that he consciously selects them. In many contexts, it will be immediately clear to a speaker which item will be taken to be the referent, and he will not bother to think about what precisely it is that will indicate this. Indeed, some of these cues are very subtle and will not be easily available to him.

33. The miscommunication is, in such a case, the speaker's responsibility. In cases in which the miscommunication is the auditor's fault, in which, say, he was not paying attention, the speaker will have said, strictly speaking, just what he intended to say, despite the fact that it was not understood. No doubt there are intermediate cases in which it will not be clear where to place the responsibility and equally unclear what was, strictly speaking, said. This is, I think, as it should be, since "what is said, strictly speaking," is an institutional notion and there is little institutional utility to providing a determinate answer for such intermediate cases.

34. Discussions of the example given in this paragraph have convinced me that my intuitions here are not universally shared. The intuition that the man pointed to is the referent and that the truth-value of what was said depends upon *his* properties is surely not as firm as are the intuitions about the Ahern case of the second section (Pure Indexicals), or the pointing examples in the third section (Demonstratives: Critical Remarks). Nor do I base my argument against the intentional theory on the present case. If my arguments in the second and third sections are correct, however, the intentional theory is no longer a contender. Given that it is not a contender, and given the sort of institutional picture that has been emerging, it seems implausible that the speaker is responsible only for those cues that he intends to communicate by. Much more plausibly, he is responsible for those that he *to all appearances* exploits.

35. Kaplan, "Dthat," p. 396.

36. Nor is it clear that Kaplan could point to the dog behind his son without moving his son out of the way, despite the fact that the geometrical line from his finger passes through the dog.

37. So Kaplan concludes in "Dthat." This is a desperate expedient, given Kaplan's program of doing the semantics of indexicals without appeal to such intentions.

38. McGinn, "The Mechanism of Reference," p. 163.

39. Ibid., p. 163. McGinn's view is that this rule represents something of an idealization of our actual linguistic practice. At least part of

what he means is that we do not always take such care in pointing as his rule requires and that we will count someone as have demonstratively referred to something even if the line extending from the pointing finger misses its target by an inch or so. Nevertheless, thinks McGinn, the reference of a demonstrative is determined by the spatial relation in which the speaker stands to the referent. See his discussion of "idealization" on pages 163–64.

40. I cannot pursue it here, but I suspect that the sort of argument I employ against Frege's view that indexicals function as surrogates for uniquely denoting definite descriptions, and against the Russellian view that "indefinite" definite descriptions like 'the table' are elliptical for uniquely denoting definite descriptions, applies against McGinn's view here as well. For the argument, see my "Indexical Reference and Propositional Content," pp. 24–25, and my "Demonstrative Reference and Definite Descriptions," pp. 41–42.

41. See the beginning of the previous section, Demonstratives: Positive Remarks.

42. McGinn, "The Mechanism of Reference," p. 183 n. 14.

43. See also the examples in the third paragraph of the previous section, Demonstratives: Positive Remarks. One might try to handle all such cases, as well as the Watt example just given in the text, as cases of anaphoric uses of demonstrative expressions. But it is hard to see how one could come up with a natural account along these lines, since, for one thing, no other reference to that individual need have occurred in the prior discourse. In any case, I sometimes, perhaps often, think that it is a virtue of the account I have provided that such cases need no special treatment. Another class of cases that comes to mind here is that of "deferred ostension." A kindergarten teacher, pointing to finger paintings done by her pupils, says, "This one is very good at writing but is not much of an artist. This one is quite good at this but is something of a behavior problem." She thus refers to her pupils with demonstratives by means of pointing to the paintings. Is this straightforward demonstrative reference, or rather a special category of "referring to one thing by demonstratively referring to something else (that represents it)"? My view allows us to treat such cases as straightforward demonstrative references. The referent is the pupil indicated by the cues. One of the relevant cues is the pointing gesture to the painting done by that student.

44. This paper was written while I was an NEH Fellow (1981–82), and I am grateful to the National Endowment for the Humanities, the Graduate School of the University of Minnesota, and the Office of the Academic Dean of the University of Minnesota, Morris, for support. I am also grateful to the Department of Philosophy of Stanford University, and especially to its former chair, John Perry, and to Patrick Suppes, Director of the Institute for the Mathematical Study of the Social Sciences at Stanford, for the hospitality shown me during 1981–82. I am especially indebted to Perry for extremely helpful discussions of

the questions I discuss in this paper, as well as for his comments on earlier drafts. Others to whom I owe a special debt are David Kaplan, for hospitality and extended discussions at the University of California, Los Angeles, and Joseph Almog, for long-suffering patience with earlier versions. The final form of this paper owes much to the comments of Michael Bratman, Keith S. Donnellan, Evan Fales, Philippa Foot, Eli Hirsch, Ernest LePore, Julius Moravcsik, and Patrick Suppes, as well as to the comments of a number of individuals present at talks I gave on this subject at Stanford, the University of California, Riverside, and the University of Notre Dame.

Essay 8

1. Gottlob Frege, "Letter from Russell," *Gottlob Frege: Philosophical and Mathematical Correspondence*, abridged ed. (Chicago, 1980), p. 169.

2. Talk of Russell's perspective (in semantics or elsewhere) is risky. There were, of course, various strands to Russell's thinking, and these, moreover, took on different emphases at different times. Nor did he hesitate to change his mind. I will isolate one important strand in Russell's thinking, a strand that contrasts sharply with Frege's approach, and one that is, at least to my mind, suggestive of a way forward. Russell emphasized these views in "Knowledge by Acquaintance and Knowledge by Description," in Bertrand Russell, *Mysticism and Logic* (Garden City, N.Y., n.d.), as well as in the parallel piece by the same name in *The Problems of Philosophy* (Home University Library, 1912, reprinted 1959, Oxford University Press).

3. Russell, "Knowledge," in *Mysticism and Logic*, p. 211.

4. Ibid., p. 223.

5. Query: Given Russell's epistemic constraint on propositional constituency, how can, for example, Mont Blanc itself be a constituent in a proposition that we can understand? Perhaps Russell, in telling us that "despite all its snowfields, Mont Blanc is actually a component part of what is asserted," indulges a desire for a dramatic example of a real thing in a proposition, or perhaps he has something else in mind. Clearly, in giving such examples, Russell needs to tell us more. I speculate, in the section "Why Russell Was Not a Neo-Fregean," below, that such examples betray a tendency in Russell's thought that is at odds with his "fundamental epistemological principle."

6. The terminology of "direct referent" derives, so far as I know, from David Kaplan. He uses it, however, in a wider way than I do here. As I use the terminology, a directly referential expression will be one that, as Russell says, is a "mere noise or shape conventionally used to designate a certain [thing]; it gives us no information about that [thing], and has nothing that can be called its meaning as opposed to denotation." Kaplan's notion, on the contrary, allows for directly referential expressions that possess descriptive meaning, indexicals for example, on Kaplan's view.

7. Russell, "Knowledge," in *Mysticism and Logic*, p. 218.

8. In chapter 1 of my forthcoming—as yet untitled—book, I argue, following Richard Mendelsohn in "Frege's *Begriffsschrift* Theory of Identity," *Journal of the History of Philosophy* 22, no. 3 (July 1982): 279–99, that modes of presentation were not the innovation of Frege's later sense-reference picture. What was new in "On Sense and Reference" (in *Translations from the Philosophical Writings of Gottlob Frege*, ed. P. Geach and M. Black [Oxford, 1966]) was the idea that modes of presentation, already available to Frege in the earlier work, might well be seen as propositional constituents and that this would make for a more natural solution to the puzzle of informative identity statements than had been available. See Gottlob Frege, *Begriffsschrift*, sec. 8, for the earlier view.

9. What I am envisaging here is the possibility that *ordinary* names could function semantically as mere tags for their referents, a position that Mill maintained, as we shall see. 'Hesperus' and 'Phosphorus' would accordingly be tags for a single planet. Russell, of course, would have rejected this idea for epistemological reasons, namely, that we are not directly acquainted with the heavenly body. The question here under consideration is, why does Frege reject the idea?

10. Russell, "Knowledge," in *Mysticism and Logic*, p. 208.

11. Frege, "On Sense and Reference," p. 58n.

12. His reasons are another matter. Russell's obscure discussion of his objection to the sense-reference approach, in "On Denoting" (in *Logic and Knowledge*, ed. R. C. Marsh [London, 1956], pp. 41–56), is not a paradigm of philosophy.

13. Both descriptions derive from Russell; see "Knowledge."

14. Nathan U. Salmon, in *Frege's Puzzle* (Cambridge, Mass., 1986), p. 64ff., speaks of such descriptions as "thoroughly descriptional," as opposed to those that are "relationally descriptional."

15. Russell is not here singling out place names for special treatment. The same holds for proper names like 'Bismarck', as the context makes clear.

16. Russell, "Knowledge," in *Mysticism and Logic*, p. 210.

17. Ibid. I am not sure why Russell, of all people, says that this description "must apply to some man." If two men share the honor of being longer lived than anyone else, so that there is no unique most long-lived man, then the description lacks a denotation, as Russell's famous theory of definite descriptions reminds us. But let us not worry about this. Russell seems willing to allow, in any case, that we can come to know that a description like 'the most long-lived of men' has a denotation.

18. The identification with *knowing who* is suggested by much of Russell's discussion in "Knowledge" and his parallel piece in *The Problems of Philosophy*. See, for example, Russell's discussion of his idea that even one who knows Bismarck only through history—and this is not, for Russell, a case of having a mere purely qualitative description that denotes Bismarck—*knows who he was* (in *The Problems of Philosophy*, p. 58).

19. Russell sometimes appears to deny that in cases like that of my son's name I can know who is in question. He says, for example, that only when I am acquainted with something can I know which thing is in question. At the same time, he clearly holds that we can know who is in question in cases in which knowledge by acquaintance is out of the question, for example, the Bismarck case mentioned in the last note. Perhaps the point is that there is a strong sense of "knowing who," according to which one knows who x is only if one is acquainted with x. But in another perfectly legitimate sense one can know who someone is if one knows enough about the individual, even if one is not acquainted with him/her. See note 32 and the accompanying text for further discussion of "knowing who." The topic of "knowing who" is extremely complicated, as recent philosophy testifies, and no serious attempt at resolving the perplexities involved can be carried out here. For a recent illuminating discussion, the general tone of which I feel sympathy for, see Steven E. Boer and William G. Lycan, "Knowing Who," *Philosophical Studies* 28 (1975): 299–344.

20. Russell's "man with the iron mask" example is confusing since the description would seem to be purely qualitative, and so Russell ought to deny that we can know anything about the denotation beyond what is implied by the description. Perhaps Russell took this description, as it is ordinarily used, to be a truncated form of another description, the latter containing a direct reference to some object of acquaintance. If, however, the description is really hybrid, then why should it differ from that concealed by 'Bismarck' in the way that Russell here claims? Perhaps the answer to this question lies in the considerations briefly discussed in note 25 below, that hybrid descriptions do not guarantee *knowing who*, or perhaps Russell has something else in mind.

21. Russell, "Knowledge," in *The Problems of Philosophy*, p. 58.

22. In the "weaker" sense of "knowing who" distinguished in note 19 above.

23. Russell, "Knowledge," in *Mysticism and Logic*, p. 209.

24. Here I adapt a remark of Russell's ("Knowledge," in *Mysticism and Logic*, p. 210): "If however, we say, 'the first Chancellor of the German Empire was an astute diplomatist,' we can only be assured of the truth of our judgment in virtue of something with which we are acquainted—usually a testimony heard or read."

25. Actually, there are varying strengths of epistemic access afforded by constellations of universals-cum-(acquainted-with-)particulars. The constellation expressed by 'my daughter', after all, should be quite different in this respect than that expressed by 'the individual, whoever that may be, who is standing closest to a point exactly 4,000 miles due west of me at the moment'. Russell would surely agree—he himself distinguishes in the passage quoted above between the "stage in the removal from acquaintance" represented by Bismarck's friends and that represented by one who knows Bismarck only through history. Russell, then, would presumably not want to say (or, at least, he might well not want to say) that in cases like 'the individual, whoever

that may be, who is standing closest to a point exactly 4,000 miles due west . . .', despite the agent's possession of a "hybrid concept," the agent automatically knows who is in question. So possession of a hybrid concept may not supply a sufficient condition for *knowing who*, and Russell never even hints at what further conditions might be relevant. In what follows I will ignore this complication and speak as if the possession of any hybrid description assures the appropriate sort of identifying knowledge of the denotation.

26. Russell, "Knowledge," in *Mysticism and Logic*, p. 209; italics added.

27. Ibid., p. 210.

28. Joseph Almog has argued in conversation that there are direct semantic intuitions—he refers to "argument by ear"—to the effect that ordinary proper names are directly referential. I find this appeal to intuition difficult to evaluate.

29. This is true even for contemporary philosophers who explicitly deny that ordinary names are surrogates for descriptions. Keith Donnellan, for example, a defender of a direct reference view of ordinary names, nevertheless argues that one must stand in a privileged epistemic relation to an individual in order to refer to it by name. See, for example, Keith S. Donnellan, "The Contingent A Priori and Rigid Designators," in *Contemporary Perspectives in the Philosophy of Language*, ed. P. French, T. Uehling, and H. Wettstein (Minneapolis, 1979), pp. 45–60.

30. Frege, "On Sense and Reference," p. 57.

31. At issue here is not Russell's, nor Frege's, use of the term 'concept' (or '*Begriff*'). I am using the term 'concept' as I have all along, to refer to the things like Fregean senses (as opposed to the things that Frege calls "concepts," i.e. the *references* of predicates, or that Russell does, i.e. universals). My point is that it is stretching things to attribute to Russell the view that hybrid descriptions express such concepts.

32. I have not forgotten Russell's view that the definite descriptions have "denotations." I return to this below.

33. See "On Denoting" for Russell's reasons for denying that the apparent grammatical structure reflects what is really going on, as well as for his reasons for the positive view sketched here.

34. There is more than one way to understand the relation between the original sentence and the Russellian reformulation. I have been taking this in the way that I think was Russell's dominant tendency. Russell, that is, tended to view the reformulation as making explicit the thought in the mind of the speaker, a thought that is misleadingly put by the original sentence. One might do it differently (in the spirit of Quine, for example) and see the original as muddled (who knows what ordinary folk think when they use descriptions, and who cares?) and the reformulation as coming as close to the original as possible while meeting serious standards of acceptability, intelligibility, and so forth. For more on this see W. V. O. Quine, *Word and Object* (Cambridge, Mass., 1960), esp. "The Ordered Pair as a Philosophical Paradigm."

Also see Russell's remarks in this Quinean direction in his "Mr. Strawson on Referring," in *My Philosophical Development* (London, 1959), ch. 18, part 3.

35. At one point in "On Denoting," after formulating how things should go according to his own theory, Russell says, "This may seem a somewhat incredible interpretation; but I am not at present giving reasons, I am merely *stating* the theory" (p. 44).

There is an interesting methodological contrast here with Frege. As David Kaplan notes in "What Is Russell's Theory of Descriptions?" in *Bertrand Russell: A Collection of Critical Essays*, ed. D. F. Pears (Garden City, N.Y., 1972), pp. 227-44: "Russell and Frege were both interested in removing the logical imperfections of ordinary language but their methods were quite different. . . . Where grammar called for entities whose nature was obscure, Frege attempted constructions, as with numbers, or a theory about the purported entities, as with propositions. Thus he sought to preserve the integrity of ordinary language with ontological ingenuity. Russell's response, at least in the case of definite descriptions, was by grammatical reconstrual and replacement."

36. Russell, "On Denoting," p. 51.

37. As I am using 'intentionality', it has nothing special to do with the problem, associated with Franz Brentano, of how it is possible to think about something that does not exist. 'Intentionality' here concerns the more general phenomenon of the "aboutness" of thought. The traditional picture to which Frege, Russell, and many others subscribe has it that thought can be about something only if that something is cognitively discriminable by the thinker.

Essay 9

1. Alvin Plantinga, "The Boethean Compromise," *American Philosophical Quarterly* 15, no. 2 (April 1978): 129-38. The quotation is from page 130.

2. The heart of the new theory is, not this notion of proposition, but rather the idea that certain sorts of terms, names and indexicals, for example, function, not to introduce a sense into the proposition, but rather to make it the case that a certain referent is under discussion. This intuitive point—that it is the referent itself, and not some descriptive characterization of it, which figures in what was asserted—might be given a number of theoretical treatments. For the purposes of this paper I provisionally adopt the Russell-Kaplan treatment.

3. Nondenoting singular terms present several different sorts of problems, some of which are not my concern here. I have nothing to say in the present paper about, for example, the crucial problem posed by negative existentials, or the related problem of apparently genuine reference to fictional or mythological entities. My motivation for discussing here only what I do discuss is (briefly) as follows. Negative existentials present problems for everyone, not just for the new theo-

rist. The problem I discuss in the text is, by contrast, a problem specifically for the new theorist, a problem over and above any general difficulties about negative existentials. Moreover, the account of negative existentials that I am tentatively attracted to—I develop the beginnings of this briefly in "Did the Greeks Really Worship Zeus?" (in this volume)—would be of no help with the problem I discuss in the text.

4. As Frege notes in Gottlob Frege, "Introduction to Logic" (in *Posthumous Writings*, ed. H. Hermes, F. Kambartel, and F. Kaulbach; trans. P. Long and R. White [Chicago, 1979]), "The object designated by a proper name seems to be quite inessential to the thought-content of a sentence which contains it" (p. 191).

5. This is essentially Frege's original problem about informative identities. The first proposition is trivial and uninformative, whereas the second contains substantive information. These propositions are, then, not the same.

6. My example here is essentially John Perry's in "The Problem of the Essential Indexical," *Noûs*, 13, no. 1 (March 1979): 3–21. In Perry's examples, formulated before the neo-Fregeans mounted their recent counterattacks, the attacker was a bear.

7. Although I cannot discuss it here, it is less than obvious that the Fregean orientation does so well with "Frege's data." See note 28 below.

8. Kaplan once argued in conversation that a "gappy proposition" was expressed. Keith S. Donnellan in "Speaking of Nothing," *The Philosophical Review* 83, no. 1 (January 1974): 3–32, says that in such cases no proposition has been expressed.

9. Tyler Burge, "Belief *De Re*," *The Journal of Philosophy* 74, no. 6 (June 1977): 338–62. The quoted remark occurs on page 354.

10. John Perry, "Frege on Demonstratives," *The Philosophical Review* 86, no. 4 (October 1977): 474–97.

11. Neither Perry nor Kaplan (see especially section 17, "Epistemological Remarks," of David Kaplan's long-awaited monograph "Demonstratives" [in *Themes from Kaplan*, ed. Joseph Almog, John Perry, and Howard Wettstein (New York and Oxford, 1989), pp. 481–563]) developed these ideas in quite the general way that I will explore here. Kaplan emphasized the application to the original puzzle of informative identities, and Perry emphasized the application to the puzzle concerning the explanation of action. Perry's remark in "Frege on Demonstratives," however, that "roles," which are pretty much Kaplan's "characters," can do the cognitive work of Frege's senses certainly suggests the generalization I explore here. The idea that this apparatus ought to be of use with regard to the first Frege puzzle occurred to Kenneth Olson and me in a discussion of these questions.

12. Kaplan recognizes this when he says, in section 22 of "Demonstratives," "proper names do not seem to fit into the whole semantical and epistemological scheme as I have developed it [for indexicals]" (p. 562).

13. Both Donnellan and Kripke have expressed skepticism about whether the view they advance is in any crucial sense a *causal* theory, Donnellan in "Speaking of Nothing" and Kripke in a talk at Stanford University in the spring of 1983.

14. This is not, of course, to say that a name cannot be *introduced* by a reference-fixing description. The point is rather that no such description stays attached to a name as the determinant of its reference. Kripke's views on this question are complex, and difficult to unravel completely. See Saul Kripke, *Naming and Necessity* (Cambridge, Mass., 1980), p. 88 n. 38. Perhaps it is not altogether clear that he is opposed to such a view. My point is that very little is clear about the historical-chain approach at this level of refinement.

15. Kaplan and Almog give different accounts of the pre-semantic role. See Kaplan, "Demonstratives," (sec. 22, pp. 558–63, esp. p. 563 n. 78) and Joseph Almog, "Semantical Anthropology," in *Midwest Studies in Philosophy*, vol. 9, ed. P. French, T. Uehling, and H. Wettstein, (Minneapolis, 1984), pp. 470–90.

16. One might try to resist the idea that these utterances differ in cognitive significance, in which case the present sort of example would not show that cognitive significance fails to be explicable in terms of linguistic meaning. One might insist, for example, as Perry did recently in conversation, that the cognitive role of these two sentences—or utterances—is the same. It is just that so much else about the cognitive states of the person in question is different in the two contexts that we can account for his willingness to affirm one remark and unwillingness to affirm the other without supposing that the very remark in question has a different cognitive value in the two contexts. Whatever the ultimate virtue of such a move, it employs a very different idea of cognitive significance than we find in Frege—or, especially significant here, in Perry in "Frege on Demonstratives," or in Kaplan in "Demonstratives." Perry, in "Frege on Demonstratives," (explicitly) following Frege, counts two utterances as different in cognitive significance if someone who understands both affirms the first but is unwilling to affirm the second. Indeed, Perry considers several examples that are essentially like the one I utilize in the text, and concludes, as I do, that the same sentence has different cognitive values. (See the *Enterprise* and *Morning Star* examples, pp. 483–84). Perry somehow never makes the connection between these examples and his thesis, expressed later in the paper, that "we can take senses to be 'roles'," that cognitive significance can be accounted for in terms of linguistic meaning. These examples, however, make it clear that "roles," linguistic meanings, cannot be made to do the cognitive work of senses.

17. One might try heroically to save the Perry-Kaplan approach by arguing that, contrary to what I take to be plain horse sense, not all (deictic) occurrences of the demonstrative 'that', say, have the same linguistic meaning. Kaplan, although he no longer holds such a view, argued in "Demonstratives" that, for example, the informativeness of

"That = that" should be explained by positing a difference in linguistic meaning or character between the first occurrence of the demonstrative and the second.

An interesting suggestion, made by a reader for *The Journal of Philosophy* who reviewed this essay, is that there is a broader notion than "linguistic meaning" that deserves to be called "meaning"—for it is very much tied to public communicative conventions—and yet may capture cognitive significance. One who understands a use of a demonstrative grasps not just the linguistic meaning but also the "meaning" of the demonstrative-cum-ostension, ostension being a rule-governed practice. This broader notion of meaning can be pressed into cognitive service. Utterances will differ in cognitive significance if there is a relevant difference in the ostensions.

This proposal captures something of the spirit of Kaplan's intuition that there is a kind of incompleteness to demonstratives ('this', 'that', 'he', 'she'), as opposed to "pure indexicals" ('I', 'now'), an incompleteness that requires a "demonstration," a pointing gesture, for example. Let me briefly mention some problems. First, ostending is inessential to the use of demonstratives, and it remains to be seen how this approach would generalize to cases in which there is no gesture, or in which there could be no gesture (e.g. demonstrative references to remarks people make or to someone who has just left the room). I discuss this and related matters more fully in "How to Bridge the Gap Between Meaning and Reference" (in this volume). Second, this broader notion of "meaning" is both too coarse-grained and at the same time too fine-grained. It is too coarse-grained because the speaker might utter the same sentence on two occasions with the same (or relevantly similar) sort of pointing gesture and still the cognitive significance of the utterances might be obviously different. It is also too fine-grained. Take a case in which "He = he" is trivial. It won't matter that the respective gestures were a bit different, or even very different.

18. Because it is so misleading to refer to singular propositions as thoughts, I have not done so in my exposition of the Perry-Kaplan view to this point. Perry and Kaplan repeatedly do so, however. See Perry's remarks in, for example, "Frege on Demonstratives," where he thinks of himself as introducing a "new notion of thought" (p. 482), and Kaplan's in, for example, "Demonstratives," sec. 17.

19. Ruth Barcan Marcus, "A Proposed Solution to a Puzzle About Belief," in *Midwest Studies in Philosophy*, vol. 6, ed. P. French, T. Uehling, and H. Wettstein (Minneapolis, 1981), p. 504.

20. As Bertrand Russell says in "The Philosophy of Logical Atomism," in *Logic and Knowledge: Essays, 1901–1950*, ed. R. Marsh (New York, 1956), "It is not accurate to say 'I believe the proposition p' and to regard the occurrence as a twofold relation between me and p . . . the belief does not really contain a proposition as a constituent but only contains the constituents of the proposition as constituents" (p. 224). Another and more radical suggestion involves denying that believing is

a relation at all. I develop this in a forthcoming paper (based on existing talks), "Bringing Belief Down to Earth."

21. I borrow the term 'anthropology', as used in this connection, from David Kaplan, who used it in his response to John Searle (at the 1982 meetings of the American Philosophical Association, Pacific Division) to characterize the nature of Kripke's study of proper names.

22. Tyler Burge, "Sinning Against Frege," *The Philosophical Review* 88, no. 3 (July 1979): 398–442. The quotation is from page 398.

23. Michael Dummett, *Truth and Other Enigmas* (London, 1978), p. 458.

24. The first of these rules, consistent with a genuine causal theory of reference, is of a piece with the views of Michael Devitt in his *Designation* (New York, 1981). The second is suggested by the view defended by Donnellan with regard to proper names and definite descriptions. Donnellan, in conversation, has argued for this sort of rule for demonstratives. The last rule is in line with the view I defend in "How to Bridge the Gap Between Meaning and Reference."

25. None of this precludes, I suppose, some sort of "implicit knowledge" of such rules. Perhaps such rules are "encoded" in our brains. This is not, however, germane to the present discussion, so far as I can see. Perhaps an omniscient god could "read" the rules directly from my brain, but I cannot. So it is hard to see how the rule can be taken to specify how I am thinking about the referent.

26. Tyler Burge, in "Individualism and the Mental," *Midwest Studies in Philosophy* 4 (1979): 73–122, argues that the thoughts and beliefs we attribute to an agent reflect not only his own "psychological states narrowly conceived" but also social facts, including facts about how his linguistic community employs its terms. It is not clear to me that the different rules I am imagining would engender a difference in cognitive states, even according to Burge. In any case, Burge's intriguing view, which clearly cannot be investigated here, appears to rest upon assumptions that I do not share about the semantics of belief sentences.

27. Michael Dummett, in *The Interpretation of Frege's Philosophy* (Cambridge, Mass., 1981), attributes this remarks to his earlier *Frege: Philosophy of Language* (London, 1973), without citing a page reference. Searle's remark is from John Searle, *Intentionality* (New York, 1983), p. vi. Schiffer's can be found on page 171 of Stephen Schiffer, "The Basis of Reference," *Erkenntnis* 13, no. 1 (July 1978): 171–206.

28. Perry, especially in "The Problem of the Essential Indexical," argues convincingly that the Fregean orientation runs into severe problems even in the area of cognitive significance. These arguments of Perry, based upon the work of Hector-Neri Castañeda, ought to make us even more suspicious about Frege's epistemological condition of adequacy. Not even the Fregean orientation, motivated by such epistemological concerns, can provide the wanted epistemological results.

29. Thomas McKay, in "On Proper Names in Belief Ascriptions," *Philosophical Studies* 39, no. 3 (April 1981): 287–303, denies "Frege's

datum" here. See also Saul Kripke's discussion in "A Puzzle About Belief," in *Meaning and Use*, ed. A. Margalit (Boston, 1979), pp. 234–83. Recently both Nathan Salmon and Scott Soames, the latter in a symposium with David Kaplan and John Perry at the 1985 meetings of the American Philosophical Association, Pacific Division, have advanced such a response.

30. For a case in which a definite description is substituted for a name, let Barbara use the name 'Mike', and let me, the reporter, use the definite description in reporting Barbara's belief to Tom. The truth-preserving substitutions that involve definite descriptions are particularly interesting, since not only Fregeans but just about everyone has assumed that such substitutions ought not to preserve the truth. This shows, I think, that we have virtually all had the wrong idea about the semantics of attitude reports. I develop these themes in "Bringing Belief Down to Earth."

31. In some cases this may present no problem for the Fregean. Jones says, "Reagan is a Republican," and someone reports him as believing that the President is a Republican. This may present no problem for the Fregean (even though, let us assume, 'the President' does not formulate the sense of the name 'Reagan'), for the reporter may be assuming (perhaps with good reason) that Jones also believes that Reagan is President and that Jones no doubt believes that the President is a Republican. The reporter, that is, may not be trying to report precisely the same belief that the believer expressed by his original utterance. This argument will accommodate certain examples but will surely not accommodate all. Similar remarks apply to the new theorist with respect to truth-preserving substitutions involving definite descriptions, substitutions that ought not to preserve truth even according to the new theorist.

Another possible move on behalf of the Fregean is to bite the bullet and insist that the sorts of substitution discussed in the text do not preserve truth. My report of Nigel's belief, then, is false, although useful or conversationally acceptable. This denial of the putative data, however, exactly parallels the move of some new theorists discussed above (note 29) and seems similarly objectionable.

32. John Perry does so in "The Problem of the Essential Indexical," pp. 9–10.

33. Nor does substitutivity cause the only problems for either approach. John sincerely says, "Vulcan is a large heavenly body." The problem for the new theorist is not one of substituting some other term for John's 'Vulcan'. The problem is that even reporting him in his own words seems to attribute to him a relation to a *nonexistent* singular proposition. Here is a problem for the Fregean: Since listeners, at least in many cases, do not know which Fregean senses speakers attach to the names they utter and, therefore, do not know which propositions those speakers express when they use names, there is a problem about how it is possible to report the beliefs so expressed. This clearly requires more

exposition than I can give here. Kripke discusses such problems for the Fregean in "A Puzzle About Belief."

34. In "Bringing Belief Down to Earth" I expand on these remarks, as well as on the diagnosis offered below. I argue that neither Fregeans nor new theorists have done very well with attitudinal embeddings. A Fregean exception is John Searle. My diagnosis has been partly inspired by Searle's discussion in "Referential and Attributive," in his *Expression and Meaning* (New York, 1979), pp. 137–61; see esp. sec. 3.4, "*De Re* and *De Dicto*." I further argue that the social character of our reporting practices, emphasized by W. V. O. Quine in, for example, *Word and Object* (Cambridge, Mass., 1960), pp. 218–19, and briefly discussed below, provides a key to the well-known puzzles, as well as to more substantive questions about belief.

35. I have in mind here not only the substitutivity data adduced by both sides but also the other sorts of relevant data mentioned in note 33 above.

36. As it has for Searle, in "Referential and Attributive." I have doubts about the final adequacy of Searle's approach to the data, but I believe that it represents an important advance.

37. Can one really study the cognitive significance of simple sentences without, in effect, studying the semantics of additudinal embedding? The answer, clearly, is yes. In doing so one will make *use* of cognitive notions but will not have to provide a semantics for the terms that express such notions. Why should one have to provide a semantics, clearly a very difficult task, in order to use the notions?

38. Belief sentences are not treated in Kaplan's "Demonstratives," for example, or in Perry's "The Problem of the Essential Indexical."

Essay 10

1. The epigraph is from Walker Percy, "The Delta Factor," in *The Message in the Bottle* (New York, 1954). I borrow the phrase "eternal structure of thought" from Tyler Burge, "Sinning Against Frege," *The Philosophical Review* 88 (1979): 398–442. The quotation is from page 398.

2. Michael Dummett, *Truth and Other Enigmas* (London, 1978), p. 458.

3. Russell, giving voice to this intuition, maintains that in order to be genuinely thinking about an object, or making a judgment about it, one must know *which thing is in question*. The "cognitive fix" requirement can be understood in a number of ways, some requiring an extremely strong cognitive relation to the referent, some requiring a more modest relation. Russell himself was quite a fanatic about intentionality (in the sense of "aboutness"). He required, or at least there was a strong tendency in his thought to require, that to really be thinking about an object, one must be *directly acquainted* with it. Otherwise one would not know which thing was in question, even if one possessed a definite description that denoted the object. Frege maintained a weaker requirement, that one possess an individuating sense. Weaker still is a

tendency in, for example, Keith Donnellan's thought, according to which some special sort of causal connection to a thing is enough to establish a cognitive fix. See Keith S. Donnellan, "The Contingent A Priori and Rigid Designators," in *Contemporary Perspectives in the Philosophy of Language*, ed. P. French, T. Uehling, and H. Wettstein (Minneapolis, 1979), pp. 45–60.

4. Indeed, argues Kripke, typical speakers may not know any more about Cicero than that he was 'a Roman orator', hardly individuating knowledge, and yet they are still perfectly competent with the name.

5. The point I am making about the typical inaccessibility of the "rules" that characterize our practices is perhaps easy to see for the case of proper names, where just about everyone seems confused about the matter. The point, however, is quite generally applicable. Consider, for example, the kind of example in which one might well suppose, and it has indeed been supposed, that the rules are much closer to consciousness. In the case of the first-person pronoun, for example, typical speakers may have a better *rough idea* of the semantic character of our practices than they do in the case of proper names. This is not to say, however, that they can discern an adequate general characterization—as opposed to a rough idea—by introspection, or even that they can select such an adequate characterization from a list of subtly different candidates. Consider Kaplan's candidate rule: the reference of the first-person pronoun is the agent of the context. Notice that 'agent of the context' is a technical term for Kaplan. For technical reasons having to do with contexts in which no one is speaking, Kaplan does not understand 'the agent' to mean the same as 'the speaker'. The typical competent speaker, I submit, will not find Kaplan's "agent" idea the obvious one. See also my paper "Has Semantics Rested on a Mistake?" (in this volume).

6. It is indeed tempting, following the suggestions of both Walker Percy and David Kaplan, in his response to John Searle at the 1982 meetings of the American Philosophical Association, Pacific Division, to characterize the semanticist as a Martian anthropologist. Do not look into the speaker's head, Kaplan advised, for an account of our practices, but import an alien who has the advantage of distance from our practices. Making the anthropological semanticist a Martian—that is, one who is not a participant in our, or perhaps any, linguistic practices—raises its own problems that, for the present, I would rather avoid.

7. My anthropological semanticist is not looking for anything like an "analysis" of the notion of "reference." He, and I—following Saul Kripke in *Naming and Necessity* (Cambridge, Mass., 1980)—take this notion to be a kind of primitive *(for the time being)*. Ultimately, I believe, we must say something more substantive about this fundamental notion, but such a study should not be thought of as preliminary to the study described in the text, nor have anti-Fregeans yet had virtually anything to say about it (excluding for the moment the minority who have been interested in the physicalistic reduction of the notion of "reference"

and who, unlike Kripke himself, claim to see in Kripke's work the makings of such a reduction). I will make a tentative suggestion: if we take seriously the idea that natural language is an institutional arrangement, it would seem natural to see the notion of reference as an "institutional notion," not any more reducible to something physical or psychological than is, say, the notion of "ownership" in some legal system. I find Searle's remarks on institutional facts suggestive here (see John Searle, *Speech Acts*, Cambridge, Eng., 1969). Perhaps it is an "institutional fact" that a certain term refers to something, a fact comparable to the fact that someone owns something, or that someone stole third base. I will pursue this theme elsewhere.

8. I owe this point to Joseph Almog.

9. See "Has Semantics Rested on a Mistake?" for a criticism of various attempts, most notably those of David Kaplan and John Perry.

10. The widespread feeling that the Fregean conception of semantics is inevitable—that semantics cannot be divorced from questions about thought and about cognitive significance—owes much, I believe, to a lingering Cartesian influence. This is not to say that contemporary neo-Fregeans are all fundamentally, or equally, Cartesian, or that they all exhibit the influence of that tradition in the same respects. They, under a number of anti-Cartesian influences, most notably the influence of Wittgenstein, depart in various and sundry ways from both the letter of Frege's law and the Cartesian spirit that I see as inspiring it. One can, however, see in such contemporaries the strong influence of the Cartesian picture, or so it seems to me.

11. My reading of Frege makes him an arch-representationalist and emphasizes the distance between his picture of language and thought and that of someone like the later Wittgenstein. I think that this is in line with a naive, straightforward reading of the main line of the Fregean texts, but this is, of course, controversial. In any case many philosophers have expressed agreement with the philosophical views of "my" Frege, and we can thus speak of the "Fregean tradition," even if, contrary to my view, Frege never did maintain this sort of outlook. Kaplan remarks that when he presented a similar reading of Frege at Oxford, the response was that first, Frege never held any such thing, and second, if he had, he would have been correct.

12. Similarly, the thought content of a sentence that contains indexical expressions depends upon which sense the speaker attaches to the indexical. In the case of indexicals, however, it may appear that Frege is no more individualistic than anyone else. Does not the reference of a demonstrative, for example, depend upon something quite individual? Even here, I believe, a more social picture is available. The reference of a demonstrative, I argue in "How to Bridge the Gap Between Meaning and Reference" (in this volume), depends not upon the individual's preferred descriptions, nor more generally upon his intentions to refer, but rather upon socially available cues, typically but not exclusively pointing gestures and things of the sort.

I am speaking here of Frege's own view. One neo-Fregean variation consists in socializing Frege's view. Such a view would be continuous with the representationalist aspect of the Cartesian heritage but would depart from its individualism. See note 37 below.

13. "The regular connexion between a sign, its sense, and its reference is of such a kind that to the sign there corresponds a definite sense and *to that in turn* a definite reference" (Gottlob Frege, "On Sense and Reference," in *Translations from the Philosophical Writings of Gottlob Frege*, ed. P. Geach and M. Black [Oxford, 1966], p. 58; italics added).

14. Indeed, as Joseph Almog pointed out to me, Frege may be seen as offering a reductive analysis of the reference of terms, reducing reference to the satisfaction of descriptively articulated conditions. Josef Stern offered the complementary observation that to speak of linguistic reference is not really to speak of the same relation as the "reference" of a sense.

15. Having made the distinction, crucial to Frege's account, between the psychological process of thinking and its objective content, I will not always be careful to observe it, at least where there is no danger of confusion. I thus take not only Frege's view but also views according to which thought contents are *mental* to be "thought driven." I want to emphasize how much all such Cartesian-spirited views have in common, despite differences about the ontological status of the contents.

16. The seminal work of Strawson should also be mentioned in this connection.

17. Ludwig Wittgenstein, *Philosophical Investigations* (New York: Macmillan, 1953).

18. As anything more than a picture which provides direction to our thinking, it is surely inadequate. The sketch it provides, moreover, may well be questioned, even by the anti-Fregeans. David Kaplan, in "Demonstratives" (in *Themes from Kaplan*, ed. Joseph Almog, John Perry, and Howard Wettstein [New York and Oxford, 1989]), and more recently Joseph Almog, in "Semantical Anthropology" (*Midwest Studies in Philosophy* 9 [1984]: 479–90), suggest that although historical chains need to be brought into the total picture of our practice with names, the chains are not to be brought into the semantics per se. That is, contrary to the suggestion of Donnellan's and Kripke's original remarks, the historical chains do not, strictly speaking, determine reference. Kripke himself recently suggested a similar view in conversation.

19. See note 35 below for a brief discussion of the so-called "ambiguity" of proper names.

20. 'Conceptual' here is not intended to invoke anything like Fregean senses, or Cartesian concepts. What I have in mind, for example, is the fact that I associate being a philosopher with the name 'Bertrand Russell'.

21. Kaplan has remarked that talk of linguistic meaning, even descriptive meaning, seems more at home when we turn our attention from proper names to, for example, indexicals. Even here, however, talk of "meaning" has probably done more harm than good, again encouraging representationalist tendencies and leading us away from the

proper emphasis on the use of language as a kind of practical mastery. Kaplan's account of indexicals (in "Demonstratives"), ground breaking as it was, had a strong representationalist flavor, a point to which I will return in the final section below.

22. See "Frege-Russell Semantics?" (in this volume) for a more detailed look at Frege's representationalism. Russell's position on this question, as noted and explored there, is complicated.

23. It is interesting that one who looks for illumination on this apparently fundamental question fails to get much help from, say, Frege.

24. See Wittgenstein, *Philosophical Investigations*, sec. 71.

25. Think here about the tendency to see an important task of philosophy as "explicating" sloppy ordinary talk and replacing it with more precise, scientifically acceptable forms of speech.

26. Perhaps you will think, but how could someone ever *learn* to apply a general term if not by somehow picking up, even if not totally consciously, which features count as the, so to speak, essential ones? This question, however, presupposes a "definition-based" picture of concept acquisition, as opposed to what we might call a "paradigm-based" picture. Having been exposed to a certain number of cases, and having perhaps been corrected on a number of occasions on the application of the term, one gets the feel for what is to count as a genuine application of the term, somewhat like the way one gets the feel for how to serve in tennis. The topic of definition-based, as opposed to paradigm-based, pictures of concept acquisition deserves more attention than it has received in the philosophic literature. For an interesting discussion see Stephen Stich, *From Folk Psychology to Cognitive Science* (Cambridge, Mass., 1983), ch. 5.

I am merely scratching the surface in my discussion. As Stich points out, there may be various kinds of cases in which the traditional picture of predicates and properties fails, and there may be very different reasons why it fails, not all having to do with family resemblances. See Stephen Stich, "Are Belief Predicates Systematically Ambiguous?" in *Belief*, ed. R. J. Bogdan (Oxford, 1986). Nor is this notion of family resemblance sufficiently clear. For example, is Wittgenstein advancing what has come to be known as a "cluster theory," or is his point about family resemblance terms a more radical one, as I suspect?

27. He might, for example, modify his picture of concepts so that the concepts themselves, or the properties, can somehow be vague. Alternatively, he might attribute vagueness only to language and not to concepts and go on to lament the great gap between the two. Finally, he might understand the "master's" inability to decide borderline cases as a lack of total, theoretical mastery of the relevant nonvague expression.

28. This last word seems just right, not only because it avoids the masculine form but also because it applies to such unlikely things as angels (if there are any). Fregean thoughts are the common treasure of all rational beings. Again, the real action, as noted above, takes place at a great remove from social practice.

29. These Wittgensteinian reflections suggest a more fundamental

criticism of Fregeanism than that typically urged by the anti-Fregeans, that *there can be no Fregean sense of terms like 'game'*. The sense of this term, for one thing, was supposed to consist in a specification of those features, common to all games, that are necessary and sufficient for the application of the term. Wittgenstein's point, though, is that there are no such common features. Games, moreover—and this emphasizes from another side why there *cannot be* a sense that has the class of games as its extension—do not constitute a determinate kind, the sort of thing that might be determined by a Fregean sense. Rather, games constitute a loose, open-ended assortment.

30. Here is another Wittgensteinian theme to be pursued elsewhere: it has been often assumed that there is a single notion, "reference," that provides the master key to the connection between words and things. But it seems far from obvious that the semantics of predicates is best understood in terms of the notion of reference. That is, it is not obvious—perhaps especially in light of the Wittgensteinian discussion of 'is a game'—that the final semantical word on predicates is that they refer to properties. Nor is it even obvious that indexicals like 'now' *refer* to times. (What are times?) The core of Kaplan's idea about 'now' was that the truth-values of utterances that contain 'now' depend, not upon anything like a Fregean sense that has a time as reference, but simply upon a feature of the context of utterance, namely, when the sentence was uttered. This need not incline us to say that 'now' *refers* to the time of utterance.

31. Kaplan's positive suggestion is to link them in terms of the Donnellan-Kripke chains of communication.

32. In "Bringing Belief Down to Earth," forthcoming (*Noûs* 1991), I develop an account of belief that is sensitive to the points made here.

33. Here, as elsewhere throughout this paper, it is "semantic reference," the conventional reference of the name, as opposed to the "speaker's reference," roughly the individual that the speaker has in mind, that is under discussion, unless otherwise indicated. For the distinction between semantic reference and speaker's reference see Saul Kripke, "Speaker's Reference and Semantic Reference," in *Contemporary Perspectives in the Philosophy of Language*, ed. P. French, T. Uehling, and H. Wettstein (Minneapolis, 1979), pp. 6–27.

34. Fregeans sometimes appeal to the fact that we also know that he was called "Cicero." This metalinguistic move has, for me at least, the flavor of an ad hoc response to save the theory. Independently, however, it is far from unproblematic. To mention one problem, the names we use often name many different people, and so, in general, the metalinguistic move, unless further supplemented, will often not provide individuating descriptions. To mention another, Cicero was not called "Cicero" by his fellows. That is our name for him. So this approach certainly needs refinement. Cf. Stephen Schiffer's remarks (pp. 110–11) in "The Real Trouble with Propositions," in *Belief: Form, Content and Function*, ed. R. J. Bogdan (Oxford, 1986), pp. 83–117.

35. More accurately, proper names as used on particular occasions have conventional referents. The name 'Aristotle' can be used to refer to any one of the people so called. On particular occasions of use, however, only one of these will be the conventional referent. This fact about our practices will make life difficult for the anthropological semanticist. He will want to enquire as to what subtle factors determine which individual called "Aristotle" is in question on particular occasions. It is sometimes suggested that this so-called "ambiguity" of names is evidence for the Fregean picture. It is far from obvious, however, that the answer to the semantical anthropologist's question will pertain to the beliefs of the speaker. It is very far from obvious that such considerations should convince us that speakers need to have *individuating* conceptions of their referents. Perhaps their beliefs can be far off the mark, but something very different makes it the case that it is this Aristotle that is in question, perhaps some features of the context, or perhaps something about the historical chain of communication. Or perhaps, to allude to the more radical Wittgensteinian tack suggested at the end of the previous section above, there is no one simple formula, a theory that will neatly apply to every case.

36. Taking seriously that proper names are elements of the public language does not, on the other hand, *entail* that the reference of names does not depend upon the properties that individual speakers associate with the name. Nor does the public-language picture entail that reference surely does not require a cognitive fix. Perhaps a practice might evolve in which the references of certain sorts of linguistic expressions are dependent solely upon the properties that the speaker associates with the expression. I think that although we cannot rule out this possibility a priori, it is not at all surprising, given the public-language picture, that names do not function in this way.

37. The general approach discussed in this paragraph, although not all of the details, was endorsed by John McDowell, in conversation, and by Gareth Evans, in *The Varieties of Reference* (Oxford, 1982). Evans writes, "The abandonment of the principle of identification [the cognitive fix requirement] at the level of saying is a trivial consequence of the distinction between what one says and what thought one intends to express. Its abandonment at the level of *belief* or *thought* would be an extremely significant move. What has happened is that the former has been mistaken for the latter" (p. 76 n. 18).

38. Another Fregean variation involves insisting that reference does require individuating knowledge, but not on the part of the individual speaker or thinker. Kripke, in *Naming and Necessity*, discusses a socialized description theory of names, an attempt to defeat anti-Fregean criticisms by socializing Frege's approach. One might, in this spirit, try to retrieve the sense of a name not from the individual speaker but somehow from the linguistic community. Such an approach would be more socially sensitive than Frege's, but it would still overintellectualize language and thought, at least from the point of view taken here. The

distinction that needs emphasis is that between an approach that makes reference depend upon the beliefs of the community and one that makes it depend only upon the community's practice. Could it not be, for example, that our current beliefs about a historical individual have become all fouled up but that the continuity of usage secures reference nevertheless? Our remarks about *him* are, in such a case, mistaken, but there remains an individual about whom we are talking and about whom we are mistaken.

39. One might, of course, insist that it cannot be that speakers are so cognitively impoverished that contrary to what the Kripke-Putnam examples suggest, we somehow *must* have available some individuating description. If the Fregean can make good on such an insistence and do so in a natural way—a tall order—then these counterexamples lose their force. Evans and McDowell, impressed by the Cartesian intuition, but also by the social character of language *and* by the anti-Fregean counterexamples, grant that we often do not have such information when we use, for example, historical names. They thus insist that in such cases, speakers, although their words refer and their sentences have truth-values, fail to express thought.

40. Again, the Fregean can insist if the speaker really has a mistaken belief about Aristotle, then the descriptions must fit him. One way to make this work would be to come up with descriptions other than the obvious ones and argue that these are really available to the speaker. I am again skeptical about the prospects for a natural-seeming answer along these lines, but I do not here explore the matter further.

41. Indeed, it may be that, in many cases, there is no one thing thought about. Even some of the cases briefly described in the last paragraph may be more appropriately described as cases in which the agent is thinking to some extent of one person and to some extent of another. I discuss this question in more detail in "How to Bridge the Gap Between Meaning and Reference" (cf. Kripke, "Speaker's Reference and Semantic Reference").

42. My own view, elaborated in "Bringing Belief Down to Earth," is that ascription of reference in thought, like ascription of belief, depends upon subtleties involving not only the situation of the thinker but also the situation of the reporter, the one who is ascribing the reference-in-thought or the belief. In other words, "about whom he was thinking" depends not only upon considerations having to do with the thinker but also upon what is relevant or important to the discussion in which the reporter is engaged. W. V. O. Quine, in *Word and Object* (Cambridge, Mass., 1960), emphasizes this sort of context sensitivity of "attitude reports," and I discuss this in "Bringing Belief Down to Earth." My view is thus doubly anti-Cartesian. First, I certainly do not think that the question of reference in thought is to be resolved by looking to the speaker's concepts. Second, and more radically, I think that there are factors that, on the more traditional picture, ought to have nothing to do with the question of reference in thought, that are really extremely germane, the "pragmatic" factors mentioned above.

43. Focusing the discussion on the identity case may well induce a solution that fails to apply to the general case. Frege's metalinguistic *Begriffsschrift* account is a case in point.

44. John Perry, especially in "Frege on Demonstratives" (*The Philosophical Review* 86, no. 4 [October 1977]: 474–97), embraced a similar view. The Kaplan-Perry idea was to retrieve modes of presentation from the "characters" of the indexicals, that is, from the rules that determine their references. 'I' and 'he' have very different characters, and this is so even when the expressions are used to refer to the same thing (and thus induce the same propositional constituent on the Kaplan singular-propositions picture). This difference in character means, according to Perry and Kaplan, that 'I' and 'he' take us to their single referent (in the case we are imagining) in different ways by means of different cognitive perspectives. 'I' presents me as (roughly) 'the speaker', and this "mode of presentation" is, of course, very different from that associated with 'he'. The two sentences 'I am about to be attacked' and 'He is about to be attacked' thus differ in cognitive significance. They can express the same proposition, but even when they do so, each presents that proposition in a distinctive way, by means of a distinctive cognitive perspective. Notice that the Kaplan-Perry modes of presentation, unlike Fregean senses, (1) determine a reference only relative to a context of utterance and (2) do not enter into the propositions expressed.

45. See "Has Semantics Rested on a Mistake?"

46. Kaplan, following Frege, wanted his semantical apparatus to yield an explanation of the cognitive significance phenomena. Kaplan's "characters," like Fregean senses, (1) are in the head, (2) determine reference (although only relative to a context), and (3) explain cognitive significance.

47. Note, in this connection, that Kaplan's approach to indexicals, while it rejects Frege's version of the cognitive fix requirement, does not reject the requirement. What is needed, according to Kaplan, is a context-relative sort of fix. Relative to a context in which I am speaking, the Kaplanian character of 'I' provides an individuating concept of me.

48. See pp. 146–47 above for a brief discussion of these examples.

49. My point here is that a mode-of-presentation-type account of the cognitive dimension is very strongly out of step with the anti-Fregean approach. This does not mean, of course, that one could not try to make the mode-of-presentation-type analysis work. Indeed, given the dominant sense that there can be no other way to explain cognitive differences between expressions, it is not surprising that one sees anti-Fregeans searching for some way, compatible with the anti-Fregean approach to semantics, to make it work. One hears in discussion, for example, the idea that the conceptual files in the Cicero-Tully case are distinct, for the speaker associates 'being called "Cicero"' with the name 'Cicero' and 'being called "Tully"' with 'Tully'. Note first that this is just the sort of move that anti-Fregeans fight vigorously when it is used in defense of a Fregean approach to *semantics*. Note second, how-

ever, that it seems plausible to suppose that there might be examples in which the same name is in question. One might pick up the name 'Paderewski' in two different contexts with the same associated information, say 'a famous Polish musician'. The speaker may have forgotten where he picked up the name, but he may well remember that there were two such occasions and that he assumed that two different people were in question, and he may begin to wonder whether there are indeed two different people, or whether Paderewski is none other than Paderewski.

There are many other ways to try to work out such a Frege-inspired approach to cognitive significance. My point here is that the spirit of the anti-Fregean outlook should strongly discourage the very attempt. Cf. David Kaplan's remarks in "Dthat," in *Contemporary Perspectives in the Philosophy of Language* (ed. P. French, T. Uehling, and H. Wettstein [Minneapolis, 1977], pp. 383–400), on the attempt to find a way to make Fregean semantics work: "I don't deny that on a phenomenon by phenomenon basis we can (in some sense) keep stretching Frege's brilliant insights to cover. With a little ingenuity we *can* do that. But we shouldn't."

50. Russell required, in effect, that the name user have the referent smack up against his mind. He concluded that co-referring names, used concurrently, could not differ cognitively—if they were really names, that is. If two expressions look like names but clearly differ cognitively, 'Cicero' and 'Tully' for example, this shows, concluded Russell, that they were not really functioning as names but were definite descriptions disguised.

51. The form of explanation I am employing applies to cases that involve indexicals as well. The approach favored by Kaplan and Perry individuated cognitive perspectives by linguistic meanings. A problem for that approach, fatal I have argued, is presented by cases in which the same indexical, with the same linguistic meaning, plays different cognitive roles. How, for example, can we explain the fact that one might react very differently to two utterances of "That is the battleship *Enterprise*"? One might, I suppose, in the case of "perceptual demonstratives" look to the visual perspectives for a way of discriminating the cognitive perspectives. Such a speaker may, however, be faced with qualitatively identical scenes and may still wonder whether the same ship is in question. We could, at this point, try stretching a bit further to recover a difference in cognitive perspective. The natural explanation, I submit, bypasses the need for such stretching. The speaker's knowledge, or beliefs, about the relevant referents is incomplete enough so that he cannot decide the question of whether there is one thing in question or two. The properties he takes the referent of 'that' to possess in the first context, and those he takes the referent of 'that' to possess in the second, neither conclusively indicate that a single thing is in question nor that two are. The relevant properties can be different (for example, if the scenes look very different), as they will be in many cases, or they can be the same.

52. Talks based upon this paper were given at the University of Notre Dame; the University of California, San Diego; the Center for Advanced Study in the Behavioral Sciences at Stanford University; and the University of California, Los Angeles; and I am grateful for the very helpful comments I received on those occasions. For reactions to earlier drafts, I wish to thank Laird Addis, Arthur Collins, Aron Edindin, Alasdair MacIntyre, Philip Quinn, Kenneth Sayre, Lawrence Simon, and Zeno Vendler. Special thanks indeed are owed to Thomas Blackburn, Richard Foley, David Kaplan, Ernest LePore, Genoveva Marti, and especially Joseph Almog.

Essay 11

1. It has become customary to refer to those of us who oppose the traditional approach as anti-Fregeans—and this is a custom I follow here—but our opposition is to many of the main lines of Russell's approach as well. Anti-Fregeans, more specifically, oppose Russell's descriptivist view of names, as well as his idea that direct reference is possible only with respect to objects of direct epistemic acquaintance.

2. It might be supposed that what motivated Frege to introduce modes of presentation were not general considerations of the sort mentioned in the text but were rather his concerns about informative identity sentences. This seems wrong. In his early *Begriffsschrift*, Frege's intellectual apparatus includes something very much like his later "modes of presentation," but the function of these is not to solve the famous identity puzzle. Indeed, even with something like modes of presentation, Frege, in *Begriffsschrift*, still feels the need for a metalinguistic account of identity to solve the otherwise apparently insoluble puzzles about how true identity sentences can have informative contents. So modes of presentation, it would seem, serve some more primitive need than the solution of the famous puzzle. For more on this point of Frege interpretation see "Two Fundamental Problems: Frege's Classical Approach," chapter 1 of my forthcoming book, and also Richard Mendelsohn's seminal paper "Frege's *Begriffsschrift* Theory of Identity," *Journal of the History of Philosophy* 22, no. 3 (July 1982): 279–99.

3. But see note 27 below for the question of how straightforward Frege's solution really is.

4. There are, as noted, other aspects of what has been called "cognitive significance" that I do not touch upon here. At most, then, I show that the intentionality intuition and Frege's famous puzzle present no problem for the anti-Fregean. These two putative problem areas, however, are at the heart of the Fregean assault from cognitive significance. It is sometimes supposed, on the contrary, that at the heart of the Fregean approach, and at the heart of the Fregean attack on the allegedly cognitively insensitive anti-Fregean approach, is Frege's treatment of belief sentences, or, more generally, his treatment of "propositional attitude" ascriptions. It is also alleged that Frege's approach yields a natural account of the semantics of belief sentences, while the anti-Fregean

is stymied here as well. I think that both of these points are mistaken but I cannot pursue it here. I do so in the afterword to "Has Semantics Rested on a Mistake?" (in this volume), and I will amplify those remarks elsewhere. See note 24 below.

5. David Kaplan's long-unpublished monograph "Demonstratives" appears in *Themes from Kaplan*, ed. J. Almog, J. Perry, and H. Wettstein (Oxford, 1989). I owe to Joseph Almog the idea that what Kaplan calls the pure indexicals supply to the conservative an easier target than the connotationless proper names.

6. See especially Kaplan, "Demonstratives," sec. 6 (part ii), sec. 14, and sec. 17.

7. While Kaplan's "characters" determine the reference, are intellectually available to the competent speaker, and are crucial to the explanation of cognitive significance (in these respects they are like Fregean senses), they do not, unlike Fregean senses, enter into the propositions expressed, and, as already noted, they specify their referents only relative to a context.

8. It is interesting to note that Kaplan's emphasis on the lack of any sort of descriptive meaning for proper names does not induce him, in his later work, to reject an approach to names that is, in my vocabulary, fundamentally conservative. I have in mind here Kaplan's recent unpublished lectures, "Word and Belief," the doctrine of which is subtle and complicated, to which I cannot begin to do justice here. Kaplan's conservatism, then, is no mere reaction to facts about indexicals, but is a symptom of a Fregean tendency in his thought. I suggest below that Kaplan's conservative approach to indexicals is far from inevitable in any case.

9. Indeed, Kaplan's treatment of indexicals is, in one respect, more Fregean in spirit than Frege's own approach to indexicals. On Kaplan's view, each indexical is associated, *by the conventions of language,* with a (quasi) sense. For Frege, of course, this was not so, and this was a defect in natural languages.

10. But see note 14 below for some discussion of the more innocuous, but not entirely innocent, thesis that reference fixing by description furnishes a paradigm of name *introduction*. Kaplan, in the case of indexicals, attenuates Frege in two directions. He relativizes the descriptive contents to contexts, in the sense explained above, and assigns to the descriptive concepts the role of mere reference fixers. Like the sècond and stronger reference-fixing thesis discussed in the text, the Kaplanian descriptive concepts are available to the users of the indexical and fix the reference for each use.

11. Other popular Frege-inspired variations less clearly avoid violating the intentionality intuition. Saul Kripke, in *Naming and Necessity* (Cambridge, Mass., 1980), critically discusses a socialized description theory of names, an attempt to defeat anti-Fregean criticisms by socializing Frege's approach. One might, in this spirit, try to retrieve the sense of a name, not from the individual speaker, but somehow from

the linguistic community, perhaps in terms of commonly held beliefs about the referent. Notice that such an approach, to the extent it deemphasizes the role of individual cognition, stands in tension with the intentionality intuition. Descriptional or not, such an approach faces the specter of semantic action at an epistemic distance. Also see note 15 below.

On a different topic, notice that the moment one assigns to the descriptive concepts the role of reference fixers, as opposed to being full-blown senses and therefore propositional constituents, one produces an attenuated description theory that, as is evident from Kripke's discussion in the first lecture of *Naming and Necessity*, is immune to the modal argument championed by Kripke, Kaplan, and others. If one sees the modal arguments as at the core of the anti-Fregean approach, as I do not, one might conclude that intellectually mediated reference is not what the anti-Fregean revolution is about.

12. Kripke, "Identity and Necessity," in Milton K. Munitz, ed., *Identity and Individualism* (New York, 1971), p. 157. Kripke does not here mean that reference-fixing descriptions are never used to *introduce* names. Indeed, he suggests that this may even be the standard case of name introduction, as I discuss in note 14 below.

13. Kripke, *Naming and Necessity*, p. 139.

14. Saul Kripke, "A Puzzle About Belief," in *Meaning and Use*, ed. A. Margalit (Boston, 1979), pp. 234–83. The quotation is from pages 243–44; italics added.

The Fregean intuition that the tie between words and things must, at some level, be descriptional seems not far from the surface in Kripke's discussion of the *introduction* of names (see *Naming and Necessity*, p. 96 n. 42). Kripke seems tempted by the idea that the paradigm of name introduction is an occasion on which a name is introduced by means of a reference-fixing description, and that baptism by ostension might be subsumed under the description paradigm. "The primary applicability of the description theory," Kripke writes, "is to cases of initial baptism."

Introduction of a name of course, is quite a different matter than the subsequent use of a name. So even if one adopts a description theory of name introduction, nothing follows about the subsequent use of the name. But why suppose that description of the bearer is essential even for name introduction? Why can't one baptize a child by pointing to it where this does not involve anything like a description? Alternatively, consider a case in which someone simply starts using a name as a name for an individual without any formal name-introducing ceremony. If asked to whom he was referring, such a speaker might say all sorts of things (some of which, we might add, could be incorrect, not affecting his reference). Doesn't it seem artificial to insist that such a speaker must be fixing his reference by description?

Kripke, in informal discussions at the University of Notre Dame during the academic year 1985–86, stood firm on the description theory of name introduction. Indeed, when faced with prima facie counterexamples to this description theory, Kripke suggested (albeit in a very tentative fashion) that "perhaps we need a cluster theory here." My own sense, which derives in part from Kripke's work, is that the suggestion that we need a cluster theory to save a descriptional picture is something about which we should be very suspicious, to put it mildly.

15. The examples of conservatism discussed so far have a Fregean—as opposed to a Russellian—flavor. These examples turn on the replacement of full-blown Fregean senses by context-relative concepts, or concepts that merely fix the reference. Still another sort of conservative strategy takes its cue from Russell's epistemic orientation. One might take ordinary proper names to be "directly referential," where Russell takes only "genuine proper names" to be so. One could no longer require epistemic acquaintance of the name user, but one could still impose nontrivial epistemic constraints. One might suggest that some sort of causal connection with the referent is a necessary condition for referring to it by name where the causal condition is somehow construed as providing a sort of epistemic connection. One thinks here of the work of Keith S. Donnellan, especially of his paper "The Contingent A Priori and Rigid Designators," in *Contemporary Perspectives in the Philosophy of Language*, ed. P. French, T. Uehling, and H. Wettstein (Minneapolis, 1979), pp. 45–60.

16. The point of adding the word 'substantive' here is to allow me to avoid the issue of whether *any* sort of knowledge or belief about the referent is required. If someone overhears a conversation between mathematicians, for example, in which the name 'Joan' is used as a name of a theorem, need the speaker know at least that it is the name of a theorem, as opposed to being the name of a woman, in order to use it and thereby refer to the theorem? If he says, "I bet Joan is tall," has he asserted something (false), or do we rather treat his utterance as radically defective? This is the sort of issue I wish to sidestep here.

17. Kripke, *Naming and Necessity*, pp. 91–92.

18. Kaplan, in "Demonstratives," and more recently Joseph Almog, in "Semantical Anthropology," *Midwest Studies in Philosophy* 9 (1984): 479–90, suggest that although historical chains need to be brought into the total picture of our practice with names, the chains are not to be brought into the semantics per se. That is, contrary to the suggestion of Donnellan's and Kripke's original remarks, the historical chains do not, strictly speaking, determine reference. Kripke himself recently suggested a similar view in conversation.

19. As we saw in note 11 above, one might try to accommodate the social character of our practices with names within a fundamentally intellectualist picture of the name-referent tie. Such an approach would be more socially sensitive than Frege's, but it would still overintellectualize language, at least from the point of view taken here. The crucial question is whether reference is to be tied to the community's *beliefs* or rather to its *practices*. Couldn't it be, for example, that our current beliefs about a historical individual have become all fouled up but that the

continuity of usage secures reference nevertheless? Our beliefs about *him* are, in such a case, mistaken, but there remains an individual about whom we are talking and about whom we are mistaken.

20. Nor does even the first-person pronoun present an easy target for Kaplan's approach. Competent speakers, it is true, no doubt possess a good *rough idea* of what contextual features determine the reference of 'I', something like "being the speaker." This is not to say, however, that they can discern the sort of fine-print theoretical characterization which for Kaplan constitutes the character rule. Consider Kaplan's candidate rule: the reference of the first-person pronoun is the agent of the context. Notice that "agent of the context" is a technical term for Kaplan. For technical reasons having to do with contexts in which no one is speaking, Kaplan does not understand 'the agent' to mean the same as 'the speaker'. The typical competent speaker, I submit, will not find Kaplan's "agent" idea the obvious one. See also "Has Semantics Rested on a Mistake?" pp. 125–26, for further discussion.

21. Gottlob Frege, "On Sense and Reference," in *Translations from the Philosophical Writings of Gottlob Frege*, ed. P. Geach and M. Black (Oxford, 1966).

22. Focusing the discussion on the identity case may, in addition, induce a solution that fails to apply to the general case. Frege's metalinguistic *Begriffsschrift* account is a case in point.

23. Kaplan's conservative-style explanation distinguishes the sentences cognitively in virtue of their different "characters," or linguistic meanings. 'I' and 'he', on Kaplan's view, present the referent under different aspects, and thus the sentences differ cognitively while expressing the same singular proposition. Kaplan's explanation applies, in any case, only to cases that involve indexicals. What to do with proper names remains an open question.

24. The question just posed in the text concerns the cognitive roles of singular terms as these occur in simple, unembedded sentences. This, I want to emphasize, is not a question about the difficult-to-understand occurrences of singular terms when these are embedded in epistemic, say, belief, contexts. That problem is unaddressed in the present paper, as I explain in note 4 above. The problem is sometimes, I think misleadingly, referred to as "Frege's puzzle," although it is not the problem Frege takes up at the beginning of "On Sense and Reference," nor is it the problem that Kaplan discusses as "Frege's puzzle" in "Demonstratives." No doubt the two problems are related, but their relation is, I believe, quite complicated.

25. See "Has Semantics Rested on a Mistake?" p. 119, for more along these lines.

26. Kripke, "A Puzzle About Belief," p. 246.

27. One philosopher's mystery is another's fundamental tool for clarification. (Perhaps this is some sort of consequence of the customary *modus ponens–modus tollens* quip.) It is interesting, in this connection, that the Fregean's fundamental piece of intellectual apparatus, senses,

is just what seems mysterious to the anti-Fregean. "What are these senses," we want to ask, "and how in the world can anything have such a nonconventional satisfaction relation to a referent?"

28. Versions of this paper were given at the University of California, Los Angeles; the City University of New York; and Rutgers University; and I am grateful to participants in those discussions for helpful comments. I am especially grateful to Joseph Almog, Tom Blackburn, Jon Kvanvig, Genoveva Marti, Chris Menzel, Gilbert Plumer, and Bernard Reginster.

Index

Index

In this index an "f" after a number indicates a separate reference on the next page, and an "ff" indicates separate references on the next two pages. A continuous discussion over two or more pages is indicated by a span of page numbers, e.g., "57–59." *Passim* is used for a cluster of references in close but not consecutive sequence.

Almog, Joseph, 118, 204, 207, 214, 222
Anaphora, 61–63, 68
Anthropological semantics, 123–26, 134–36, 153, 158, 212, 217
Anti-Fregean outlook, 6–8, 136–49 *passim*, 156, 166, 170–71, 176, 221
Aquaintance, epistemic, 86–88, 91–94, 96–98; direct, 107, 156, 160, 173. *See also* Russell, Bertrand
Attitudinal embeddings, 127–30, 211

Belief sentences, 127–31, 165, 171
Benacerraf, Paul, 15–17, 183
Burge, Tyler, 113, 123, 209

Cartesian perspective, 136–39, 142–52, 155, 158

Cartwright, Richard, 10, 11–15, 17–19, 182–83
Castaneda, Hector-Neri, 29–33, 38, 185f
Causal theory: of names, 32, 116; of reference, 70, 193–94
Character, *see* Kaplan, David
Cluster theory, 165–66
Cognitive content, 133–41 *passim*, 149, 152
Cognitive fix, 106–8, 133ff, 146–68 *passim*, 173–76 *passim*
Cognitive insensitivity, 159, 161
Cohen, Morris R., 184
Context of utterance, 22, 26–27, 47, 53–79 *passim*, 83, 114
Convention, 4, 80, 148; conventional application, 75–77; conventional referent, 140, 147

Definite description, 20, 28–54 *passim*, 58f, 91–109 *passim*, 128; referential-attributive dis-

230   *Index*

tinction, 35–39, 44–51; indefinite, 40–44, 46–49; property attributing use, 50–52; referential use, 52, 57–58
Demonstratives, 3, 69–85 *passim*, 91, 94, 163, 168; and Frege, 113; rules for, 125–26. *See also under* Reference
Denotation, Russell's definition, 105–6
Devitt, Michael, 73, 194, 209
Donnellan, Keith, 5, 20, 32–33, 69, 109, 166–70; referential-attributive distinction, 35–40, 49–52 *passim*, 185–89, 195–96; historical chain approach, 116–18, 125, 135–40 *passim*, 214; intentional theory, 184–85; speaker's reference, 195–98
Dummett, Michael, 1, 123, 126, 132, 137

Evans, Gareth, 217

Family resemblance, 143–45
Frege, Gottlob, 1–8 *passim*, 20–35 *passim*, 40–44 *passim*, 52–70 *passim*, 86–94, 101–44 *passim*, 152–77 *passim*; outlook of, 7, 21, 113, 136–58 *passim*, 161–66, 170–73; sense-reference model, 52, 87, 93, 106, 109, 123–24, 131–37 *passim*, 152–53; insight of, 112; data of, 112, 119, 127, 153–57, 168–75. *See also under* Puzzles

Grice, H. P., 39f, 51, 191

Historical chain of communication, 5, 117–18, 125, 135, 139–40, 167, 193, 214, 224. *See also* Donnellan, Keith; Kripke, Saul
Hume, David, 87

Indexicals, 3, 21–28 *passim*, 43, 70–78 *passim*; pure, 72–73, 76–78, 85, 194f; McGinn's view of, 83ff; Perry-Kaplan approach to, 116–19, 163–71 *passim*, 214–15, 220
Informative identities, 8, 89, 109, 113–19 *passim*, 124, 159, 168–69, 176. *See also* Puzzles: Frege's
Intentionality intuition, 106, 133, 146, 155, 158–63, 166
Intentional theory of reference, 71–83, 194, 196
Intentions, speaker's, 24, 60, 71, 75–76, 80–83

Kaplan, David, 3, 69, 109, 201, 206; character, 3, 163, 219, 222, 225; singular propositions, 44, 51, 110, 120–23; pure indexicals, 72, 76; demonstratives, 81f, 113–16, 187, 198, 208; indexicals, 116–20, 144, 184–85, 220; treatment of cognitive significance, 118–23, 127; conservative strategy, 162–64; rules, 212
Katz, Jerrold, 22
Kripke, Saul, 3, 5–6, 20, 69, 109, 222–23; and referential-attributive distinction, 37–40; historical chain approach, 116–18, 135–40 *passim*, 166–67, 207, 214; reference without discriminating knowledge, 133, 146–47, 171–72; reference fixing by description, 164–65, 223–24; speaker reference vs. semantic reference, 186–87, 189, 196–98

Language: vitality of, 2, 4–5, 138–39; public, 140
Lockwood, Michael, 37f

Marcus, Ruth Barcan, 20, 121, 161

Index   231

McGinn, Colin, 77, 83–85
McKinsey, Michael, 196
Meinong, A., 59, 61
Mendelsohn, Richard, 202
Mill, John Stuart: names as tags, 5, 20–21, 69, 109, 116–18, 125, 133–36 passim, 153, 161, 163; connotative vs. nonconnotative terms, 27–28; reference as pointing, 35
Modality, 3, 166, 181
Mode of presentation, 88–90, 108, 133, 150, 154, 157, 161, 168; Perry-Kaplan approach to, 113–16, 163, 171, 219. See also Sense

Nagel, Ernest, 184
Naturalism, 139–46
Natural language, institutional character of, 72, 80
New theory of reference, 69, 71, 78, 109–10, 112, 131, 205
Nondenoting singular terms, 111, 114, 205
Nonexistent objects, 59–62, 64–68, 192–93

Ostension, 20, 81f, 208

Parsons, Terence, 59–68, 192–93
Peano's axioms, 14–15
Percy, Walker, 132ff
Perry, John, 56, 109, 113, 116–23, 127, 151, 154, 219; and cognitive significance, 207ff; linguistic meanings, 220
Platinga, Alvin, 110, 161
Plato, 138
Practice, social, 4, 6, 134–42 passim, 147, 167, 174
Proper names: and Frege, 20, 134–35, 147; and Mill, 20, 27–28, 35, 69, 133, 153; genuine (logically proper), 29–33, 88, 91–93, 97–102 passim, 107, 109, 173, 224; ordinary, 29f,

91–109 passim; and Kripke, 165–66, 171
Propositions: and sentences, 1–2, 9–10, 22–25; propositional opacity, 31; propositional content, 39f, 144; determinate, 44–48 passim, 53, 58; singular, 44, 51–58, 110–16, 120–23, 128, 145, 153, 169; general, 51f, 58; Frege's 86–88; Russell's, 92, 96, 103–4
Putnam, Hilary, 69, 108f, 136, 139, 147, 172, 194
Puzzles, philosophical, 7; cognitive significance, 8, 113, 123, 161; informative identity, 8, 89, 113, 119, 124, 152, 159, 168–69; Frege's, 110–12, 114–16, 119, 152–57; nondenoting singular terms, 114, 205; belief sentences, 127–31, 165, 171; subtitutivity, 130, 210

Quine, W. V. O., 22–23, 26, 182, 204, 218

Reference: singular, 20f, 35; determinate, 43–48, 53, 70, 81; demonstrative, 43–48, 50–53, 81–85; implicit vs. explicit, 47; failure, 59–68; to nonexistent, 59–68; pretended, 63f, 68; direct, 70, 86–94 passim, 99–100, 106–7; intended, 75–82; fixing by description, 117, 164–65, 171; referential dualism, 160; speaker's vs. semantic, 186–89, 196–98, 216
Representation, 4f, 137–43, 147, 154; representational character, 4, 105; representative theory of conception, 88–89; representationalism, 88–94, 101–6, 139–44, 153–57
Rules, 142, 167, 209, 212
Russell, Bertrand, 7, 26, 109, 159, 162, 177, 201; theory of

descriptions, 35, 39–53 *passim*, 171; propositions, 86–87, 122, 129; knowledge by acquaintance, 87–98, 106–7, 156–57, 160, 163, 173, 203, 211; hybrid descriptions, 93–103 *passim*, 204; denotation, 105–6, 185; singular propositions, 110, 153, 169. *See also* Propositions: singular

Salmon, Nathan U., 50f, 54–57, 190–91
Schiffer, Stephen, 126
Searle, John, 126, 165, 213
Semantics, 6–8, 31–32, 39, 45; and content, 51, 57–58. *See also* Anthropological semantics
Sense, Fregean, 2–6 *passim*, 20, 30–33, 52, 87–91, 112, 138, 141; of indexicals, 20, 117; sentential, 44, 87, 138; new theorist rejection of, 124, 154, 166, 171–73; context relative, 163–64

Sentences, 2, 9–26 *passim*; and propositions, 2, 9, 55–56; eternal, 11–26 *passim*; as complete formulations, 11f, 21f
Significance, cognitive, 3, 7–8, 109–32, 153–55, 161, 168–72 *passim*; of language, 109–10, 123, 158–62 *passim*; of sentences, 112; of names, 125, 131
Stern, Josef, 214
Stich, Stephen, 215
Strawson, P. F., 35, 37, 40, 45, 153, 186

Thoughts, Fregean, 1, 21, 26, 44, 53, 86–87, 120, 138, 145; new theorist's, 121–22; silent, 151
Truth-value, 9, 21, 25, 37–40 *passim*, 52, 55

Vitality of language, 2, 4–5, 138

Wiggins, David, 37f
Wittgenstein, Ludwig, 2, 4–8, 71, 126, 138–46, 215–16

Library of Congress Cataloging-in-Publication Data

Wettstein, Howard K.
  Has semantics rested on a mistake? : and other essays / Howard K. Wettstein.
    p. cm. — (Stanford series in philosophy)
  Includes bibliographical references and index.
  ISBN 0-8047-1866-0 (cl.) : ISBN 0-8047-2527-6 (pb.)
  1. Semantics (Philosophy) 2. Languages—Philosophy. 3. Frege, Gottlob, 1848–1925. I. Title. II. Series.
B840.W45 1991
121'.68—dc20   90-19721
                                                            CIP

This book is printed on acid-free paper.

The authorized representative in the EU for product safety and compliance is:
Mare Nostrum Group
B.V Doelen 72
4831 GR Breda
The Netherlands

www.ingramcontent.com/pod-product-compliance
Lightning Source LLC
Chambersburg PA
CBHW021807220426
43662CB00006B/219